During the four years Roger
Finance in the fourth Labour G
the most far reaching structura
has experienced. Roger Do
Member of Parliament. In the third Labour Government
between 1972 and 1975 he was the youngest Cabinet
Minister for nearly half a century with the Broadcasting,
Post Office, Housing and Customs portfolios. Since his
retirement at the 1990 election, Roger Douglas has
travelled as an international consultant advising on
privatisation and structural reform in countries as various
as Russia, Brazil, Mexico, Pakistan, Canada, Peru,
Vietnam, China, Australia, South Africa and Singapore.
Much of his consultancy work is on behalf of the World
Bank. In New Zealand he has advised private sector
business and public sector corporations.

He has published two previous books: *There's Got to be a
Better Way* (1980) based on his Alternative Budget released
while in Opposition and *Toward Prosperity* (1987).

Random House New Zealand Ltd
(An imprint of the Random House Group)

18 Poland Road
Glenfield
Auckland 10
NEW ZEALAND

Associated companies, branches and
representatives throughout the world.

First published 1993
Reprinted 1993, 1994
© Roger Douglas 1993
ISBN 1 86941 1986
Printed in Australia

UNFINISHED BUSINESS

ROGER DOUGLAS

RANDOM
HOUSE
NEW ZEALAND LTD

Contents

Acknowledgements

There are a number of people to whom thanks are due for their contributions to this book.

First, to Louise Callan, who wrote the book with me and who took drafts in various stages of readiness and, with diverse bundles of additional material, made a coherent whole of them. My thanks also to Bevan Burgess, who drafted both the section on SOEs and Chapter 11.

I had great assistance in the actuarial work and general number-crunching for the many tables in Chapter 12 from Rodney Hide and John Erickson. Rodney also deserves thanks for his wider reading and comments on the rest of the text. Acknowledgements are also due to Trevor Lynds and Aetna Health NZ Ltd for permission to use material in Chapter 6.

There were a number of people who took the time to read the early drafts — Roger Kerr, Brian Nicolle, Murdo Beattie, Alan Gibbs and Glennis Douglas. I am also grateful to Peter Holle from Canada for his observations. All these people were generous with their analysis and comments. I incorporated some of their suggestions and disagreed with others. Therefore, none of them can be held responsible for the final contents.

A huge thanks is due to Margaret Cosgrove and Pauline Elmes for the typing and retyping of countless drafts and for so intelligently deciphering my handwritten notes. The final text is the better for the careful editing given it by Max Rogers.

Grateful acknowledgement is made for the use of the quotation in Chapter 3 from *Triumph of Politics* by David Stockman published in 1986 by Harper Collins Publishers in the USA and by The Bodley Head in the rest of the world.

And, lastly, thanks to my old friend and colleague, Trevor de Cleene, with whom I debated the concepts at length but to whom I still have not dared to show the text.

Roger Douglas
August 1993

Foreword

We need an unconstrained, unrestricted, full-fledged, unspoiled market economy, and we need it now ... We want to achieve the transition from a state-dominated economy to an economy based on the private sector, private initiative and private entrepreneurship ... We are increasingly convinced that our country, or any other, is less unique than is often claimed ... The basic economic laws are valid across continents, economic systems, as well as ideological beliefs ... The 'third way' [between central planning and the market economy] is the fastest way to the Third World.
Vaclav Klaus, *Czechoslovakian Minister of Finance, 1991*

This book offers a vision of the way New Zealand could be in the year 2020. It offers practical policies and politics rather than theory. In particular, it looks at what helps and does not help the disadvantaged. Its goals can be checked against a set of assumptions about growth that most would consider conservative. A founding principle of the book is that it is people who are important, not institutions. Its policies are based on the concept of individual choice and personal responsibility, within a supporting framework of social and economic policy. In that context, responsibility means providing for yourself and your family to the extent you can afford to.

It therefore rejects the doctrine promoted by the Alliance and supported by many in the Labour and National Parties that the poor are less well educated, less competent and unable to make decisions for themselves. This argument has always appalled me. I represented the people of Otara, in Auckland, when it was New Zealand's poorest suburb. They wanted what everyone else wants — a job, a home, a good education for their children, access to health care, security, dignity, pride, a sense of self-worth. What they didn't want was to be told what to do, to have options taken away from them, to be left with no power, no control over their lives.

This book deals with the plight of the disadvantaged and the adverse impact their situation has on the rest of the population. Delivering real gains to them is crucial because that automatically delivers something of value to everyone else. There are a number of points to be made:

❏ While income is obviously important to disadvantaged people, it is not enough to remedy their situation.
❏ Their deeper need is for opportunities and the incentives to make real advances themselves through their own efforts.
❏ By helping the disadvantaged to achieve independence and contribute more to society, we not only transform their future but we also improve everyone else's.
❏ These gains have a vital role to play in creating a fair society.
❏ The alternative is a society with a permanent underclass of alienated people with no stake in prosperity or social harmony.

The book begins with our situation as it is now: a country with unemployment at high levels, heavy indebtedness, where high interest costs eat up a huge percentage (15 per cent) of the government's income while at the same time it has heavy and expensive commitments in health, education, social welfare, housing, retirement income (superannuation), policing, defence and the justice system. Although this book is about the New Zealand situation, the scenarios, lessons and answers it contains could equally apply elsewhere. New Zealand is not the only country experiencing serious problems with national debt, taxation and the high and escalating cost of social programmes, without any apparent improvement in the services they provide. There appears to be little or no accountability and little choice for the people who use the services — the programmes' customers.

This book does not recommend that the government

withdraws from these activities. It assumes that no government in the developed world would permit a situation to exist where children do not have access to education, citizens cannot get health care, where people do not have an income when they retire or because of some adverse event such as sickness, an accident, or unemployment. Rather, it advocates that governments should concentrate more on creating an environment where there is choice, competition and diversity. I regard the creation of competition within and between the private and public sectors as of the utmost importance. Achieving key objectives and goals in areas such as health, education, housing, retirement income and social welfare is critical. The means of their delivery is left open to allow normal market forces to operate with individual consumers free to buy the service that best suits them and their needs.

The book also takes certain things for granted. For instance, that government does not itself need to be a provider of services. Ownership often distracts from what is really important. As owner of Air New Zealand, the government controlled the number of aeroplanes flying into the country. Profits and jobs in one company took precedence over profits and employment in tourism as a whole. Governments would do best by keeping foremost in mind the interests of taxpayers and consumers — the small people — not those of producers and special-interest groups. Therefore I have not assumed, for example, that health and education are the exclusive domain of either the public sector or the private sector. Instead I have begun by assuming that patients, parents and students should be able to choose for themselves.

I have assumed that there should be no rule or special assistance that favours one sector over the other. The consumer will decide. I have assumed, too, that in order for these policies to work there will have to be an element of compulsion. That will be opposed by many, despite the fact that we have it now — compulsory taxes pay for services such as health, education and retirement income. Under the new system the government would continue to make payments compulsory but would collect them in another way whenever a person could afford to pay. When a person could not afford to pay directly for a service, the government would give them a grant from a general taxation pool. Then they, like everyone else, would have total choice and responsibility for the purchasing decisions they make.

Ultimately, in changing from one system to another, there is a period of transition. There can be difficulties when negatives from the old system are still present and the benefits of the new have not yet appeared. I have tried to deal sensitively with transition issues, providing security to those who would find the period of change difficult. The rules governing any transition that takes place should be as fair as possible, with short-term costs as clear as possible. Changes do not take effect overnight. Those with young families would have a free ride into the new system. There would be huge incentives for people just entering the work force with their earning lives in front of them. Those in mid life with adequate income would have to face the transition without major incentives or sweeteners. However, the measures I am recommending would ensure that on retirement they would have the security of superannuation and health care.

Finally, the book assumes that there is no satisfactory solution to a country's problems, including class warfare, unless it is seen to be solving the problems of the disadvantaged. The book also assumes that the public can be trusted to understand the real situation of the country and what needs to be done to solve its problems. And it assumes that they can and should be told without trying to dupe them, or to cocoon them in cottonwool. Unemployment, race relations, crime, health, education, housing, welfare, debt and the economy remain the key issues in New Zealand. These issues are all linked. We cannot look at and deal with each one in isolation. Poor parenting, lack of motivation, inadequate skills, unemployment, lack of opportunity and a lack of economic growth are all parts of the same syndrome. They all reinforce each other. Any programme that is going to solve these problems — and they are solvable — has to provide goals and dreams and a practical commonsense way to deliver them within a reasonable time frame. I believe the programme outlined in this book demonstrates how.

1   Old Arguments, Basic Assumptions

> *Free marketing and deregulation are not right wing policy
> stances. They are the policies of those who believe in
> individual liberty and the availability of choice in a com-
> petitive environment. Right and left wings are of the same
> political ilk. They believe in controls and dictatorial
> government. There was, for example, no difference between
> Hitler and Stalin.*
>
>   Aubrey Begg, Labour MP for Awarua, 1972–1975

A few years ago now, one of the country's high-profile
business leaders remarked to a friend of mine that I was a
political 'wet'. 'What do you expect?' my friend replied.
'Roger is a Labour Minister of Finance in a Labour
Government.'

I don't think I've ever regarded myself as either 'wet' or
'dry', although I have been labelled as both at different
times. For anyone inhabiting the farther regions of the
political right or left, my policies and the beliefs that
underpin them are never likely to win favour. But that
does not mean I have no allegiances of my own. I have been
a member of the New Zealand Labour Party almost all my
life and a Labour representative in Parliament for 21
years. My ancestry is Labour — not just my mother and
father, but their fathers before them. When I retired from
Parliament in 1990, I was conscious of the ending of a
tradition unbroken for three generations. Until that day,
for more than 55 years there had always been a member of
the Anderton-Douglas family on the Labour side of the
House. It was a continuum I broke with regret. My political
beliefs and my general philosophy of life are all products of
that Labour line.

There are some inside and outside the Labour Party who
find that hard to accept. They do not see me as

representing their idea of Labour. Most major political parties these days are broad churches, to use a popular phrase. Their members hold many shades of belief. From time to time arguments about those differences cripple a party. If they are out of power, there is no more effective way to keep them off the government benches. When they are in power it makes them ineffective as a government and is a sure path to defeat. Almost always the arguments are about means. During lulls in the skirmishing, opponents can usually be heard pledging themselves to the same objectives.

I don't think my ambitions for this country differ greatly from those of the Labour movement, and many others as well. Six years ago, I enumerated the goals of every Labour government for our society:[1]

❒ A reasonable standard of living for everyone.
❒ Access to a good education and good health services, regardless of income.
❒ A job for everyone who is able to work.
❒ A social welfare system that allows people to reach the level they can and want to achieve, and where the assistance provided does not make those who receive it dependent on it but instead opens the way to self-support.
❒ A society which gives people opportunities for self-fulfilment.

Where I came to differ from some parts of the Labour movement (and some sections of the National Party, too, going on recent performance) was in how we went about achieving the society we all wanted. Like many others in many parties in many countries, my ideas on the means to these ends have not been static. As our goals began to recede, no matter how strenuously we pursued and expanded the instruments of social and economic policy introduced by the first Labour Government, I was forced to consider the possibility that those policies were no longer

[1]Roger Douglas and Louise Callan, *Toward Prosperity, People and Politics in the 1980s: A Personal View.*

the answer. The more I looked at how they were working, and at the distortions that had crept in over the years, and howthose distortions had produced results never envisaged by the original architects, the more change seemed necessary. It was obvious. If what we were doing wasn't working, then we needed to find another way to get what we wanted.

At the beginning, however, I was not so different in my thinking from my colleagues. When I first entered Parliament I believed in the ability and rightness of governments to pick winners in business and industry. I saw no problem in their being involved in the market-place in a hands-on way. I thought they could encourage economic growth by directing government money and private funds into selected sectors or industries. What they couldn't manipulate that way, they could control by statute and legislation. In my maiden speech in 1970, I criticised the breweries for raising the price of beer and recommended that the government institute a form of price control. I also had a lingering regard for the policy of using import barriers to promote industrialisation, and so diversify an economy that was far too reliant on producing raw agricultural products. But I knew, too, through my own experience in business, of the problems created by import controls. In that same maiden speech, I also urged the government to allow New Zealand exporters to invest overseas, rather than restricting them from doing so.

For a third-generation member of the Parliamentary Labour Party, the corollary to all the business of economics was people: providing them with security against unforeseen financial hardship, the opportunity to improve their lives and the lives of their children, and the means to make the most of their opportunities. That meant not just the safety-nets of State assistance to the sick and unwillingly unemployed, but the provision of a satisfactory standard of health care, education and housing for everyone. Taking care of business was supposed to create the funds to make all that possible.

My ideas on government's role in building a stronger

economy began changing during my first six years in Parliament. They moved progressively away from the policies that were rapidly turning the New Zealand economy into the most regulated outside communist Europe. There were many reasons for casting off those old beliefs, but there was one I kept returning to. It was supposed to be the justification for the government's increasing intervention in the economy to gain our social goals. But I saw the policies weren't helping the poor, the disadvantaged and those on lower incomes. The unwelcome truth was that they actually made the situation worse for the less well-off.

For instance, import policies were meant to protect the average New Zealander, ensure jobs that might not exist otherwise, and regulate the supply of goods. The down side of import controls was that we paid way over the odds for items as diverse as cars, television sets and shoes. Having paid more than we should for those items, we had less to spend on other goods, thereby costing jobs elsewhere in the economy. If you had to pay $70 for what could have been a $20 pair of shoes, that was $50 you no longer had to spend on other things. We created jobs where we were least efficient and lost jobs where we were relatively efficient. Workers in Australia, Britain and the United States spent a substantially smaller proportion of their incomes to buy the same items, and had a greater range of goods to choose from. Having money didn't mean you could buy what you wanted either. Import controls, high import duties and severe restrictions on how much money New Zealanders could take out of the country meant that even if you could afford them, you were effectively prohibited from buying the goods you wanted.

The change in my attitude to social policy happened at the same time. When I entered Parliament, and for some time after, I continued to accept the old argument that if something wasn't working, the way to fix it was by allocating more money. For instance, the best way to help the disadvantaged was simply to increase spending on education and health. During the 21 years I worked as an

MP, I saw government expenditure in social services increase by 100 per cent over and above the high inflation of those years. Yet the standard of the services got worse, not better.

The fact that a bigger budget rarely fixes a problem was what David Stockman, President Reagan's Budget Director during his first term of office, tried to drive home to those in the White House, and more especially to those on The Hill. He could never understand why the same logic and financial imperatives that operated in the real world were steadfastly ignored by governments. Why, he asked, was the Pavlovian response to a policy that wasn't working always a request for more money? Why didn't people consider that maybe the problem was the policy, and stop funding it altogether? Then they could set about finding a policy that did work. Like Stockman, I no longer believe that more money is the answer. If we are serious about our social goals, we should be asking the really basic questions in a number of areas — health, education, housing, superannuation.

In fact, a growing number of people from a wide cross-section of society are doing just that, and there is noticeable agreement on the answers. It is remarkable that there is now little divergence in the New Zealand business community about what still needs to be done for the economy. There is similar accord between the government's economic advisers, the OECD and the financial markets. In health and education, people are emerging who favour the new ways. Public opinion is also changing. For example, a 1992 NRB McNair survey for the Ministry of Education showed that more than 50 per cent of Maori parents and guardians think Maori private schools provide a better education for their children.

The old politics of the so-called economic right and left are meaningless — the political landscape has changed so much in the last 10 years. There are new groupings, new divisions. What we have now are internationalists — the realists — and the isolationists or protectionists. The former understand that the world is more and more becoming a single market and want to be part of it. The second group hanker for the past. They want to put up barriers and pretend that they can operate outside the global market. Both groups are represented in the main political parties around the world, whether they are labelled 'left' or 'right'.

By the time I became Minister of Finance in 1984 I had decided that governments didn't have to run things. Their role was to design an environment that positively encouraged the people they represented to go out and run things. The story of Air New Zealand and airport terminal facilities illustrates this well. It shows only too clearly that governments are not good at getting things done. The government, together with the Wellington City Council, owned the passenger terminal at Wellington airport. The terminal had been a factory for De Havilland aircraft and things had gone pretty much downhill since then. It was a slum gateway to the country's capital city. For 10 years, government and the council had been in committee arguing about renovation, costs and who should pay what. Yet, within 10 days of the announcement that Ansett was starting up in the domestic market, Air New Zealand had found the money to start work. Those of us who used the airport regularly could finally enjoy modern air travel. We, too, could have an airbridge to reach our plane instead of having to walk across the tarmac without an umbrella in Wellington's wind and rain.

I believed that the kind of environment I wanted to create, and the economy that then developed, would be able to support our social goals. New Zealand began a process of economic change which radically altered the way government and the private sector thought and operated. From 1984 to 1987, those changes succeeded in creating a new confidence in the economy, both at home and abroad. They also earned this country widespread respect for the unflinching way we addressed the substantial problems New Zealand faced. Along the way, politicians, bureaucrats and the public took a crash course in economic realities and began an ongoing discussion on ways and means. However, that discussion became increasingly fractious and early economic confidence sustained a number of knocks when the government's sense of purpose was seen to waver.

The first dent in confidence was caused by Prime Minister David Lange's imposed tea break in 1988. While policy that was in the pipeline gave the impression that things were still happening, future economic policy was put on hold indefinitely and the government began to distance itself from what had taken place over the previous three years. The National Government, voted into office at the end of 1990, revived that sense of confidence; but a series of U-turns in policy and the government's failure to improve New Zealand's poor fiscal situation will once again begin to undermine local and overseas trust in our economic future.

The concern is justified. The predictions of doom coming from politicians of all parties and from all quarters are self-fulfilling if they are unopposed. At the moment they reverberate loudly in a vacuum left by the government and Labour opposition. This confusion of voices and messages falls into four basic categories. First there are the 'whingers' — the voices of the past selling a seductive message of nostalgia. They espouse a return to the old days and old discredited ways. Next there are the centralists who believe that means are more important than the ends; for example, that the State must be the provider of health care, whether it does it well or not. Then there are the misguided rather than wilfully blind and those who are more than a little politically opportunistic. They hold a finger up to the electoral wind and then find the policy that will win them enough voter approval to keep them in power. Finally, there are the silent — those who are not willing to stand up in political circles for what they believe and who have largely opted out of the economic and social policy debate. They are locked into party systems where if they say too much they are punished by loss of ranking or their parliamentary seat. It is no wonder the public are anxious, irritable, uncertain of what is expected of them and what they can expect from government.

The doom-sayers are right in one thing only — this

country's troubles are not over. The job is far from done. They are absolutely wrong in their prescription to reimpose policies which created our problems in the first place and so undo everything that has been achieved. Just as damaging is the National Government's apparent decision not to respond to this dismaying chorus and its paralysis in policy-making. As each day passes, the need for government, and to a lesser extent the Labour opposition, to counter the prevailing mood of gloom grows more urgent. They should be providing the kind of leadership and direction the country so badly wants.

Some of what we hear from doom-sayers like Jim Anderton, Winston Peters and others is driven by the dark gremlins of ego and power. Some of it is a hankering for times past, a desire to turn back the clock, an exercise in nostalgia instead of constructive thinking. What they don't realise, or don't want to recognise, is that the 'good old days' were a myth. Theirs is a rosy view of life which was never as it seemed. The problems New Zealanders face now are not the result of changes made over the last nine years or of the 1987 stockmarket crash. Those factors merely highlighted the difficulties New Zealand had accumulated over a period of 40 years. A report by the Monetary and Economic Council in 1962 found that between 1949 and 1960 the New Zealand economy earned the unfortunate distinction of having one of the slowest annual rates of growth of productivity among all the advanced countries of the world. From 1960 to 1984, New Zealand's average growth rate in productivity was 1.2 per cent, lower than any other country in the OECD. Japan was averaging 5.8 per cent and the EC countries 3.3 per cent per year. Real wages in New Zealand were no higher in 1987 than in 1960, whereas workers' wages in Japan went up by 175 per cent and wages in Australia rose by 70 per cent in real terms in the same period. New Zealand's puny achievements were the result of slavishly following policies that are again being advocated. I cannot see why they will help the disadvantaged now when they failed to do so last time.

Over the years, we have played a game of brinkmanship with the national economy. We attempted reforms, but each time it got tough, we backed off. Every time we reverted to more of the old ways our problems intensified. Despite the constant economic discussions of the past nine years, there is still only a limited understanding of just how bad our situation is — the size of our problems, how dramatic the changes will have to be in order to solve them, and how long it is going to take. Doing what we've done before — looking for a quick, less uncomfortable way out instead of fixing the problems at their roots — will have consequences that hardly bear thinking about. This time it would push us up to and over the economic brink.

However, the news is not all bad. We have made some real progress over the last nine years. Today, New Zealand's inflation is at its lowest level for decades — as low or lower than nearly all our trading partners. Labour productivity would appear to have grown by nearly 6 per cent annually over the past three years. By comparison, the OECD estimated labour productivity growth in Australia at 0.9 per cent a year between 1979 and 1990. The real exchange rate of the New Zealand dollar is now at roughly the same level as it was after the 20 per cent devaluation in 1984. The tax system has been overhauled. Agriculture is no longer dependent on the State. Quantitative import controls have been virtually abolished. The financial sector is largely deregulated. Government departments' monopoly rights have been removed and internal product markets, such as Telecom, have been significantly deregulated. State business enterprises are now commercial. The public and private labour markets have been reformed. Growth is slowly emerging from recession and New Zealand is more competitive than at any time in the last 30 years.

It is in other areas that our remaining problems show up graphically and indicate serious imbalances in some of the polices still being followed. Unemployment has risen to dangerous levels. Successive governments have failed to control government spending and allowed the rate of taxation to increase relentlessly. Despite the 100 per cent rise in social expenditure over the last 20 years, we cannot claim to have much to show for it. There certainly has been no real improvement in the quality of our spending, especially for the disadvantaged groups. We are spending more and more just to stand still. In the commercial sector, New Zealand continues to shelter some major import-competing industries such as cars, footwear and textiles, as well as protect large parts of the public sector. As a result, the adjustment costs — unemployment, pressure on exporting and regional disparities — remain higher than they should be. On top of all this is the fear that with social policy areas obviously in trouble, despite repeated real increases in spending, no serious effort is being made to ensure that we get better value for the money being spent, apart from changes in health, which will bring only limited improvement.

Over the next 36 months, unless the government is seen to take back the initiative, confidence in our economy will start to erode again. I am not advocating measures to bail out those companies or sectors hit by the changes but rather decisive action of the kind we had during 1984 to 1987 and again in late 1990 and early 1991. Its absence has raised doubts: Is the government split? Has it lost its way? Does its unwillingness to tackle social policy in a concerted way mean that fiscal restraints have been put aside? There will always be doubts about any government's resolve to enact measures which will catch political flak. New Zealand cannot afford the uncertainties being created at the present time. A small country with an undiversified economic base such as ours will always face the temptation to back down and become interventionist. To do so now would be a disaster.

If we continue to do no more than what is already in the pipeline, the following scenario is probable: Two to three years from now companies will be more and more reluctant to invest until political uncertainties have been resolved and they have clear signals of the country's economic direction. A continuing budget deficit will finally put pressure on interest rates. Jobs will not increase as fast as they should; only our debt and public sector spending will continue to rise. The deficit may expand even further and talk of a budget surplus will be laughable. Finally, any residual confidence in the economy and its future will disappear. To do no more than we have done to date will be to risk another major crisis in four or five years' time — a crisis that would force us to make massive unplanned cuts to social spending or to increase taxes substantially, possibly both. The policies of instant miracle workers like Peters or Anderton would then prove dangerously attractive to many people.

The country cannot afford an irresolute government like the one we have now, or a Labour government that wants to go back to the policies it pursued in past years, or an Alliance government that advocates policies even worse than those that brought us to our knees in 1984. New Zealanders need to separate the rhetoric from the reality. In taxation, income maintenance and in the social services, our present institutions are failing to achieve our economic and social objectives. The tax system still demands that many workers on low incomes pay unreasonably high rates of tax. Despite improvements to the social welfare system, some beneficiaries continue to face intolerably high marginal tax rates. It is impossible to defend a system that makes a low-income working family receiving modest income support pay the highest effective marginal tax rates in the country. New Zealand's system of providing assistance is failing badly. While many benefits go to those in real need, other payments by the State do not. After years of ballooning government spending and increases in debt-servicing costs, the taxpayer no longer has the discretionary dollars to pay those who don't need assistance. There are citizens not being protected who need protection — *they* have to be our priority, rather than those who can take care of themselves.

We must reassert a commitment to policies like those in the 1985–86 tax-benefit reforms and the ill-fated December 1987 package. We must act on a broad front in order to protect those who are most vulnerable and battered by economic adjustment. We must stimulate investment and job creation by strengthening incentives and eliminating impediments to growth and productive effort. We need to create a climate that encourages confidence and assists and rewards independence and effort. In other words, we need to break the dependency cycle which encourages some people to look to the State for support when they could be making it on their own.

2   Bad Housekeeping

Debt finance is a politician's dream: it's a scam by which popular programmes — and their concomitants, votes and campaign lucre — are financed by saddling future generations with the costs. When the federal government finances a programme by issuing thirty-year debt, it is taxing kids who aren't yet old enough to vote; indeed, it's taxing the unborn children of unborn children. If these glimmers in their mothers' eyes could speak, they might adapt the old Revolutionary slogan to their predicament and cry, in unison: 'No taxation without gestation!'

James T. Bennett and Thomas J. DiLorenzo, *Official Lies: How Washington Misleads Us*

Adam Smith would not approve and neither would John Maynard Keynes. At the beginning of 1993 every New Zealand household owed at least $60,000. The interest on this debt is $100 a week minimum, or about $5200 a year for every family of four. If principal is repaid at 5 per cent per year, the family has to find a further $2800. The total for the two is $8000 per year. But the worst part of it is that the debt is the government's, yet one way or another, you and I will have to repay it. Whether repayments come from existing taxation or increased taxation, we will need to find that money for the next 20 years. The size of the debt and the ongoing annual deficits are the foremost reason why New Zealand has to complete the process of reform begun in 1984. The situation is such that we do not even have the option of stopping where we are now. The country cannot go on running deficits of $2 billion plus. There are other reasons, and good ones, why the reforms proposed here should be implemented, but the debt and deficit are the most pressing.

Until the end of the Second World War, economist Adam

Smith's support of a balanced budget — what is prudence in the conduct of every private family can scarcely be folly in that of a great kingdom — was very much the prevailing view of governments, intellectuals and the general public. But there were other reasons given for supporting a balanced budget. Among the principal ones was that failure to balance the budget and the continual running of deficits meant current spending would be financed at the expense of future generations. The government in effect would move forward some of the cost of current spending to future taxpayers. The unfairness of this legacy generally inhibited governments from incurring deficits.

Another reason was advanced by the Swedish economist, Knut Wicksell, as early as 1890. He argued that if governments ran deficits then citizens were not being given clear information about the costs and benefits of programmes which they were being asked to support as voters. Informed choice requires direct knowledge of both the costs and benefits of proposed expenditure. If much of the cost could be transferred to a subsequent generation, citizens would select more government expenditure than if they had to carry the true costs of the benefits they received. This commitment to a balanced budget was not as naïve or rigid as some modern commentators like to suggest. There were times, such as war or the Great Depression, when deficits were incurred. It was understood, within the general principle, that temporary and limited deficits and surpluses could not be avoided.

Attitudes to the balanced budget began to change in the 1930s with John Maynard Keynes. According to Keynes' new theory, government's role was to balance the economy, not the budget. The government had the ability, through its taxation and expenditure policies, to influence overall economic activity.

Therefore, in times of economic distress, it was obliged to intervene. This meant, of course, that from time to time the government would have to run a deficit. It was to be regarded as a balancing element within the system — to quicken the economy during periods of economic depression and act as a brake when the economy became overheated. However, it was certainly not Keynes' idea to run continuing deficits.

Keynes' expectations about what a deficit can accomplish were far more conservative than those of many of his later disciples. In 1937, at a time when unemployment in the United Kingdom was 11 to 12 per cent, the London *Times* published an article by Keynes entitled 'How to Avoid a Slump', in which he urged that government spending be levelled off:

> *Three years ago it was important to use public policy to increase investments. It may soon be equally important to retard certain types of investment, so as to keep our most easily available ammunition in hand for when it is more required . . . just as it was advisable for the government to incur debt during the slump, so for the same reasons it is now advisable that they should incline to the opposite . . . just as it was advisable for local authorities to press on with capital expenditure, so it is now advisable that they should postpone whatever new enterprises can reasonably be held back.*

Distribution of demand and not its total level was the problem. Government spending was crowding out the private sector. A few years later, in 1946, he wrote of the 'deep under-currents at work, natural forces one can call them, or even the invisible hand, which are operating towards equilibrium' in the economic system. 'I find myself moved, not for the first time', wrote Keynes in *The Economic Journal,* 'to remind contemporary economists that the classical teaching embodied some permanent truths of great significance, which we are liable to overlook because we associate them with other doctrines which we cannot now accept without much qualification.' Keynes was not an economist who believed in a deficit for all seasons.

New Zealand's record with debt is not good. According to a Department of Statistics' review of debt levels over the past 100 years, the country's public debt has never been low by international standards. We had our first 'think big' experiment under Sir Julius Vogel which led to a huge debt and the long depression of the 1880s and early 1890s. Once government spending was under control again, succeeding governments proved to be prudent housekeepers even after the introduction of the Welfare State. Throughout the 1960s government spending fluctuated between 26 and 29 per cent of Gross Domestic Product (GDP) and at the beginning of the 1970s stood at 27.7 per cent. During the same period, deficits seldom exceeded 3 per cent of GDP, although that was correctly regarded at the time as being too high.

New Zealand governments developed truly spendthrift habits in the 1970s and maintained them for the next 20 years. Between 1971/72 and 1975/76 government expenditure rose from 28 to 38 per cent of GDP. Deficits blew out to 8.6 per cent of GDP in 1975/76 under the Rowling government and to 8.6 per cent in 1978/79 and 9.1 per cent in 1984/85 under the Muldoon government, election years in all cases. By 1983/84 spending exceeded 40 per cent of GDP and it is currently around the same level despite a reduction in industry assistance and the exclusion from government accounts of major trading activities (SOEs).

At the beginning, the rise in government expenditure as a percentage of GDP was caused by higher spending on social services and debt-servicing costs. Since the mid-1970s there have been a number of pressures:

❐ A deteriorating financial balance resulted in growing public debt and increased debt-servicing costs. This was accentuated by government taking over major project debt ('think big' projects).
❐ The economy's poor performance caused higher numbers of beneficiaries (unemployment benefits, with some spill-over to the domestic purposes and sickness benefits).
❐ Wage increases (above the rate of inflation) in the public sector increased spending on health, education and other government services.
❐ Political decisions increased the real cost of programmes (e.g., national superannuation, the introduction of DPB and higher ratios of teachers to students).

❐ A change in demography pushed up spending on superannuation and tertiary education while a decline in the number of school-age children did not bring a proportional reduction in the cost of education programmes.

The government's real net debt (total debt less offsetting government financial assets and inflation) tripled between 1974/75 and 1978/79 and tripled again between 1978/79 and 1984/85. It rose a further 35 per cent by March 1990.

Between the year ending March 1978 and the year ending June 1990, the New Zealand government's real public net debt increased by $31.9 billion dollars. Last year alone (the year ending 30 June 1992) the government's operating accounts showed a deficit of $5149 million, about 7 per cent of GDP, or $5884 per family ($113.15 a week). Government liabilities exceeded government assets by $15,080 million at 30 June 1992. Should New Zealand's debt be called up, the government would be bankrupt. A government is no different from any other borrower; the more it borrows in relation to its income potential, the more it puts itself in the hands of its lenders.

However, the causes of New Zealand's current economic woes can be traced back long before the 1970s. The apparently sound figures of the 1950s and 1960s masked destructive behaviour. The 1993 report, *OECD Economic Surveys:* New Zealand, summarised this and later periods:

> *Throughout 1950 to 1985 the New Zealand economy was one of the most highly protected within the OECD. It lacked labour force skilling, suffered from rigid factor and product markets and supported high effective tax rates. In addition the Government's persistent tendency to accommodate external shocks resulted in high and variable rates of inflation. In these conditions investment was often misdirected and there was little competitive pressure to control costs in what has been described as a 'cost-plus economy'. The result was the accumulation of capital ill-suited to providing sustained per capita income growth.*

In the 1950s our standard of living was one of the best in the world, yet the 1962 report of the Monetary and

Economic Council recorded that between 1949 and 1961 New Zealand had one of the slowest annual rates of growth in productivity of all the advanced countries. The poor performance of the 1950s continued throughout the 1960s and 1970s. Our growth rate averaged 3 per cent over the 1960s. This seems high by today's standards but 3 per cent was one of the lowest growth rates in the world during the 1960s, and it didn't improve. From 1960 to 1984, New Zealand had the slowest rate of productivity growth in the OECD. The impact of the country's poor performance hit home in the 1970s. The two oil shocks and international stagflation exposed the chronic weaknesses of the economy with a vengeance.

At the start of the 1970s the economy was tightly regulated and narrowly based. Farmers were heavily subsidised and manufacturers were assisted by border protection, mainly through import licensing. Unemployment began to increase. There was a series of general wage and price freezes. The government's response to the oil shocks was to borrow in order to increase subsidies to exporters and invest in energy development. Inflation surged upwards: the rate was 50 per cent higher than the OECD average through most of the 1970s and 1980s. On 22 June 1982, Prime Minister Rob Muldoon announced a 12-month freeze on all wages, prices, rents, interest rates, dividends, directors' fees and professional charges. At the end of the 12 months, the freeze was extended for another 12 months and then for a further 8 months. The economy languished, swamped by debt and regulation. Job losses continued to grow; by 1984 nearly 130,000 New Zealanders (including those on special government work schemes) were unemployed. Yet real wages had not risen since the early 1960s. Foreign commentators knew the cause to be poor policy and in 1984 *Euromoney* magazine gave the Muldoon government the 'wooden spoon award' for economic management.

New Zealand's real income (GNP) per head in 1986 placed it 19th on a list of 25 high-income countries in the World Bank's 1991 World Development Report. Its income was only 40 per cent of Switzerland's at the top of the table and 50 per cent of Japan's, second in the table. But in the years just after the Second World War, New Zealand's per capita income was comparable to Switzerland's, and Japan was a low-income country. More relevant, however, is the relative growth in real income per head in the 25 years between 1965 and 1989.

New Zealand's growth rate of 0.8 per cent was well below all the other high-income countries with the exception of Kuwait, on –4.0 per cent. It was half that achieved by the United States which at 1.6 per cent had the next lowest average rate of growth. Switzerland's per capita income growth had been 4.6 per cent and Japan's 4.3 per cent. In 25 years, New Zealanders had increased their economic pie by 20 per cent; the Japanese meanwhile had increased theirs by 175 per cent.

Poor productivity translates into poor wages. New Zealand workers were no better off in 1987 than they were in 1960. In comparison, the Japanese worker was 2.75 times better off and the Australian worker 1.7 times better off. New Zealand is now a relatively low-wage country. It is often said that money isn't everything, but most people would consider that their situation had improved if their real income doubled. New Zealand's lacklustre performance over the years has meant that New Zealanders are much poorer than they deserve to be.

New Zealand's economic performance has been inferior no matter which indicator it is measured against. No nation that wants a high standard of living can afford the type of economic government we have had for much of the last 40 years. One yen and one mark now buy 6.9 and 4.7 times more New Zealand goods respectively than they did in 1970. That is one measure of New Zealand's relative fall in its standard of living compared to other countries. Many of the social pressures evident today are much more the result of what happened during the years up until 1984 than in the years since then. Poor performance was a direct consequence of poor policy.

A sound fiscal policy, where expenditure and revenue

are in sync, is a basic factor in any healthy economy for the following reasons:

❒ Government spending and taxation have a powerful negative influence on incentives and relative prices right through the economy and affect how resources are allocated and wealth is generated. As governments have expanded their role in the economy this century, this influence has grown enormously.

❒ Taxes divert resources from the private sector to the public sector. When resources are used in public sector projects that yield a lower return to the community than they would earn in the private sector, the welfare of the whole community is reduced.

❒ Government spending and taxation decisions alter the distribution of income, affecting spending, savings and investments.

❒ Fiscal policy (government spending) interacts with monetary policy (money supply) and so influences the level of inflation and nominal and real interest rates.

❒ Governments' spending, taxing and borrowing decisions may, in the short term, influence the total level of activity in an economy. However, the direction and strength of the influence is uncertain and any positive short-term effect is likely to be neutralised by larger negative long-term consequences.

❒ Fiscal policy affects the level of certainty and confidence in the economy.

In the 1950s, 1960s and 1970s, New Zealand government policy propped up inefficient industries with subsidies and import protection. The 'Fortress New Zealand' approach guaranteed a second-rate performance. There was no need to compete and therefore no need to strive to be efficient. Businesses kept on as they always had and New Zealand stood still while the countries we like to compare ourselves with passed us by.

A country that wants to increase its rate of productivity needs productive businesses; and businesses can only be productive by staying efficient. This is a constant process as new information and new ways of doing things are continually discovered, rendering previous practices inefficient and obsolete. Efficient enterprises soon find they become inefficient if they don't change. The American economist Lester Thurow considers the closing of inefficient factories and plant to be the best of all investments:

> *While there are many voices calling for more investment, the process of disinvestment is even more important. Eliminating a low productivity plant raises productivity just as much as operating a high productivity plant . . . To close a low productivity plant also makes it possible to move workers and capital that have been tied up in this activity into new, high productivity activities . . . Paradoxically, the investment of investments is disinvestment.*

One of the enduring myths about the reforms begun in 1984 has been that they were done to benefit big business. In fact it was the previous policies that protected and benefited big business. The removal of protection cost major companies tens of millions of dollars as they were forced to restructure their operations. In some cases businesses were forced to close once the protection of import barriers was taken away. A couple of years ago, in a debate on tariffs, businessman Alan Gibbs described his own experience of this:

> *I have been involved in manufacturing almost everything — stapling machines, forklift trucks, washing machines, refrigerators, crockery, TV sets, bricks and bras. Many of these businesses never made a contribution to the New Zealand economy. A typical example was the television assembly industry. We would go to Japan and explain to wide-eyed Japanese that our government wanted us to assemble their TV sets in New Zealand. They could hardly believe their ears. They said no one assembles Japanese TV sets. 'Do you have cheaper labour?' they asked. 'Make your own tubes? Transistors? Anything?'*
>
> *'No,' we said. 'We just have to make them in New Zealand; and because there are only a few of us permitted to do this, we make good money doing it.'*
>
> *After much time and explanation and shaking of heads, the Japanese finally agreed to sell us the bits to assemble*

their sets in New Zealand. However, they explained this was very costly. They were making tens of thousands of sets a day and we only wanted parts for a few thousand a year. At great cost they contracted outside people to come in, take assembled sets apart, sort out all the pieces we needed and put them in boxes. They got engineers to write out all the instructions in English for reassembly, and shipped them on their way. Naturally someone has to pay for this, and on average they charged us for the parts, as a special favour, 110 per cent of the price of the finished goods all boxed and ready to go to the retailer. We then opened a factory, imported much machinery, paid the highest wages in the neighbourhood, employed the most intelligent engineers to decipher the instructions, used a great deal of electricity, and finally produced a TV set with negative New Zealand content at twice the imported price . . .

New Zealand is not a rich enough society to waste our talents this way. We must do what we are good at and buy what others are better at.

Alan had also been involved in the late lamented Crown Lynn Pottery, and he considered the effects of tariffs there to be much more destructive, as New Zealand *should* be able to have a successful crockery industry:

Based on the infant industry theory and very talented lobbying, Crown Lynn was able to obtain protection for 70 per cent of the New Zealand crockery market. You would think that with this base of business we could build an industry that would be internationally competitive. Unfortunately, the more protection we obtained, the more we needed. The problem was that rather than concentrate on a few products and develop real skill and talent in depth, we tried to make the whole spectrum of crockery to supply that 70 per cent of the New Zealand market. We concentrated on the home market because it was easier and guaranteed. We made everything, but we were master of none.

By the time we had to stand on our own feet (having been an official infant industry for 45 years) we found we had dispersed our talents. In addition, under this protection regime, our management let their guard down and our unions were able to entrench totally uneconomic work practices . . . Protection destroyed Crown Lynn, and all those jobs. I believe New Zealand could have an internationally successful crockery industry, but only when someone is prepared to stand up to the world and build a team with the talent and desire to be winners in this huge, open, competitive market.

New Zealand's inefficiencies were not confined to a cosseted commercial sector. They abounded, and still do, in the social services. Every time there was an opportunity to reduce spending, the government found a new special need to keep staff in jobs. For example, when school rolls fell, we discovered special needs to keep teachers employed. Falling rolls were not seen as an opportunity but as a problem. The problem was surplus teachers, and it was solved by making more work without considering whether ministering to 'special needs' was the best use the teachers could be put to; and asking whose needs it was were special. At the same time, rising student numbers in the universities meant that more lecturers were needed, so the budget had to be increased there.

Inefficiencies in social services penalise workers and consumers just as much as those in the private sector. Workers are affected because they pay taxes that support the services. Inefficiencies mean they have to pay more to maintain a certain level of service. Meanwhile, consumers of social services suffer because the services are of poorer quality than they need be. Opportunities to improve them go begging as efficient practices are not found and acted on.

The pain of waking up to 40 years of mismanagement has been significant — financially, emotionally and intellectually. It has produced a nostalgia for an imperfectly understood past, and a group of politicians who promise to take us back there. What is needed to counter this nostalgia, wilful blindness and childlike dependency is a 20-year vision of the future, and regrettably there are no politicians in Parliament today who are producing one.

In the 'good old days' New Zealand was going nowhere. It was not just the economy that was stagnant; the dead hand of government lay over most aspects of life. The pubs shut at 6 pm and restaurants could not serve alcohol, except in the food. There was little choice of goods in shops, and what was available was overpriced and often of inferior quality. There were long waiting lists (up to two years) for new cars, and tight restrictions on taking money out of the country. People could buy minor goods from overseas, such as magazines or clothes, but it was a time-consuming process to purchase one NZ$2 postal note at a time until the required amount had been collected. The airlines were regulated and air travel prices were high. Ministry of Works road men up and down the country leaned on their shovels, and a Prime Minister of the day ordered a group of deaf-mute Japanese mountain climbers off Mt Cook because they didn't fit the government profile of who should climb mountains.

New Zealand has come a long way since 1984, but much remains to be done. Productivity is up, and wages, which have stagnated for so long, are starting to show limited improvement. The gain to consumers is there to be seen as competition brings more choice, lower prices and better quality. Once again there is the prospect that the next generation will be better off than the present one. But only if the reform programme proceeds. The Porter Project reported that 40 years of mismanagement had left problems so deep and grave that we literally have to build a new economy. Michael Porter warned that a period of intense discomfort still lies ahead if we are to escape falling to third-world status.

The central problem confronting New Zealand is the government's ongoing inability to control its spending. Politicians find it easier to spend rather than save money. Interest groups all plead for more money; none plead for cuts. Government expenditure has risen dramatically while the economy has stood still. It is now 39 per cent of GDP (in 1974/75 it was 28 per cent). Government not only takes in a huge and growing share of the economy's wealth, it also persistently spends more than it takes in. The result is continual deficits and growing debt. The deficit for 1992/93 is over $3 billion and government debt stands at 66 per cent of GDP. The debt represents over $14,000 for every man, woman and child. But that figure rises to more than $15,000 per head if contingent liabilities such as ACC underfunding are included. The inability to control government spending is the weak link in the reform programme.

DEBT'S DAMAGE TO NEW ZEALAND

The government's debt is the accumulation of government deficits and surpluses. Our debt to GDP ratio is the fourth highest in the OECD.

Figure 1: Debt trends — per cent of GDP, fiscal years (July to June).

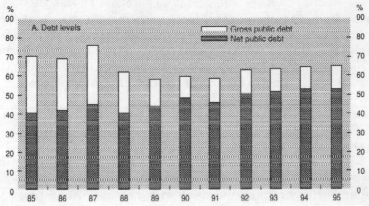

Source: New Zealand Treasury, *OECD Economic Surveys.*

Debt servicing in the year ended June 1992 cost the government $4415 million ($6814 million if you include foreign exchange losses). This is equivalent to 14 per cent of government expenditure or 16 per cent of government revenue. For every dollar taken in personal taxes, 29 cents is needed to service the debt. The cost of the debt to someone paying $10,000 in income tax is $2900 and the position is expected to get worse over the next few years.

New Zealand's present level of debt contributes to:

❐ High debt-servicing costs: at present more than $1 in every $7 of the government budget is being spent on debt servicing, which limits the government's ability to act in other areas.

31

❐ The current account deficit, since almost half of our debt is owed externally.

❐ The financial deficit, as debt must be serviced.

❐ Pressure on interest rates, caused by government borrowing requirements.

❐ Inflationary expectations.

High levels of public debt raise the risk premium that is part of all interest rates, thereby raising the cost of capital and discouraging investment, and so lessening international competitiveness for New Zealand businesses. The country is more vulnerable to external shocks such as a decline in terms of trade. Debt servicing crowds out other public and private expenditure. The servicing cost of $4.5 billion a year is a major expenditure item — greater than the total amount spent on health services. New Zealand should be aiming to reduce net public debt as a percentage of GDP to the average for OECD countries by the year 2000. In 1990, the average was 31 per cent, but as other OECD countries are aiming to reduce their net debt, the target figure is likely to be lower by 2000.

If New Zealand does not reduce its debt, its problems will remain and almost certainly worsen. The pressure to spend will continue and debt will increase. According to Treasury, the cost of servicing existing debt is forecast to rise over the next three years (1993–1996). In the 1992 Budget, the department noted that 'although a substantial amount of public foreign-currency debt has been retired as a result of asset sales in recent years, currency movements and other factors have tended to increase the level of public debt'.

The alternative, reducing the financial deficit and public debt, would bring permanent reductions in debt-servicing costs, improve the current account deficit, lower interest rates and diminish inflationary expectations. There would be attendant benefits:

❐ Reduced debt to GDP ratios would improve New Zealand's credit rating and lower interest rates.

❐ Lower interest rates would provide lower mortgage rates,

giving more people the chance to own their own home.

❐ A more favourable environment for investment and business competitiveness would create more jobs and raise real wages.

❐ The government would have greater flexibility in making expenditure decisions, particularly when debt servicing costs were permanently reduced.

There are three ways to correct the government's balance sheet — an increase in taxes, the reduction of government expenditure and the sale of some of the government's commercial assets which are not fulfilling any particular social purpose.

The costs to the economy of the first option — increased taxes — outweigh any apparent benefits. Taxes have already risen dramatically. In 1973/74, tax took 26 per cent of the national income. It rose to 30.7 per cent under the Muldoon Government and had reached 36 per cent by 1988. It had declined marginally by the year ending June 1992. If tax had stayed at the 1973/74 level, a family earning $30,000 would have $3000 more to spend. The loss of that $3000 represents lost jobs in shops, factories and service industries right across the country.

Tax is a net benefit to the community when the value the government delivers by spending our money exceeds the damage done in taking it. As tax levels increase, every extra dollar taken from the community begins to create a rising additional indirect cost. High tax rates bring problems of evasion, disincentives to work and increased collection costs. Overseas studies show that the marginal cost of raising an extra dollar of tax revenue is between $1.20 and $3. In addition, if tax rates rise there is a need to compensate those at the lower end of the income scale, leading to increased government expenditure.

The best approach to ridding the economy of deficits and debt is a combined programme of asset sales and a reduction in government expenditure. The latter is the most lasting in its effect. Asian countries, whose economies produce higher savings and investment ratios than New

Zealand's, generally keep their government expenditure below 30 per cent. In the last few years several countries have reduced their government spending as a proportion of GDP. Expenditure to GDP ratios for Japan, Germany, Austria, Belgium and Ireland in 1990 were below those recorded in 1979. Sweden is working to reduce its expenditure from 55 per cent to 40 per cent of GDP. New Zealand should be aiming to reduce its government expenditure to the early 1970's levels of 25 to 30 per cent of GDP no later than 1997. However, there can be much greater improvements in economic performance by reducing that level even further. This book shows how to reduce government expenditure and improve services at the same time.

The sale of government assets to date has had two purposes — to help pay off some of the debt and to prevent the accumulation of fresh debt. However, if government is running a deficit, the money from the sales will go to close that gap first. This is what has been happening in New Zealand's case: a lot of the money from earlier asset sales went to fund the deficit, not pay off debt. But if those assets had not been sold, today's debt would be even greater.

Even State-Owned Enterprises (SOEs) with their remarkable efficiency savings of 20 to 50 per cent have had occasion to call on government funds. Despite their success, SOEs are half-way houses, and local and overseas experience suggests the gains they have made in efficiency and productivity are not necessarily sustainable. First, fully commercial disciplines cannot be applied. Secondly, governments are always short of cash and cannot fund expansions. Governments will, however, bail out SOEs at taxpayers' expense, as has already happened. And there will always be enormous pressure on governments to interfere in businesses that operate in a politicised environment. These facts undermine the commitment of the commercial boards and managers of SOEs. Conflicting objectives are introduced, productivity falls and the organisation effectively returns to the way it operated as a government department.

Ultimately, privatisation is the only answer. In a 1992 study, the World Bank concluded that 'private ownership makes a difference. Some state-owned enterprises have been efficient and well managed for some periods, but government ownership seldom permits sustained good performance for more than a few years. There is a higher probability of efficient performance in private enterprise'. The private sector makes mistakes too but the pressures to correct them are greater. The reasons for better performance in a privatised SOE include capital market disciplines, the threat of takeover and bankruptcy, freedom from political interference, and the ability to develop a clear corporate strategy. Those incentives need to be backed up by a competitive business environment and appropriate regulation in a limited number of cases when monopoly problems may occur after privatisation.

Widespread fears about the effects of privatisation have proved groundless. Overall, prices have not gone up; in fact, in real terms they have gone down, and the gains from the earlier corporatisation have been consolidated. Government businesses which have been sold, such as Air New Zealand, Government Print, Telecom, the Rural Bank, and Petrocorp, are all giving a far better service to consumers. Nor have the gains been at the expense of overall employment across the whole economy. Overstaffing in the public sector has cost jobs elsewhere through excessive public sector charges, direct and indirect, that had to be paid by the private sector. Finally, many of the former SOEs were liabilities, not assets.

The government needs to separate its core functions from the public sector businesses which are there primarily to provide marketable goods and services. Privatisation of the latter would remove the confusion about roles and objectives. It would further ease the problem of debt and debt servicing costs at the same time as adding productive businesses to the economy.

In order to achieve the reduction in debt now needed, the government will have to run surpluses, and those surpluses should be accomplished without resorting to tax increases.

We need to build on what we have achieved to date and plough back the early rewards to reduce both unemployment and debt. Extra employment means major gains in equity and output; debt reduction brings economic security and future investment. If economic growth was boosted to and maintained at 4 per cent per year, the economy would grow by 50 per cent every decade.

It is plain that New Zealand's current debt and deficit levels cannot continue. It is also fairly obvious that something has to be done to reduce them, and that fiddling with $5000 here and $10,000 there is not enough. The debt now requires radical action. It is part of what is driving us to make the kind of reforms discussed in this book. But major reform, as I know well from personal experience, is one of the most difficult things for a government to achieve. Major change requires everyone to look to the long term. However, the pressures of political life too often produce political myopia.

3   Politics versus Change: A Case Study

By the time of the Cutting Room session that Friday afternoon, the issue was so superheated that I decided I had to invite Haig to my office beforehand in an effort to calm things down. But it was not a calm man who walked — stormed — into my office that day. It was General Haig, and he had come, in military parlance, to take names and kick ass.

'I am truly shocked by these leaks,' he began. I was momentarily speechless. The proposition that they had come from me was so preposterous that it worked. I let it drop because I couldn't bring myself to believe that he believed it himself.

Seeing that his opening salvo had produced the desired effect, he ordered a cease-fire. He then told me that while he was not unmindful of the need for budgetary 're straint', he and no one else was 'in charge of policy'. For the time being I could only wonder how he could so easily separate budgetary restraint from policy, inasmuch as the two are inextricably linked.

. . . I made some stiff remarks to the effect that the Reagan Revolution in economic policy couldn't just stop at the water's edge. I urged him to look into the can of worms his bureaucracy was rushing him into defending. But he never heard a word of it. In his mind, the whole issue had boiled down to what is known in Washington as a turf battle.

David Stockman, *The Triumph of Politics*

The party was conservative, the country the United States of America, but the story told has parallels in virtually every Western democracy. David Stockman was Ronald Reagan's Budget Director during Reagan's first four and a half years in the White House. He was one of the authors of the 'Reagan Revolution' — a revolution which, contrary to popular belief, Stockman says, never really took place. Among the reasons for its failure were the inability or refusal of the politicians to understand the basic laws of revenue and expenditure, and their unwillingness to change what they had said the Republicans wanted to change. Faced with the need for major spending cuts across the board, politicians from both houses (Congress and Senate) and both parties (Republican and Democrat) found reasons to plead that every department, every entitlement, every project, every State, was an exception. Once again, pork-barrel politics won the day. The exception, and the lobby group, ruled. Compromise and loss of nerve put even patently obvious areas to cut government spending off limits.

In this country, National and Labour politicians have succumbed to the same pressures, and misunderstood or ignored economic linkages in much the same way that David Stockman describes. My experience of this took place between late 1987 and the end of 1988. It was another version of what can happen to those involved in trying to effect real change which breaks the old game plans. There was one significant difference, however, between David Stockman, who was a one-term congressman with a seat on the Commerce Committee when he was made Budget Director, and myself, when I became Minister of Finance: I knew politics a lot better than he did. So perhaps I should have been better prepared for what happened.

Speaking notes for Cabinet:

Cabinet members agree that a financial deficit at the projected level of $3.2 billion would damage the economy and be politically fatal. But getting the deficit down is not the only critical issue of this Budget. How we get it down will make or break the economy in the period from now through to the election. We may seem to be debating nothing more than the choice between the convenience of raising additional revenue and the unpleasantness involved in cutting our expenditure. But within that financial question, like the kernel hidden in a nutshell, there is a choice of much more fundamental importance to the government, the economy and the people of New Zealand: Will the Budget deepen and extend the present recession past the limit of economic and political tolerance, or will it take us towards a sustainable recovery of economic growth and employment?

For us as a government, it is a life and death choice. We

cannot survive if we make decisions which ignore our opportunities to assist the economy and instead wilfully push it deeper into recession. In considering the choice so far, members have tended to focus almost all their attention on the cost to public sector employment and services if they take the expenditure-cutting route. These have to be taken into account, but they are less than half the picture. The recovery and our own political future are both at risk if we concentrate myopically on those costs alone. A still larger cost will be imposed on the private sector if we fail to adjust our spending.

That was not Ruth Richardson talking to her National Party Cabinet colleagues before the 1992 Budget. It was what I had to say to my Cabinet colleagues in the Labour Government prior to the 1988 Budget, when faced with a deficit similar to this year's (1993). That the fiscal problem still remains is the genesis for the policies outlined in this book. The fiscal situation (the gap between government expenditure and revenue) and what we should do about it, was at the heart of much of the dispute between Prime Minister David Lange and myself during late 1987 and the whole of 1988.

When I first brought the December 1987 tax and benefit package to Cabinet, the local financial markets were reeling from the collapse of the stock market. The financial and business sectors, and the public, were suffering a sudden loss of confidence in each other and in the economic situation generally. With things beginning to fall apart around them, they looked to the government to ascertain the strength of our economic credibility and to see whether we still had the resolve we had shown in our first three years in office. There was a perception that we had been coasting since the election in August 1987. It prompted questions about what we were going to do next, or whether we were going to do anything at all. I felt that it was important that we continued to promote policies which encouraged people to look ahead and keep investing. The first significant occasion on which the public, and the business sector in particular, would look for disunity or a loss of faith in our past policy decisions was the annual

Labour Party conference in November 1987. In the event, the party conference passed, giving the appearance (despite an attack on the government by the left wing of the party) of a unified team, headed by a Prime Minister who had confidence in his Cabinet colleagues and his government's policies.

Meanwhile, Cabinet was considering the traditional New Year announcement of economic intent: would bringing it forward help stabilise the economic situation, and what should it contain? Any economic package presented to Cabinet had to take into consideration more than the fall-out from the worldwide crash of financial markets, the loss of confidence and the desire for government to take a lead. We had a situation where nearly 40 per cent of New Zealand households with full-time salary and wage earners would be better off if they gave up their job in favour of the benefit and a little part-time work on the side. In terms of tax, households earning less than $30,000 a year — some 300,000 to 400,000 — faced marginal tax rates of between 48 per cent and as much as 100 per cent on each extra dollar earned. These problems had existed for years, but deserved and needed to be tackled immediately. The questions for Cabinet to consider were what policies would serve the country best under these circumstances and set us up for the future; whether those issues should be dealt with gradually or in a very obvious change; and when they should be announced?

Starting with the latter, I believed that it was essential we make an economic statement before the chief executives of the major companies and other business leaders and advisers broke for Christmas. During that period they reviewed their business plans for the coming year, talked to each other and collectively reached a view of the economy which would influence the attitude they took in 1988. If they knew what we were planning, they would know what they could do and needed to do. On this at least everyone was in agreement. The speed of implementation was more contentious. With the markets jittery and a general feeling that Labour's plan of reform had ground to a halt, the temptation was to ease in change over a period of five years or more with the hope of reducing the risks, political and economic.

Nevertheless, what I was looking for was a major change in incentives and behaviour. Bringing in the new policies over a lengthy period meant the incentives would be spread so thinly as to be almost invisible. If people were hardly aware of the changes, their response would be equally tentative. Without a dramatic shift in people's attitudes to production, saving, investment and spending, I believed we would face a fairly severe recession in the coming year.

However, it was the content of the package that provoked most resistance, and the way I had gone about designing it. Urgency caused me to neglect much of the inter-portfolio discussion which I normally ensured took place when we were considering major changes which involved several ministers and departments. Just as Congress and the Senate had complained that their roles in the budget process had been hijacked and that the President and David Stockman were expecting them to be no more than a 'rubber stamp', so some of my Cabinet colleagues felt I had trampled uninvited over their patches. They viewed the resulting policy proposals with some understandable resentment.

The tax and benefit package had three components. First, a 23 per cent flat personal income tax for everyone. Secondly, a practical insurance scheme in the form of a guaranteed weekly minimum income for those, with children, who worked full time. It would ensure they always ended up substantially in front of those who relied solely on the benefit, by a cash-in-hand margin of $70–80 a week. Thirdly, high-income earners would begin to pay more towards the cost of some government services, for example, health, and to pay for them directly. My intention was to cut out the middleman — government as tax gatherer and funding agency — and let high-income people use the extra money they had under the new tax rate to reimburse government service providers themselves.

After a rough start, the various ministers and

departments involved stopped grumbling and got down to work. We were on a tight schedule. Cabinet reached a collective decision on the package's content on 14 December. The policies were due to be announced three days later. The Prime Minister then expressed doubts about some aspects of the policy Cabinet had approved. At a meeting on 16 December, the day before the launch, certain elements which he was unhappy about announcing at that time were removed, to be released later. One resulting omission which I felt was particularly unfortunate was the level of the Guaranteed Minimum Family Income (GMFI). People would no longer be able to judge the real value of the package to low-income families, who are generally considered traditional Labour supporters, and for whom Labour is meant to have a special concern. More than once I suggested that if the PM was really unhappy about what we were proposing, it would be better to cancel the launch of the policy. Each time, he said that not only should we hold to the timetable, but that he intended to come back early from holiday to sell the policy. So, on 17 December, just before the House rose for the Christmas break, the package was duly announced.

At the beginning of January, David Lange returned to Wellington as he had said he would. But instead of promoting the policy, he began an extensive correspondence with me expressing doubts about the whole package. By the middle of the month he was asking me to join him in putting the entire programme on hold while we opened it to extensive public debate. I refused, and in any case, we had no mandate from Cabinet to overturn a Cabinet decision. Just before I left for an economic conference in Europe, he informed me that an analysis of the numbers in the package by a working party on income maintenance had cast doubts on the package's sustainability. I checked their calculations. Their analysis was defective, and I asked that no decisions be made until I got back from Europe in two weeks' time. I offered to arrange for some Treasury officers to talk to him and his staff and to go through the numbers with them. I would also go through the package with him again in detail on my return. The Prime Minister agreed but he didn't take up my offer of Treasury help. A week later, without warning me or anyone else in Cabinet, he called a press conference and cancelled the GMFI proposal and the nominal single tax rate.

It was an expensive decision in a number of ways. It cost low-income families up to $120 extra cash-in-hand a week; the media began a long-running soap about a government in disarray; and the public lost faith in the government's sense of purpose. They were also left with the distinct impression that Labour's economic policy, 'Rogernomics', was about benefiting the rich at the expense of the poor. There was little I could do to improve the situation when I got back. To have tried to do anything overtly, in a public sense, to patch things up would have made matters worse. We then devised a compromise. Instead of a 23 cent flat tax rate, we introduced a three-tier system with effective rates of 15 cents, 28 cents, and a top rate of 33 cents. If we had started where we ended up, then this would have looked like the next step in our programme of reform. After all, the top rate had been 48 cents. It was an improvement on the old system, but because of how we had arrived at it, all the politics surrounding it were negative. It looked like broken promises. And because they were a compromise, those rates caused some problems in other areas.

By June 1988, we were in the early stages of preparation for the Budget. Then, out of the blue, Treasury informed us that they had revised their initial forecast for the fiscal deficit, upwards. It was now $3.2 billion. The size of the new total came as a shock to everyone in Cabinet. They were in a mood to shoot the messenger; understandable but not useful. It was pointless to blame Treasury for the total. They had simply done the sums. We were the ones who were responsible for the deficit, and therein lay a great irony. The decisions we had taken in our first three years in government had meant that the once pervasive cost-plus mentality was no longer tolerated. Farms and firms had all had to become competitive and efficient, domestically and internationally, or go to the wall. We said that while we would help with the first wave of adjustment costs, we would not intervene thereafter to save them. We also promised the community that in squeezing out inflation and inefficiency we would be economically neutral. We would protect low-income people, but we would not play favourites. We would act in the interests of the nation as a whole.

However, the government's refusal to get public spending under control was not economically neutral. It was a form of intervention, and it hurt the general community, the private sector and local government. We *were* playing favourites, and it had cost us all. The savings made by the State-owned enterprises provided the evidence. The old Forest Service had lost $70 million cash in its last year operating as a government department; by 1988 it had the same production levels, a third of its former staff and it was turning in a profit of $40 million cash. Coal Corp mined the same amount of coal with half the staff and had just made its first profit in decades. The Airways Corporation had rethought their $200 million modernisation plan and found they could have a very satisfactory development for $130 million less. SOEs in general found avoidable waste of anywhere from 20 per cent to 50 per cent in the old government departments.

In the rest of the public sector, costs were rising faster than inflation. Net defence spending (the bane of David Stockman's life) had been $660 million in 1983–84; by 1988 it was projected to reach $1478 million unless something was done. Non-benefit spending by Social Welfare had more than doubled in four years from $257 million to $545 million. Maori Affairs spending had risen by 200 per cent in two years from $61.5 million in 1986–87 to $186 million. If Maori Access was excluded, the increase was still 100 per cent. There was more, much more. If some private sector lobby group intent on protecting its own interests, had made demands on government that increased the financial strain on sectors already under pressure and unprotected, we would have told them to get lost. Yet here we were, sitting round the Cabinet table, and we were the lobby group. Cabinet ministers and their departments convinced themselves that when they indulged in cost-plus behaviour it was somehow socially, economically and politically desirable. What we had required of the private sector, we were not prepared to apply to our own departments.

A Labour government in particular finds it hard to face the fact that public sector waste hurts low-income people most of all. It obviously reduces the resources available for them. It also reduces the number of jobs the economy should be able to offer them. To take an extra $1 from the private sector and put it into the public sector costs more than $1 — something between $1.20 and $3. Those extra cents are known as 'dead weight loss'. Total income in the economy is reduced. Then, unless the money is used in the public sector at least as productively as it would have been in the private sector, its effectiveness is decreased further. And when low-income workers are pushed into unemployment, the perversity of the benefit structure deprives many of them of the financial incentive to move off the benefit and back into the workforce when they have the chance. That increases the fiscal problem too.

With Treasury's new forecast before us, I believed we needed to make some major cuts in public spending. The issue at this point was not about whether the State should be a big or small player in the economy. It was about even-handedness. I suggested that if Cabinet accepted an appropriate base figure to aim for, then how and where ministers went about making cuts within their own portfolios was less important to me provided they were sound from a medium-term perspective. The most important point was that if we didn't address the deficit this time, in this Budget, then the economy and the public would be very unforgiving.

While various ministers were mulling over options, the six most senior members of Cabinet met privately to discuss the new deficit numbers. We worked through a very broad range of possibilities. David Lange and I both had proposals on how the deficit should be tackled. First of all the Prime Minister wanted us to place the blame on Treasury, to obscure the size of our over-spending by drawing attention to the size of Treasury's forecasting error. He wanted a public enquiry. The rest of us disagreed. He also proposed tax increases, including a 5 per cent increase in company tax, a 5 per cent increase on the top personal tax rate, a 1 per cent increase in the main tax rate on the majority of the population, and the raising of GST to 12.5 per cent. The tax increases were rejected, too, although a couple of his other proposals were picked up. I had taken a large number of options to the meeting and saw some of them bite the dust. In the end, however, we decided to follow my overall line to cut expenditure.

The proposal went to Cabinet and the expenditure paper was approved. The Prime Minister said hardly a word during the discussion. There were still a couple of matters to settle on the revenue side — whether we had some indirect tax increases and user-pay charges which would pull in another $100 million; but basically, by the time Cabinet finished, we had fixed the fiscal problem for that year. The revenue questions were left to the Cabinet Policy Committee (CPC) on the Wednesday following Cabinet. The CPC meeting began one and a half hours early with David Lange circulating the same proposals that he had taken to the senior ministers' private meeting — a public inquiry into Treasury's mistake and his increases in taxation. Some people at CPC had not seen the paper before this as it had never been to Cabinet. CPC rejected the paper outright and asked that all copies be withdrawn from circulation. It was not an official Cabinet paper and they wanted to avert the danger of it leaking into circulation. They thought that additional taxes on a community and business sector already hard-pressed would only make adjustment more difficult and painful. Cabinet had already made its decision to reduce the deficit as far as possible by cutting waste and expenditure that brought little benefit to the community.

We were the people who time and time again, department by department, had authorised spending increases which in many cases amounted to twice the rate of inflation. We were the people who had increased total taxation by $3 billion in real terms on 1983–84 levels and pushed up tax by more than 6 per cent of GDP in four years (tax revenue went from 30.4 per cent of GDP in 1983–84 to 36.8 per cent of GDP in 1988). While it was mainly needed to close the fiscal deficit we inherited, it was also required to fund those real increases in government expenditure. The money had been taken from the private sector, and the companies, enterprises and individuals from whom we had taken those extra funds had been forced to cut back on their own activities to an extent that was the equivalent of 6 per cent of GDP. If we took the tax option promoted by the Prime Minister, we would then be moving no less than 9.2 per cent of New Zealand's total gross domestic product from the private sector to the public sector. We would be asking thousands of private sector businesses, large and small, to lay off their staff because we weren't prepared to make cuts in our own.

Over the period between the private meeting of senior ministers and the CPC meeting in late June, I argued that how you get the deficit down is just as important economically, socially and politically, as by how much. Had we not acted, our net expenditure was expected to rise by 13 per cent from $24.4 billion to $27.6 billion, twice the rate inflation was running at that time. We had been going to take an extra $3.1 billion from our GDP. The total increase in the gross domestic product for that year in nominal terms was only $3.3 billion. No less than 96 per cent of the increase in national income would have been diverted through higher taxes or increased borrowing to cover government spending. That would have left only 4 per cent — $0.139 billion — available to the whole private sector of the New Zealand economy, a reduction in real terms.

Trimming government expenditure was essential. David Lange had quite correctly pointed out that our reductions in spending would not be cost free. They would inevitably involve some public sector redundancies. But the case

against losing jobs in the public sector because
unemployment was already too high could not be made. For
every unproductive public sector job saved in an economy
at a fragile point in its adjustment, more than one job
would be lost in the private sector. There was no way we
could expect to win the election in 1990 with this
combination of high-tax and high-spending policies.

Despite Cabinet and CPC decisions, the Prime Minister
and his office were not convinced. They planned a public
statement along the lines that Treasury had bungled the
fiscal estimates, I was partly to blame and as a result the
possibility of my resigning could not be ruled out. The plan
was then leaked to TVNZ's late news programme. Next the
Prime Minister sought an urgent speaking engagement at
the Wellington Press Club, where he intended to talk about
the $3.2 billion deficit and the government's determination
to keep it in check. To keep on talking about a deficit of
$3.2 billion when Cabinet and the CPC had already okayed
the spending cuts which would bring it down to $1.2 billion
was senseless. It was likely to damage confidence.

I finally managed to see the Press Club speech on the
morning it was to be given, as it was being prepared for
distribution to the media. I found that none of my or the
Secretary of Treasury's advice had been taken. As well as
frequent references to a $3.2 billion deficit, it also talked
about the need for more revenue. The decisions we had
already taken to bring the problem under control were
barely mentioned. All I was able to do at this stage was
make a few technical corrections. I warned the Prime
Minister's office that our still weak financial markets were
likely to be alarmed and react accordingly. If they started
wobbling, I told them I would have little option but to take
whatever action I thought appropriate.

The inevitable happened. I faxed a detailed statement to
the markets late that night in an effort to clear up some of
their confusion. Unfortunately, as relations between David
Lange and myself deteriorated, this action was represented
as an attack on the Prime Minister after I had agreed to
the contents of his speech. Any stabilising effect my

statement to the markets might have had was soon undone with this new story running in the media.

The Labour Party conference in September 1988 presented the party and the public with a united front again. The Prime Minister publicly endorsed what the government and its ministers had done up until then. But behind the scenes things were far from cohesive. In a major speech given the previous week in Australia, the PM had announced that the pace of change was now slowing down. In his words, it was time for a cup of tea. His statement caused intense speculation about the direction of our economic policy and just how firm my grip was on the Finance portfolio.

On his return, the Prime Minister told me he could not work with me any longer. One of us would have to go. I did not feel I could voluntarily step down. I talked with the Deputy Prime Minister and three other senior Cabinet ministers, and we agreed not to take the matter before Cabinet on the week of the party conference, in case it cast a cloud over that event. Instead we would, if possible, formulate recommendations for the post-conference Cabinet meeting. But early on 29 August David Lange handed me a letter asking me to resign as Minister of Finance. The matter was not discussed at Cabinet that morning but it was raised, as agreed, at the meeting immediately after the party conference. Cabinet indicated by an overwhelming majority that I should retain my portfolio. Despite this, the Prime Minister persisted. After complicated negotiations that night, I retained Finance, assisted by David Caygill and Mike Moore.

There was no way to hide the battle and bleeding that had taken place. The greatest casualty, however, was the economy. The future direction of our economic policies was left in doubt for the business community and the public. When Richard Prebble, one of my staunchest allies, was sacked from Cabinet it became obvious to me that the Prime Minister was more interested in his personal vendetta with his Finance Minister than he was about the damage being done to the country. I realised the issue would need to be brought to a head at some time. What follows is my review to Cabinet, after Richard's departure, of the crucial issues controlling the fate of the fourth Labour Government.

The issue of how best to manage the business sales programme has been raised. That is a relatively minor matter which decides itself almost automatically by due Cabinet process. The issue has also been raised of whether Richard should have been sacked from his SOE portfolio, or whether he should have gone quietly, as he offered to. These questions are past history. The deed and the damage have already been done. Our job in Cabinet and Caucus is to solve the problems of the future. New Zealand's future depends on us winning in 1990. Our track record as a government in the past year has been pathetic. The opinion polls reflect that. Nobody knows any more what we are doing or where we are going. Worse than that, we don't know ourselves. We cannot rely from one month to another on what the government is doing, or what it may do next. We have no more certainty than the public.

The problem does not originate in either Cabinet or Caucus. The Cabinet has a reliable decision-making process which is endorsed by Caucus. The problem arises because on a substantial and growing number of occasions, the Prime Minister has unexpectedly overturned decisions or announced his own policies as fait accompli. He has done so without seeking public service advice and without consulting or advising Cabinet or Caucus. Indeed, without advising even Geoff Palmer [Deputy Prime Minister]. As Ministers, we seem to find ourselves at the mercy of an agenda which has never been laid out before us or the country and to which, as a Cabinet, we have never given collective agreement.

For a year we have responded by loyally defending decisions and positions which in fact threw us and the country into confusion. What loyalty did we get back in return? Our professional integrity has been placed on the line time after time, defending decisions we had no hand in making. The consequences are self-evident. It is impossible for us to adopt and put into action consistent policies, or to keep the confidence and approval of the general community. We are seen as being ceaselessly at war with each other. Cabinet is never given the chance to resolve any of these matters. We are left without even the chance to paper over the cracks.

What is the problem? Does the Prime Minister not believe

in the Cabinet process? Does he automatically take it for granted that he has a monopoly of wisdom in cases of disagreement? Has he some difficulty in allowing other people to review the quality of his case? Can he not bear the idea of losing? On two occasions recently he changed agreed policy without warning because he said the issues were stopping him from sleeping. Could he not have talked about it to us in Cabinet? It is no longer a matter of personalities to raise these issues. They have become crucial to the fate of this government and its policies. If we cannot, as a Cabinet, develop, promote and implement consistent, reliable and predictable policies, the recovery is dead in the water, and so are we as a government.

I may as well have saved my breath. By then Cabinet was mesmerised by the question, 'What happens to us if David Lange goes?' Yet Cabinet had not been the first to ask the question. The Prime Minister was repeatedly raising the issue of his leadership, by his actions and his words. The previous Saturday, at a press conference after the sacking of Richard Prebble, he told the media he believed the government had no answer to the question, 'Who's next as leader?' I believed the real question had become, 'What happens to us if David Lange stays?' After the events of the previous 12 months I was convinced that the Prime Minister didn't really care what happened to the economy. He was prepared to sink the ship in what he had come to see as a turf war between himself as Prime Minister and me as Minister of Finance.

Cabinet was paralysed. The year's hostilities and uncertainties had sapped their energy. They didn't want to lose me but they could not imagine the government without Lange as PM. If we both stayed, there was no way for things to get better. The effects on the country would be entirely negative. In the end I could see no option but to leave Cabinet. There was a chance that a more united government would calm some of the public's doubts about our competence.

Unfortunately, the doubt and loss of confidence remained after I relinquished the Finance portfolio. It was knocked again when Lange got his way and GST was

increased from 10 per cent to 12.5 per cent, as he had
proposed in 1988; particularly because there was largely no
off-set for the most vulnerable in society, which Labour
governments had always ensured in the past. Nor did it
improve when he stepped down as Prime Minister six
months later. National's victory in the 1990 election
changed that for a period. Confidence stretched and
expanded. But in their second year in office they too began
to be perceived as split and uncertain of their economic
direction. By 1993 people talked openly about who had the
upper hand, which faction was in the ascendancy, who was
winning. The turf battles continue.

Since my earliest years in Parliament, I had been
interested in reforming the government expenditure, tax
and benefit systems. It was not until 1984 that I had the
chance to influence them substantially, and my interest in
government expenditure and revenue did not cease in 1988.
It became an item of unfinished business. In the
intervening years I have had time to think about a whole
range of interconnecting issues that impact on the
government as taxer and spender. Those issues include
what a government should do and should not do — its role;
how a government collects the revenue it wants; the
incentives it creates on the way; the best way for
government to assist the disadvantaged without
patronising them; the search for personal responsibility
and the creation of opportunity. Those are the real issues,
not the power and personality wars which so often obscure
and overtake them. But the politics cannot be ignored. Part
of the art of major government reform in a democracy is to
make those changes politically practicable. That is what I
have attempted to do in the chapters that follow.

4   Care and Responsibility

Fifty years ago we recognised that there were people among us who needed extra help and made a decision, as a nation, that those needs should be met. Even if we have a perfect economic system, there will still be some who fall out of it for a variety of reasons and for varying periods of time. At the end of the 1930s we established a welfare system to act both as a safety net and a base from which people could re-enter productive society. Part of that system was a number of institutions whose role was to act as conduits for aid given by the community, through the Government, to those who were in need. But something has gone terribly wrong with the system, and the institutions, as society has changed around them.

Roger Douglas, *Toward Prosperity, 1987*

The welfare system established in New Zealand at the end of the 1930s inevitably involved the government's tax, expenditure and benefit systems. As time passed, government expenditure expanded far beyond anything envisaged in the thirties, and the tax and benefit systems became expensive, convoluted, burdensome and wasteful. They no longer were fair or equitable. Decades of fiddling around the edges simply created greater anomalies and more problems. By the late twentieth century, the most disturbing question about social welfare and the poor and disadvantaged was not how much it cost but what it had bought. Reform was long overdue when Labour took office in 1984. A much broader, more radical approach was needed — one which took account of the connections between the two systems and the way they influenced people's behaviour. It had to be an approach that kept the balance between efficiency gains and equity considerations and avoided poverty traps as much as possible. Any reform also had to recognise that New Zealand is operating in a world market for products, skilled people and business investment. The 1985 and 1988 tax-benefit reforms were a move in that direction, but there is still a long way to go.

To achieve the right kind of system requires an uncomfortably honest look at the present system — why we agree to help some people, what we want to accomplish, and the constraints on how we 'help' people. American social scientist Charles Murray has said of the social programmes instituted under the 'new wisdom' of the 1960s that they were not just a 'blunder on purely pragmatic grounds' but also wrong on moral grounds, no matter how noble the intentions have been:

> . . . It was wrong to take from the most industrious, most respectable poor — take safety, education, justice, status — so that we could cater to the least industrious, least responsible poor. It was wrong to impose rules that made it rational for adolescents to behave in ways that destroyed their futures. The changes we made were not just policy errors, not just inexpedient, but unjust. The injustice of the policies was compounded by the almost complete immunity of the élite from the price they demanded of the poor.

Murray's argument is that the fault of today's social welfare programmes is strategic; that social policy helps set the rules of the game — 'the stakes, the risks, the payoffs, the tradeoffs, and the strategies for making a living, raising a family, having fun, defining what "winning" and "success" mean'. He maintains that although governments and the general population think of social welfare as an economic transfer from the haves to the have-nots, an alarming number of non-economic transfers are from poor to poor. When poor, young offenders are put on probation, the people left most at risk are the poor in their neighbourhood. When job-training programmes are set at the level of the least competent, they take away from the most competent trainees the opportunity to reach their potential. When social policy ranks some jobs as too menial to ask anyone to do, those who prefer to do that work rather than go on welfare have their basis for self-respect taken from them.

If taxpayers are to agree to economic transfers (benefits), Murray considers that they can legitimately ask of the government doing the redistribution that it be right — that the taxpayer's resources are large enough overall and the recipient's too small; and that the transfer is successful — that it has the desired effect. But he warns that governments and general society need to remember two factors. First, by their nature, transfers are treacherous. They can be needed, useful and justified, but they should be approached like a dangerous drug — not to be used at all if possible and no more than necessary otherwise. Secondly, compulsory transfers between one poor person and another are, as a general rule, uncomfortably like robbery. When a government takes money from the very rich to give it to the very poor there is room for error. With non-economic transfers from poor to poor there is no margin for error at all.

Social policy's purpose is not to salve consciences at the expense of those society wishes to help. The defence of 'good intentions' is no longer credible. A fundamental rethink of social policy is needed. Personal and family responsibility and support should be placed first once more. The focus needs to shift from the State as the chief, and sometimes only, means of help to that of the safety net when all else has failed. Too many years of the State attempting to take care of every problem, every situation, eventually weakens an individual's sense of responsibility — first for fellow members of society, then for relatives and family, and finally even for him or herself. If the State has been taking a substantial portion of each person's income to fund its role as universal caretaker, then people begin to feel they've done their bit and that all care and responsibility now lie with the government/State. The ultimate effect is a less-caring society. The overriding question of all social policy must be: Under what conditions can we reasonably expect a welfare transfer to accomplish more good than harm? The answer directly affects any reform of the tax-benefit system.

This chapter deals with government income and

55

expenditure, particularly in areas (such as housing, defence, social welfare and labour) not covered in other parts of the book. New Zealand should not be clinging to systems which can still be improved dramatically through tax policies which channel savings into productive investment and assistance measures which help those who really require it — low-income families. We need a tax-benefit system which guarantees a decent standard of living without sending out the wrong signals which discourage work and encourage dependency. No other worthwhile reform is possible unless those disadvantaged through no fault of their own are adequately cared for and have the opportunity to move to self-help.

At the heart of my proposals is a greatly enhanced Guaranteed Minimum Family Income (GMFI). Right from the outset this will be accompanied by a two-tier, personal income tax system designed to strengthen the incentives to earn and to invest while removing the financial load that high marginal tax rates impose on low-income groups. Families with children at school will be given a substantial tax-free income allowance before they are required to pay any tax at all: a basic $32,000 for families with one child at school, and $10,000 for each additional child at school. For those families whose income falls below these levels, a cash grant (voucher) of $1 for every $3 shortfall in their income will be provided for educational purposes. This will ensure that low-income families are immediately better off, not only in dollar terms but in the choices available to them in, for example, health and education.

These measures, together with the GMFI and associated health, superannuation and education reforms, will be real steps to ensuring fairness. The aim is to put the underprivileged in the same position as anyone else as far as is possible. You can give people $1000 a week but that won't make them feel good about themselves. Any form of assistance must leave them with their dignity intact. It should still allow them to make the sorts of choices available to those around them: to save for their retirement, to have access to good health care and to choose the sort of education they want for their children. To that end, the following are needed:

1. Improved targeting of health, education, housing and welfare benefits so that limited resources are directed to those who really need them instead of helping those who can take care of themselves.

2. Major changes to superannuation policy which, while providing an improved minimum income in retirement, will enable virtually all New Zealanders to provide for themselves.

3. Government surpluses and on-going asset sales to enable New Zealand to solve its debt problem and stop debt draining our economy as it does at present.

4. A programme of tax reform which gives individuals and companies the maximum incentive to earn and invest while shouldering their fair share of any remaining government expenditure and debt commitments.

5. Continuing public sector reform, so that costs are restrained and government departments listen to their ultimate owner — the public.

6. Easier entry to occupations so that social mobility is improved and consumers get better value and more choice.

7. Continuing deregulation so that sectors within the economy are unable to protect their interests at the consumers' expense.

8. Continuing *tariff reform* so that ordinary consumers are able to buy the products of their choice, and so that viable New Zealand industry can stand on its own feet.

All these measures are constructed to work together to achieve the major social objectives. At the same time they would restore many New Zealanders' confidence in our social and economic future. Each of the measures is outlined below, together with the problems they are designed to solve and the projected effect of their implementation.

TAX-BENEFIT AND INCOME-SUPPORT REFORMS
The most urgent priority facing New Zealand and many

other countries is to encourage the creation of jobs and to encourage people to take jobs. In simple terms, we have to make it worthwhile for people to work and to invest. This is also one of the primary objectives of our income tax and income support systems: to redistribute income fairly and efficiently in a way that provides everyone with an adequate income; and to protect the most disadvantaged while at the same time preserving incentives to work and to achieve for those who are able to do so.

In practice, however, the present structures do not meet these objectives. In many ways they have the opposite effect. The 1985 and 1988 reforms of New Zealand's taxation and benefit structures were major steps towards strengthening incentives, improving the system's fairness and efficiency and making the two parts work better together. The system had evolved over the years in an *ad hoc* manner with little regard to whether or not it worked to achieve its original objectives. The existing system, while vastly improved, still destroys the incentive to work and fails to tax or redistribute fairly. It still gives privileges to some while robbing others of their independence and initiative. In some cases the assistance is simply not effective in meeting the needs of those who receive it; in many it is not efficiently delivered. The reforms proposed here, in promoting both fairness and incentives, will effectively solve most of our remaining problems.

Personal Income Tax

What is wrong with the present regime? Our income tax system, while substantially better than it was eight years ago, does not spread the tax burden as well as it could according to people's ability to pay. The top rate of 33 per cent now applies to all incomes from a level just above the average wage. Too many low-income tax payers, particularly families, face high marginal tax rates. The last dollar of a person's income is taxed much more heavily than the first; yet the last dollar is the discretionary dollar. A tax dollar extracted from the last dollar of income is more costly than a dollar raised from initial income because of

the impact it has on people's decisions and behaviour —
how much they work, earn and save, how and where they
invest, and how much effort they put into evading tax. In
the end, we cannot be sure that higher tax rates raise more
revenue. The following examples illustrate some of the
problems:

❒ Why do we insist on taxing middle-income people
heavily, only to give their money back to them in some
way? Wouldn't it be better to dramatically reduce taxes for
these people and let them buy the services they need
directly, e.g., education and health. This would allow
government to concentrate on those who need help.

❒ Where is the incentive for a low-income earner to move
up the income scale? A worker supporting a spouse and one
child, and getting family support and housing assistance,
can face an effective marginal tax rate of more than 70
cents in the dollar. High marginal tax rates destroy
people's incentive to work overtime or to take higher-
paying jobs with more responsibility.

❒ Wage and salary earners lose on every count. Although
they are automatically caught by PAYE, other groups may
pay little or no tax because they can arrange their affairs to
avoid it, either through the cash economy or through some
of the remaining loopholes open to big business and top-
bracket income earners.

❒ High-income earners can also reduce their tax bill
through family trusts or income splitting.

Any reforms should have as their goals the efficient
collection of taxes with the least interference in people's
lives, a fairer system, and the encouragement of productive
jobs and economic growth. To those ends I propose:

❒ No personal income tax for families with children, up to
certain specified income limits (see Annex 1 — Family
Assistance: Education, at the end of this chapter). The size
of the tax-free income allowance (TFIA) will depend on the
number of children at school. Any income above the TFIA
will be subject (in the year earned) to tax, at the highest
rate of personal tax for that year.

❏ A top rate of personal income tax of 28 cents in the dollar. This rate will decline to nil as other measures to save government expenditure take effect.

❏ An increase in the level of personal income to be taxed at 15 cents in the dollar from $9500 a year to $12,000 a year, equal to a tax reduction of $325 a year, to compensate taxpayers without children for the cost of their personal health-care cover.

❏ A family grant for part-time workers who do not qualify for the Guaranteed Minimum Family Income (GMFI) and do not receive any government means-tested benefits, to ensure that those people are not adversely affected when compared to those whose main income is from means-tested benefits.

The effect of lowering, then flattening and finally eliminating the personal and company tax rates will be dramatic. It will radically improve people's incentives to work, spend, save, invest and innovate, and in the process generate jobs and growth. Confidence in the economy will be greatly improved.

The tax changes will be complemented by an income-maintenance scheme. Together they will meet the objectives which our present tax-benefit system fails to achieve. The accompanying income-maintenance measures will have the effect of making the lower half of the income-tax scale progressive and the upper half of the scale proportional. Some people will clearly gain less initially than others. But in any reform of this magnitude it is incredibly important that people weigh up the long-term benefits for themselves and the country as a whole. No one's income situation is static. People's ability to support themselves varies during their lives. Nevertheless, there is a basic pattern: lower income and expenses to begin with, a period of high earnings and higher expenses during the child-rearing years, and finally reduced income and outgoings in retirement. Those who will not gain immediately from the proposed changes will still benefit at a later stage as their income situation changes. Any assistance needs to take this pattern into account rather than attempting to target all low, taxable income. Low income alone is not the best guide to need. People will have a low taxable income for a variety of reasons. The proposals in this book take those factors into account.

The tax-benefit and income-support reforms, with the other changes proposed, will give New Zealand a fiscal surplus within three years. This will be possible largely through the elimination of poorly targeted government assistance.

Margins Between Beneficiaries and Workers

The present tax-benefit system actively discourages beneficiaries from working. It fails to reward those who make the effort to move off assistance and return to the workforce. Inadequate margins between what beneficiaries receive and what they could earn act as barriers to those who might otherwise be able to find work. They trap people in poverty and State dependence. If people do help themselves, they risk being further disadvantaged: in many cases those who work earn less than people who remain on benefits. A large number of full-time wage and salary households earn less than the gross equivalent of the benefit paid to a household with two adults and a child with additional earnings of $60 a week. This situation is grossly unfair. The incentives in the system encourage people to go on to a benefit and stay there. The result is disastrous, both socially and economically.

To turn this situation around, we need a system that makes people want to get a job, puts those in employment ahead financially and ensures that the advantages of working are maintained. This requires:

❐ A Guaranteed Minimum Family Income (see Annex 1 — Family Assistance, for full details) significantly higher than the present GMFI for families with a full-time wage earner. It will ensure a minimum disposable weekly income of $380 for a couple with one child, $390 if both adults work, and $340 for a full-time working solo parent with one child. These levels are increased by $25 per week for each additional child.

❒ An end to the present family support system. It will be replaced by the new GMFI.

❒ The GMFI to be indexed to movements in the wage rate and any increases made annually.

❒ GMFI payments to go to the non-earning or lower-income partner in a two-adult household.

❒ The introduction of a GMFI for single people working full time:

Age 18–24	$170 a week
Age 25 and over	$190 a week
Married couple	$290 a week

❒ An abatement rate (IRD special tax rate to replace existing tax rates) of 50 cents in the dollar up to $200 of earned income, thereafter 92 cents in the dollar for those still receiving benefits.

The implementation of all these measures will give clear margins of $50 to $80 a week between households who rely on earnings from employment and those who rely entirely on benefits. There will be strong incentives for people on the fringes of the workforce to move into full-time employment and to remain in work rather than fall back on government assistance. This means a significant reduction in dependency traps while those who really need help will receive much more through GMFI.

However, if these measures are adopted, there will have to be fairness in other parts of the economic system. In the past 20 years, the cash economy of New Zealand and many other countries has grown enormously. It has been another way to avoid paying high income tax. For instance, household spending figures in 1983–84 revealed a surprisingly large number of people whose weekly expenses were two or three times more than the low income they said they were earning, and they were not heavily in debt. The introduction of the Goods and Services Tax (GST) exposed a lot of previously undeclared income but more recently the problem has started growing again, with the increase in weekend markets and tradespeople doing jobs for cash. It is difficult to police this practice through the person earning the undeclared income. Some responsibility has to be put back on to the people who are paying the tradesperson or organising the weekend markets.

One possibility is a withholding system, where someone employing a tradesperson, for example, withholds tax from their payment if the tradesperson does not give his or her GST number. For those who continue to deal in cash without following correct procedures there will have to be stiff penalties, on both parties to the transaction. Benefit fraud will be minimised by making all benefit payments through the Inland Revenue Department, with Social Welfare acting only as the approval agent.

An Effective, Efficient Assistance System
It is essential that assistance is given to those who need it in the most effective and efficient way. Not to do so is to waste money at a time when we cannot afford it, and provide those we want to help with less than we could. Some of our present structures are far from efficient or effective, even though effectiveness is certainly one of their objectives. There are four areas where reform is particularly needed — health, education, superannuation and housing assistance.

Health
New Zealand's present system of providing primary health care in particular, but also secondary care, is discriminatory, inconsistent and heavily biased in favour of certain forms of treatment. The people who most need care are often those with least access to it. At present, the well off pay little more for basic medical care than those who can least afford it. Because the government subsidises everyone's medical expenses, those who really cannot afford medical care are not receiving enough help.

The present system is still heavily weighted in favour of the use of prescription drugs and other specifically subsidised forms of treatment. Drugs, for example, are still very heavily subsidised, but no subsidies are given for other forms of care, particularly health maintenance. Those who practise preventive medicine, who promote ways to maintain good health rather than just treating illness, are shut out of the system. In addition to this, the present structure and a range of regulations severely limit the ability of many health professionals such as pharmacists and nurses to provide competitive health care.

We need a system that doesn't discriminate between different forms of assistance and different health providers. It must place fewer restrictions on those who can provide care. The system described in Chapter 6 would remove the discrimination and restrictions and help the disadvantaged and those who are shut out of the present system. At the same time it would reduce the government's direct outlay for health care by more than 50 per cent in Year 1 and, over 25 years, cut it back to virtually zero.

Superannuation
National Superannuation, once called guaranteed retirement income, is the government's largest expenditure programme. The estimated net cost for 1991/92 was $4387 million. This represents 33 cents of every dollar of personal tax revenue collected. The number of people reaching the age of retirement each year is at present around 13,000. This will reach 25,000 in the year 2001 (65 being the retirement age from 2001 onward). The number will climb to just short of 50,000 by the year 2020. As a result, the number of retired people in relation to the number of people in the workforce will increase steadily. Under current policy, the percentage cost of National Superannuation when compared to the total personal income tax take (currently calculated at $1 in three by the Minister of Finance) will continue to climb unless tax rates are increased or something is done to stem the cost, such as reducing pension levels. The cost of superannuation has been a major factor in successive governments' inability to balance the budget.

Chapter 7 looks at what New Zealand should do about

superannuation. It describes how we can reduce its cost to government by around 70 per cent over a 30-year period and at the same time ensure that people in retirement are better off than they are today.

Education
Two of the traditional reasons put forward for the government being involved in providing or arranging the provision of education are that:

❐ Education is a public good of such merit that the government should ensure people have access to it, and
❐ Government involvement is a means of ensuring that the poor can afford education, thereby reducing social inequality.

However, despite government being the major provider of education as well as its funder, there are a number of problems with the present policy. Financing the education of virtually all children by first taxing parents to raise the money and then giving the money back as subsidies that pay for their children's schooling, makes little sense and has negative effects on work incentives. Similarly, government financial support of all students (and the elderly and unemployed) discourages many families from investing time and money in their children's values and training because parents and children do not depend as much on each other.

Another problem with the present policy concerns the efficient use of educational resources. Resources are not directed to those areas of education which return most to the community because there are no signals, financial or otherwise, that indicate consumer demand. Educational organisations do not have to satisfy those who use them in order to get funding, so there is relatively little incentive to respond to parents' and students' needs. The mismatch between school-leavers' skills and the demands of the labour market reflect these underlying problems — problems which are caused in large part by government having a virtual monopoly in education.

There are also few incentives to minimise costs. In addition, government involvement is failing in its second *raison d'être* — social equality. It is apparent that middle- and upper-income groups are more likely to succeed educationally than those from lower-income groups. This raises the question of just how effective education has been as a vehicle for ensuring equal opportunities.

Chapter 5 outlines what New Zealand should do to guarantee that education is available to everyone, and that it provides what people want and need. It shows how we can reduce direct government outlays immediately by more than 75 per cent and yet ensure that educational results are improved dramatically, especially for low-income disadvantaged children and those with disabilities.

Housing

The private sector has made few serious forays into the market for low-cost rental houses because Housing New Zealand dominates this sector. The result has been a limited choice of accommodation and excessively high rents in private rental housing. While the provision of an accommodation benefit, with the GMFI and tax measures, will make affordable housing available to most people, there will always be a need for special assistance to help the disadvantaged or those who suffer a sudden change in circumstances and need rehousing.

Housing Corporation assistance tends to continue to go to households even after they are no longer on a low income, even though households in greater need are not receiving adequate assistance. This situation can be improved by community and local special needs housing assistance. The devolvement of some State houses to community groups will improve housing assistance for the disadvantaged and groups with special needs, for example, the disabled, the aged, half-way houses and emergency housing. Up to 15,000 houses will be passed to community groups over a period of time. It will create a housing pool that can be managed by those closest to and therefore best able to solve housing problems. If this were done, the remaining Housing Corporation pool could be sold for private rentals or ownership.

In summary, the above measures to reduce, flatten and finally eliminate personal income tax, to reform income-support systems and to substantially improve education, health and superannuation are the central part of my proposals. Other complementary measures will be required to achieve a fairer and more secure economy.

Indirect Taxes
The introduction of GST in 1986 has given New Zealand one of the most efficient and equitable general consumption taxes in the world. It has also made possible many worthwhile reforms of income tax, income maintenance and the previous wholesale sales-tax system. Nevertheless, some remaining special excise taxes and stamp duties still create distortions between different products and services and raise costs, for example, of petrol. I believe we could help lock in the lower inflationary expectations of today, and so speed up the drop in real interest rates, by setting a predictable path for further cuts in the indirect taxes that remain, even if those reductions were a number of years into the future. Chapter 12 outlines the proposed path for reducing indirect taxes. The following is a summary of what is proposed:

❏ *Stamp Duties* still remaining will be eliminated within five years.
❏ *Alcohol and Tobacco Tax* will be reduced or removed as health insurance premiums reflect health risks, and as the fiscal situation permits.
❏ *Petroleum Tax* will be cut in half by the end of Year 10, leaving a user-charge tax that relates only to the cost of Transit New Zealand in its maintenance and development of roads. Alternatively, TNZ could be restructured into a State Owned Enterprise and another funding system introduced to replace the petrol tax, such as direct charging of road users.

TARIFF REFORM

There will be a steady ongoing programme of tariff reductions. This ensures that our economic resources are employed in areas that are internationally competitive without special assistance. It will also bring down prices in the industries directly affected and keep pressure on prices by increasing competition. Competition will aid the export sector and other lightly assisted industries by helping reduce any remaining costs that penalise them when higher levels of protection are granted to others. By the year 2000, it ought to be possible to be a long way towards removing all remaining tariffs and subsidies to industry.

Tariff reform will help create jobs. Contrary to popular opinion, industry protection does not mean job protection. The main stimulus to job growth is already apparent in the more competitive cost structures of our export industries, the result of tariff reductions and the removal of licensing. This growth in employment can be expected to continue to favour the regions more than the main centres since export industries form the largest part of the economic base in the regions.

REGULATORY REFORM

There is another area, long overdue for reform, where we can make rapid progress towards our social and economic goals — occupational regulation. Existing regulations often restrict employment opportunities, protect providers at consumers' expense, limit competition and innovation and reinforce occupational obstacles to social mobility. The higher cost of regulated services reduces the income of others. New Zealand needs to give people more choice in the price, type and quality of the services they use; and break down artificial barriers which limit the growth of new employment opportunities. Areas where reform will yield rapid and significant gains should be given priority, for example, occupations associated with housing, from real estate agents and drainlayers to lawyers providing conveyancing services. Reform of existing regulations will remove the monopoly they have in a range of work which could reasonably be done by less-skilled members of the labour force. Dismantling occupational barriers will bring the same noteworthy results as reform in areas such as the taxi industry already has. Another heavily regulated group is the producer boards — the Dairy Board, Meat Board, Apple and Pear Board, Kiwifruit Marketing Board and Wool Board. The boards' exclusive control or heavy involvement in processing and/or marketing is supposed to ensure producers get the best price for their goods. In fact, the distortions caused by the regulatory systems of the producer boards make it very difficult to maximise revenue, at a cost to the individual farmer, the agricultural and horticultural industries and the whole economy.

Regulatory reform aims to make sheltered occupations more responsive to the community's needs, and ensures that consumers are adequately protected from adverse results.

LABOUR MARKET REFORM

The tax and income maintenance reforms, in addition to their positive effects on employment, investment and attitude, will complement New Zealand's recent industrial relations legislation. The changes brought by the legislation are an essential factor in the move to a healthy and strong economy. However, there are still areas, such as the courts' role in the new labour market, which can be improved. Also, the introduction of a minimum income level, described in Annex 1, will enable the minimum wage legislation to be repealed, or minimum wage levels reduced to the rate of the appropriate benefit. This will give many currently unskilled, unemployed people the opportunity to find work, receive training on the job, acquire skills, and still receive a reasonable net income. The cost to government of unemployment will be reduced.

To increase the incentive to look for work, I believe we need to look at the period that the unemployment benefit is paid to someone out of work. Many OECD countries now pay the maximum benefit for a limited time, for example,

Germany pays 52 weeks of unemployment insurance (UI), Austria 30 weeks UI, United Kingdom 52 weeks UI, Japan 30 weeks UI and the United States 26 weeks UI. Those who have not found work at the end of the prescribed period are then placed in training programmes or on a lower rate of benefit.

The economy needs to perform well if we are to get rid of unemployment but there is no reason why New Zealand cannot return to a state of full employment, when anyone wanting a job should be able to find one.

DEBT AND ASSET MANAGEMENT

On 30 June 1992, New Zealand government debt stood at $48 billion, 64 per cent of GDP. The country's debt ratio is one of the highest in the OECD. Servicing that debt is expected to cost over $5 billion by the year ending June 1995, up from $4.4 billion in the year to June 1992. Moreover, those figures do not account for any exchange losses on foreign-denominated debt. That is a fiscal loss. Our debt overhang has the following adverse effects on the country:

❐ Our credit worthiness is reduced, which means we must pay higher interest rates.

❐ The premium which overseas investors demand affects in turn local borrowers, householders and businesses. The Crown's debt has a direct impact on the cost of the interest rates of every mortgage, hire purchase and credit card.

❐ New Zealand's flexibility in responding to changing fiscal and economic circumstances is impaired, since we must pay our interest bill.

❐ The need for government to take money from the capital markets crowds out other borrowers who are looking for finance for investments which would create jobs and growth.

❐ Servicing our high debt requires high taxes with negative implications for incentives and productivity.

❐ Ongoing borrowing is running up bills for our children to pay.

Over the next 10 years, an average of around $3.5 billion a year in debt will fall due for repayment. We have to choose between:

(i) Borrowing that amount each year, along with any deficit for the year, on the domestic and international capital markets, with a consequent risk of further deterioration in our credit standing and terms of borrowing, and upward pressure on interest rates; and

(ii) Running surpluses and selling assets to repay debt.

The best option for this country is the second course.

The proposals on debt repayment and interest cost reductions outlined in Chapters 8 and 12, if followed, will reduce New Zealand's debt by 30 per cent within 5 years, by 65 per cent within 10 years, by 90 per cent in 15 years, and will pay off the debt entirely within 20 years. The cost of servicing that debt will drop even more dramatically, falling by 30 per cent within 5 years, 75 per cent within 10 years, 98 per cent within 15 years and reach nil by the end of Year 20. We will have freed up $1200 million by Year 5, $3400 million by Year 10, $4500 million by Year 15, and $4600 million by Year 20. Those savings would be used to lower personal taxation. A reduction in debt and servicing costs also takes a lot of pressure off real interest rates. They can be expected to be among the lowest real rates in the world; and lower rates mean more investments and hence more jobs and high real wages.

We have to be realistic about our debt. If we try to avoid the issue and continue to run large deficits, it is only a matter of time before we will be forced, by the international banking community, to adopt measures to reduce it. Much better for New Zealand to initiate a programme of managed debt restructuring than be forced to do so.

The benefits of the programme are obvious. For each $1 billion of debt we currently pay 9 per cent interest on average. For each $1 billion of equity we have in State assets, we average little more than a zero rate of return. The vast bulk of the debt New Zealand carries is from funding the excesses of the Muldoon administration's poor fiscal management, foreign exchange losses, 'think big' and subsidies. Yet there are politicians and others who would do it to us again. The proposed programme of asset sales and the yearly surplus after three years would enable New Zealand to repay most of its debt as it matures.

PUBLIC SECTOR EXPENDITURE

New Zealand needs to eliminate the financial deficit, that is the budget deficit excluding revenue, from loan repayment and/or asset sales. In fact, we need to run a surplus in order to help repay past debt. This would further relieve pressure on interest rates and the exchange rate so as to give even greater advantage to the export sector and producers generally, and ensure that asset sales were used to reduce debt rather than fund current consumption. New Zealand has successfully decreased some areas of spending over the last eight years. However, decreases in those areas have been offset by real increases in others, particularly social policy spending, and by expenditure 'creep' across a wide range of core government activities. Debt servicing costs are still high and expected to grow over the next two to three years.

Increasing taxes to fund increased expenditure is not costless. Taxation takes more out of the economy than simply the tax dollars raised. It decreases productivity, diverts valuable resources into tax avoidance and distorts investment decisions. These costs intensify as tax rates rise. Since 1984, New Zealand has greatly reduced the cost of the tax system by making it more neutral and by broadening the tax base; that is, by clamping down on the opportunities for evasion and allowing tax rates to be reduced. Nevertheless, the economic costs of the present levels of taxation remain relatively high.

In order to have the proposed tax reductions, it will be necessary to tackle the government expenditure side of the equation. The measures outlined below will cut government expenditure by $23 billion or 70 per cent over a 35-year period. The reduction in Year 1 is around $7 billion. The reductions in expenditure that follow will not be gained at the expense of the quality of the product delivered or service provided. Both the quality and the range of products and services will be improved, especially for those on low incomes.

Proposed Reductions

The figures shown here are the final amounts expenditure would be reduced by, in some cases in one or two years and in others over periods up to 20 years. Tables showing the reductions on a year-by-year basis are in Chapter 12.

Government Employee Superannuation   *$720 million*

As all new government employees entering any departmental superannuation scheme will have to be fully funded on a year-by-year basis, the unfunded liability of government employee superannuation will decline to nil over time. To hasten the process, government departments with employees not yet retired with unfunded superannuation liabilities will be required to make up the unfunded portion with an up-front payment in the year of the employee's retirement.

Inland Revenue Department   *$200 million*

With GST ultimately the only tax applying in New Zealand, Inland Revenue administrative work would be dramatically reduced. New operations, for example, collecting compulsory superannuation and health payments, will be paid for on a user-pays basis by insurance companies and superannuation funds, while the Social Welfare Department will pay the IRD what it costs to pay Social Welfare benefits.

Defence   *$340 million*

Expenditure will be reduced by $340 million to reflect the real need in the 1990s, and operational and administration efficiency.

Labour   *$380 million*
Expenditure reductions reflect the smaller programmes required as unemployment falls and user-pays takes effect in other areas, for example, ACC payments.

Family Support Payments   *$500 million*
No longer required as a result of the introduction of the GMFI, and the reduction of personal income tax to nil for families with children at school up to an income level where family support payments no longer apply under current policy.

Tax on Benefits   *$650 million*
Benefits in future to be paid out on a gross basis from which compulsory superannuation and health savings for retirement will be deducted as well as yearly health, ACC and sickness insurance paid. Expenditure levels on various benefits have been increased to reflect this change in policy.

Unemployment Benefits   *$1150 million*
Reduction in expenditure reflects lower unemployment as the policies in this book are implemented and a time limit is placed on eligibility for the maximum unemployment benefit. The overall result will be improved incentives to work (as a result of GMFI and gradual reductions in personal taxation to zero) and improved employment opportunities (as a result of higher levels of investment brought about by lower interest rates and higher returns on capital because of lower taxation).

Domestic Purposes Benefits   *$700 million*
Reduction in expenditure for the same

reasons as those applying to unemployment benefits, plus stricter criteria. (See Annex 1.)

Sickness Benefits   *$260 million*
Replaced by compulsory ACC and sickness insurance.

Other Welfare Benefits   *$300 million*
Reduced as the gap between benefits and wages increases and work opportunities grow.

Education   *$4200 million*
Reductions explained in Chapter 5.

Health   *$3900 million*
Reductions explained in Chapter 6.

Superannuation   *$5200 million*
Reductions explained in Chapter 7.

Interest on Debt   *$4600 million*
Reductions are explained in Chapters 8 and 12.

New Zealand needs to show that it is solving its fiscal problems in a permanent way. One-off decisions to reduce expenditure are not enough. They will continue to be swamped by other increases in expenditure unless we remove the underlying pressure on spending. The reforms outlined above do this, while at the same time ensuring that low-income families are provided for by targeting payments to them so that they can provide for themselves. They are placed on almost the same footing as higher-income groups as a result of being given access to the financial resources that allow them to choose. The government will no longer be taking from people through taxation resources which would be used more productively if left in their hands. Hence the immediate reduction in direct taxation to nil for all families with children at school, except the better off. These measures will have important positive effects on fairness and the quality of government expenditure. They will reinforce all the other measures proposed in this book.

❒ First, they represent real and sustained reductions in government expenditure. The savings would endure with positive benefits for the deficit. In fact, they would put the New Zealand budget in surplus within three years and, along with asset sales, would be responsible for a dramatic year-by-year reduction in debt until it reached zero at the end of 20 years.

❒ Secondly, they focus on what works for the taxpayer and consumer and therefore on what structures are needed by the government to best service their needs.

❒ Thirdly, they remove protection from one of the last remaining sheltered sectors of the economy, the highly protected government social services area.

They are not cuts for their own sake. They will contribute to the country's drive to end waste, correct incentives throughout the economy and dramatically improve the opportunities of the underprivileged. Although they deal with the main items of government expenditure, obviously there are other significant areas of expenditure such as Justice and Police. I cannot see these altering the numbers we have been talking about to any great extent. That does not mean that there couldn't and shouldn't be some major reorganization in the other departments, with much improved productivity and service to the public as a result.

BENEFITS OF TAXATION AND SOCIAL WELFARE REFORMS

1. Many people in the community will face lower marginal tax rates and be given vastly improved incentives to create and search for jobs. When they get an increase in gross income, they will get virtually the same percentage increase in disposable income, rather than a much lower increase as happens at present. Ultimately, people will pay no personal taxes at all.

2. Assistance programmes will be more even and provide

fairer levels of assistance.

3. There will be clear margins between the disposable income of households who rely on full-time earnings and equivalent households who rely solely on benefits.

4. There will be real gains in general economic confidence and in the community's view of prospects for economic growth and employment.

5. There will be a marked reduction in dependency traps for people on benefits or receiving housing assistance as they see the prospect of a real gain in income from a move to employment.

6. The measures will create an economic climate which increases fairness as well as growth. They will contribute significantly in the medium term to a better fiscal position which would improve New Zealand's relative international position.

7. The basis of the measures is to make changes in the climate determining the creation of and demand for jobs. The income margins for people who work and the effective reductions in marginal tax rates are the centrepieces of the overall proposal. The measures aim to sustain the present position of people who do not have jobs and at the same time give them much better incentives to look for work. The lower marginal tax rates on people who already earn income from employment and/or businesses will, over time, provide them with much greater motivation to increase their incomes and expand their businesses to create more jobs.

8. Thus, just looking at the immediate cash effect of the measures on people is misleading. This would concentrate too much attention on the transition and not enough on the overall dynamics of the situation after the transition is complete. The proposals remove unfair differences in treatment, provide a better margin in effective income terms for people who work, and lower effective tax rates for as many people as possible.

9. The transitional effects cannot and should not be ignored but they have to be seen in the light of these larger objectives. What may be seen as adversity is often in fact a

correction of present unfairness.

10. The higher tax rates are, the less people have to look after themselves and the more they become dependent.

SUMMARY

For many people, the introduction of the measures just outlined will mean the difference between the chance to make it on their own and permanent dependence on the State. For those who really need the State's protection and assistance, it means more effective support delivered in a fairer and more sensible way. For many it will mean a more equal opportunity to participate in society and to reap the rewards of their efforts. For others, the measures will be a catalyst that enables them to establish innovative new enterprises. For New Zealand as a whole, it would be a giant step forward towards a sound economy and a prosperous future. The measures will work together to create a climate of confidence — an environment where effort is assisted and rewarded, where productive investment is encouraged, and viable new jobs are created. They will reinforce New Zealand's economic credibility, its commitment to a consistent policy direction and its intention to solve its fiscal difficulties once and for all. They would equip New Zealand to face the future with confidence and a sense of security.

Annex 1

INCOME SUPPORT

Family Assistance

1. The introduction of a Guaranteed Minimum Family Income (GMFI) payable two monthly to couples with a single full-time wage or salary earner, employed for a minimum of 35 hours a week on average during the year, and with one child, at a level of $380 per week ($19,769 per year) with that level of income increased by $25 per week for each additional child ($1300 per year).

2. The introduction of a GMFI payable two monthly to couples with one child where both are earners, one full-time and the other working a minimum of 15 hours a week on average during the year, at $390 per week ($20,280 per year) with the level of income increased by $25 per week for each additional child ($1300 per year).

3. The introduction of a GMFI payable to single people working full time with one child, at $340 per week ($17,680 per year) with the level of income increased by $25 per week for each additional child ($1300 per year).

4. The introduction of a GMFI payable to single people working full time as follows:
Under 25 — $170 per week ($8840 per year); 25 plus — $190 per week ($9980 per year). Married couples with no children — $290 per week ($15,080 per year).

5. The GMFI payment to couples with children would be made to the non-earner or lower income partner.

6. The amount of the GMFI is calculated on the basis of the previous year's income and time spent in employment.

7. The GMFI ceases when any member of the household begins to receive either National Superannuation or other Social Security benefit payments.

8. Households that, but for 7 above, would have been eligible to receive GMFI would become eligible again immediately such superannuation or benefit payments ceased.

9. Other than for 7 above, a household receiving GMFI would continue to do so for a 12-month period. Whether payments continued would depend upon another application being made and the household's circumstances at that time.

10. To limit abuse of the scheme, the maximum GMFI payment to any household would be the difference between the GMFI level and the corresponding benefit level.

11. The value of any fringe benefit provided by the employer would be included as income to the employee for the purposes of calculating the GMFI entitlement.

Social Security Benefits

1. The current before-tax benefit, plus any additions, would become the new benefit payable to individual beneficiaries.

2. Seven per cent would be deducted from this benefit to cover the beneficiaries' superannuation and health-in-retirement insurance policies. The remaining 93 per cent would be paid to the beneficiary provided he or she produces evidence that he or she has taken out appropriate health, accident and sickness insurance for that year.

3. Where beneficiaries do not provide evidence that they have taken out appropriate insurance policies for themselves and their children, this will be done for them by Social Welfare and reclaimed through deductions over the 12-month period the policy is operative.

Assistance to Young People

1. All benefits and allowances for young people under the age of 18 will be abolished and support for young people aged 16 and 17 without income, whether in school, Access, tertiary education, DPB or unemployed, will be directed to those parents in the lower-income bracket through the GMFI scheme, with an extra $10 a week added to the basic level of GMFI payable under the Family Assistance programme (sections 1, 2 and 3, at the beginning of this Annex).

2. Emergency assistance for those estranged from their families will be available.

3. All young people who are full time in school, Access, tertiary education or unemployed and aged 18 and 19, and all people in tertiary education and Access aged 20 and over, will be paid a weekly allowance of $70 for a maximum of three years after the age of 19. The exception will be beneficiaries aged 20 and over on courses of less than six months: they will stay on the benefit.

INDEXATION AND ABATEMENT OF INCOME SUPPORT
1. Indexation of GMFI to be on an annual basis in line with the percentage movement in a wage index.
2. No income threshold will apply before the abatement rate of 50 cents in the dollar is applied to additional income up to $200 per week. Beyond $200, the abatement rate will be 93 cents in the dollar.

NATIONAL SUPERANNUATION
1. The current tax surcharge rate will be reduced by 1 per cent a year for 10 years and then eliminated.
2. A National Superannuitant couple with children will be eligible for child support payments to a level which ensures that they are no worse off than married income-tested beneficiaries.

EDUCATION

Means-tested Beneficiaries and Those Eligible for GMFI
1. A cash grant (voucher) for educational purposes will be provided on the following basis:
   Pre School — up to $2500 a year.
   Primary School — up to $3500 a year.
   Secondary School — up to $4500 a year.
2. University and tertiary education — a government guarantee for any borrowing undertaken by children of parents who have generally had low incomes during the years of their schooling.
3. A cash grant (voucher) for educational purposes will be provided for parents not on a means-tested benefit or

81

GMFI on the following basis:

❐ $1 for every $3 shortfall in the parents' income.
❐ Any shortfall of income to be calculated on the following basis:

Tax-Free Income Allowance

	Single-Parent Family	Two-Parent Family
1 child	$29,000	$32,000
2 children	$39,000	$42,000
3 children	$49,000	$52,000
4 children	$59,000	$62,000

For example, the Tax-Free Income Allowance for a two-parent family with two children at school will be $42,000. A family with an income of $30,000 will deduct that from the TFIA. The shortfall in their income is $12,000. The shortfall is divided by three. The family, therefore, will be entitled to an educational cash grant (voucher) of $4000.

5   Learning to Succeed

No public policy issue is more important to any nation than education. Education is the process by which a society transmits its accumulated knowledge and values to future generations. Education makes economic growth possible, in the first instance by ensuring that each new adult doesn't have to reinvent the wheel — literally. By passing on what it has already learned, the present generation enables the next generation of philosophers, scientists, engineers, and entrepreneurs to stand on the shoulders of giants and see even further. And only by educating its young people about its history, its literature, and its values can a society — a nation — be said to have a culture.

David Boaz (ed.), *Liberating Schools — Education in the Inner City,* 1991

For more than a decade now, many countries around the world have been debating educational reform. The education portfolio, once a political graveyard, has been used by politicians as diverse as Margaret Thatcher and Bill Clinton as a stepping stone on their way to the top. In many Western countries, education's high profile is largely the consequence of a growing dissatisfaction with its end results, together with the development of a world market for labour as well as goods and services. Once countries competed for control of natural resources to acquire wealth and power — competition that drove exploration and colonisation in earlier centuries. Now they strive to produce a better-educated workforce in order to become rich or to stay rich. A nation's wealth in the foreseeable future will rely to a large extent on the quality of its labour force.

All countries are short of skilled and educated people. Developed countries predict a big fall in demand for unskilled labourers and a significant increase in demand for high-grade administrators, scientists and skilled workers. They want workers who are not just proficient in one or two areas but who have the ability to update techniques, learn new methodologies, and stay flexible and innovative as technology changes, which is happening with increasing speed. Over the last 30 years, in many developed countries with inflexible economies, each economic downturn has pushed more and more uneducated workers into unemployment. A shrinking number have made it back into the labour force when the economic situation has improved. For those still in work, the earnings gap between the poorly educated and the well educated is getting bigger.

In the past, people could leave school with no qualifications and find ready employment that paid relatively well. There was no need for students to get a better education, no pressure on schools to provide one. Automation and globalisation have changed all that. The former is not new. For the last 200 years, machines have been replacing people — all that is needed is a few highly skilled technicians to operate them. In the latter case, small companies and giant corporations can and do set up business wherever they find the workforce that suits them best. They often split their operations between countries with low-skilled, low-wage workforces and those with highly skilled, high-income labour pools.

New Zealand is part of this globalisation of the job market, and is increasingly affected by it. Therefore, it matters that only 35 per cent of 18-year-old New Zealanders are still in education compared with 85 per cent in Germany and 95 per cent in Japan; that only 25 per cent of our total adult population have schooling to a senior secondary level when the OECD average in 1988 was 35 per cent; that more than 38 per cent of New Zealand's workers lack any formal educational qualifications while in Germany the figure is only 25 per cent. At the beginning of 1993, 80,000 of the 100,000 long-term unemployed in New Zealand had no higher educational qualification than School Certificate. The economic effects of the New Zealand situation are only part of the problem. The costs in the physical and emotional health of those people failed by the education system, and the costs to society as a whole, are huge.

Concern about education is not confined to politicians. For parents, students, educationalists, business leaders and the general public there are two recurring questions: What makes a school successful? and, How can we reduce educational failure? While many countries face the same problems of rising costs and falling or static standards, there is no agreement on how to improve things. In fact, many of the prescriptions contradict each other. But there are some common themes as well.

In the Education Reform Act 1988, Britain introduced a national curriculum, and schools began competing for pupils. The element of choice for parents and students was increased by creating some new schools — city technology colleges (CTC) — and allowing existing schools and further education colleges to 'opt out' of the control of their local education authorities. Sweden has introduced an internal market into its education system — only part of its overall break with 'the Swedish model' of economic management. Denmark, with per capita funding for technical colleges, has made huge improvements in vocational training and has long had deregulated secondary education, which allows a form of free market. In the United States, where there is no core curriculum, calls for national tests, parent choice and vouchers are growing more insistent. Singapore has league tables to stimulate competition between schools. Japan strongly disapproves of league tables but, like Korea, wants to decentralise its education system by delegating power to local government.

In New Zealand, the *Picot Report* and government White Paper, *Tomorrow's Schools,* led to parent boards, the beginning of bulk funding and the breakup of the old Department of Education into the Ministry, the Education Review Office (ERO) and a number of regulatory agencies such as the New Zealand Qualifications Authority. Decentralisation and greater autonomy at district and school level may have been the stated aim of the reforms, but they have not eventuated in practice. The National Government pushed out reform a little with the removal of zoning and teacher registration, but overall it has been a Clayton's devolution of power. The old department simply metamorphosed into two new departments (the Ministry and the ERO) and several new agencies, and most of the departmental bureaucrats were re-employed, with increased salaries.

The common concern in Western countries has been a perceived, and in a number of cases measured, decline in educational standards over the past 30 years. At the same time, the amount of funding invested in education has increased dramatically in real terms. In New Zealand there was a 40 per cent real increase (after inflation) in education spending between 1984 and 1990. In 1990/91 we spent 6 per cent of our gross domestic product on education, which places us in the top half of the OECD education expenditure tables. In 1993 it cost the government about $4000 per annum for a pupil at a State school. (The government contributes between $392 and $720 a year for each private school student depending on class level but often gets back nearly as much or more in GST on annual fees that range from under $3000 to $9000 and more for students who board.)

During the last couple of decades politicians here, like their counterparts in other countries, have sought to improve standards by constantly injecting more funds. But money hasn't worked, which has been a hard lesson to learn. For instance, Germany spends a lower proportion of its budget on education (9.1 per cent) than any other OECD country but has an education system that is regarded with envy. In 1988, 13.5 per cent of New Zealand's total public spending was on education (the OECD average was 12 per cent). Education costs were 5.2 per cent of GDP when the OECD average was 4.8 per cent. Canada spends a higher proportion of its GDP, 7.2 per cent, on education than any other country, Japan a lower proportion, 4.9 per cent, yet the former is not conspicuously successful while the latter is far from unsuccessful. The United States is still absorbing the shock of discovering that in maths the average 18-year-old in Japan out-performs many of the top 1 per cent of American students of the same age. South Korea has classes twice the size of Britain and still regularly tops that country in academic olympiads. Around the world, researchers have tried to find a correlation between the amount spent on schools, students and teachers and how well students learn. Years of study, starting with James Coleman et al's now famous 1966 American report, *Equality of Educational Opportunity,* have been unable to establish any consistent relationship between school performance and a wide range of school resources. The possible exceptions were at the extremes, in cases of gross abundance or extreme deprivation.

New Zealand, like many other countries, decided some time ago that educating its young was important for the country as well as the individual. Therefore, it was worthwhile for government to become involved. Its involvement eventually covered every area, from financing education to regulation and actual provision. After health, education has become one of the biggest businesses in New Zealand. With the steady shrinking of the private education sector, it is now largely a State industry and, like other government institutions, it has developed the same characteristics — a massive bureaucracy and at the school level a standardised service for everyone. There is no attempt, except in the most limited way, to serve individual students' needs. The intention has been to ensure everyone has equal access to school education. However, making sure every child has a place in the classroom doesn't constitute access. As time has passed, all groups have become losers — the disadvantaged, the desperately bored bright child and also the under-extended average child. Education, once regarded as the escape route from poverty and deprivation, a key to advancement on all levels, now traps the losers in an underclass. In the world today a child who can't read and write properly, can't add and subtract, can't think logically and creatively, will be left behind by the rest of society.

Our educational establishment has long contended that New Zealand has an education system that is one of the best in the world. Over the years there have been changes intended to make education more effective. But, by and large, concern from outside the profession, from parents, students, politicians and employers, has met with complacency and aggressive admonitions to leave education to those qualified to deal with it. Measures of the system's success, both national and international, are fewer than in many other countries, and there is simply no basis for reliable statements about New Zealand's overall education performance.

What we do know is that national gains in reading and writing between 1968 and 1990 have been small. Any other industry would be embarrassed by such a lack of improvement in quality over so long a period. Tests in arithmetic and algebra, now 12 years old, put us in a cluster of lower-ranking countries, behind Britain in the middle of the tables. The Netherlands and Germany ranked high, and Japan was way out in front. Twenty years ago we were close to the top of the science tables, but by 1988 we were awarding the lowest percentage of engineering degrees in the OECD (5 per cent) and our percentage of science and engineering degrees, as a proportion of all degrees completed, was 21 per cent. France was at the top of the tables with 40 per cent, and Spain last with 14 per cent. According to the Ministry of Education, science and engineering degrees are an indication of how well a country can respond to technological change. Much-quoted scores on New Zealand's good international performance in reading and literature date from 1970. More recently, the effectiveness of our reading recovery programme has been much vaunted. But why has such a programme become so widely needed; and why, despite even this programme, do universities and polytechnics each year find it necessary to provide an increasing number of remedial classes in reading and writing for first-year students?

New Zealand education is failing those it should be helping the most — the economically and socially disadvantaged, Maori and immigrants from the Pacific. Between 1968 and 1991, education resources and teacher training increased substantially. If more money and more resources, more highly trained teachers and more changes in the curriculum haven't helped noticeably, then we must look elsewhere.

Overseas study has concluded that the most important factors in how well a child does at school are the student's ability, the school organisation, the family background and peer group influence, in that order of importance. Education policy can help people realise that parental and student attitudes are key factors for success; however, its effect on school organisation is more direct. By organisation, I mean how all the resources poured into the system — funding, teachers, administrators, buildings, equipment — are utilised. Instead of trying to find correlations between how much is paid in and the level of educational achievement at the end, an increasing number of people inside and outside the system are looking at how these resources are used, how schools are run. According to United States professors, John Chubb and Terry Moe, there are three organisational factors which are true of schools that are good at educating their students: ambitious and clearly defined school goals; a strong leader with a greater interest in teaching and education than administration; and a strong sense of professionalism throughout the school. Principal and teachers all contribute to policy and decisions, there is mutual respect, strong team spirit and a belief among the teachers that what they are doing can make a difference. There is nothing surprising in their findings. Seven other case studies in the United States[1] showed a remarkable consensus on the importance of school factors such as strong leadership, orderly climate, high expectations, achievement-oriented

[1]Weber (1971), Brookover et al (1979), Rutter et al (1979), Venesky et al, Glenn, California State, Brookover and Lezotte.

89

policy and time on task. United Kingdom research by Mortimore et al (1988) reaches the same conclusions about the organisational characteristics that are likely to lead to greater achievement. The answer to the researchers' question — Do schools matter? — was a definite yes. Mortimore found that an effective school is beneficial for all groups of pupils, whether they come from a more privileged or a disadvantaged background. An effective school, according to his study, is characterised by: educational leadership at a distance, in which maintaining records on pupils' progress is an important resource; a positive and enthusiastic atmosphere backed up by the involvement of the head and parents; and structured and well-regulated teaching.

Good organisations of any kind tend to display such qualities as high expectations, good leadership, collegial decision-making and regular self-evaluation. Those characteristics are reinforced in schools by the popularity that comes from educational success — the demand from parents and students for places in schools that are succeeding. The key question, then, is: What sort of policy environment would be most likely to encourage the development of organisational characteristics that lead to high achievement? A large part of the answer, and central to what I propose, lies in removing government as an intermediary between parents and students and educational institutions.

Chubb and Moe found that the required characteristics are difficult to develop if politicians and bureaucrats are interfering. The school and principal need to be given autonomy. Schools that have little control over curriculum, instruction, discipline and hiring and firing are likely to be measurably less effective in their organisation than schools with greater control of these matters. There is obviously some variation. Schools with students who are well behaved, above average in ability, and from relatively well-educated and informed families are more likely to organise effectively despite their lack of autonomy. The same cannot be said for centrally controlled schools where students do not have most of these background advantages.

It was in American urban schools with the lowest achievements, in the most run-down and violent neighbourhoods, that the revolt for change began in the 1970s. Poor parents wanted the same opportunity to choose where their children went to school as wealthier parents who could move to where public schools were good or send their children to private schools. Up until then, the conventional wisdom had been that choice would disadvantage the poor even further. Polly Williams, a State representative in the Wisconsin legislature, totally disagreed:

> Choice empowers parents. It allows them to choose the best school for their children. It doesn't say, as the 'educrats' do, the poor people are too dumb (they use the word 'uninformed') to make choices. Poor people are the same as rich people. They may not have as much money but they have the same desires and the same needs. And poor people make decisions all the time. They decide where they are going to live, what grocery store to buy from, where to shop for clothes — they decide everything, but all of a sudden, the bureucrats claim that they don't have enough sense to make a decision about the education of their children.

Polly Williams is an African-American, a Democrat, a former welfare mother and chairperson of Jesse Jackson's Wisconsin campaigns in 1984 and 1988. A six-term representative, she holds the record for the highest number of votes in State legislature elections — in 1986 it was 94 per cent. Williams pushed the Milwaukee voucher plan through the legislature, securing $US2500 vouchers for a few inner-city public school students to use in non-sectarian private schools.

Like choice, vouchers have been portrayed by the educational establishment as the spoilers of public education, an embodiment of everything that threatens it and the least well off. That was not how Williams and inner-city parents saw vouchers. When you consider the educational statistics in Milwaukee, it is amazing that Williams had to fight so hard to be allowed to try an alternative. Sixty per cent of the city's ninth graders (14-

year-olds) did not complete high school and, according to Williams, of the 40 per cent who stayed and walked across the stage to receive their diplomas, only 10 per cent could read. 'For what amounts to a 90 per cent failure rate we pay $US600 million a year to support Milwaukee public schools,' she has said. 'That averages out to about $US6000 per student.' Another telling fact was that 62 per cent of the teachers and administrators in the city's public school system chose not to send their children to public schools. Commenting on the Democrats in the State legislature who refused to back her, Williams says, 'They say they're liberal, but whenever it comes to empowering black people, they stab us in the back. We want self-determination, not handouts and dependency.'

Williams knew the power of her opponents — the teachers' unions, the bureaucracy and the educational establishment — and didn't try to beat them head on. Instead she mobilised at grass-roots level, going directly to the parents. They attended meetings in their hundreds and started turning up at the State capital, shocking the politicians who, like the educational bureaucrats, also believed 'the poor didn't care'. The voucher plan was passed but its political and bureaucratic opponents are trying to marginalise it by restricting it for the time being to a small trial. At the moment the plan applies only to 1 per cent of Milwaukee public school students, just under 1000 children.

David Boaz, quoted at the beginning of this chapter, asks how many industries use the same basic structure of production they used 200 years ago. The school day and school year are still geared to the rhythms and requirements of an agricultural society when people's lives were much shorter, and career opportunities were limited. In the classroom, the teacher still stands in front of a group of students and lectures. Students are encouraged to specialise, although the great majority will change careers several times during a working life that could last as long as 50 years. It is difficult to know whether this is the best, most productive way of doing things when there is little with which to compare it. The present systems are not flexible or innovative enough to throw up alternatives which provide real comparisons.

Choice is the basis of flexibility, innovation and variety; and the most important autonomy of all is parent/student autonomy. Choice links consumer and provider directly, with consequential incentives on schools. Parents can use 'exit' (moving their children from schools that are not producing good results) as well as choice to encourage high performance. Schools are then held accountable by the people who use them, not controlled from above by bureaucrats. Everything else flows from this point.

Choice is the key to the kinds of reforms needed to improve the educational achievements of all New Zealanders and particularly of minorities and the disadvantaged, as they are the ones that the current system is failing most. Nearly as badly served are especially gifted children who are too often treated as a threat to 'equality of outcome', which is a mistaken distortion of 'fair and equal access'.

Choice in the New Zealand system would raise our standards of educational achievement under pressure from both teachers who would see new opportunities, and parents and students who would move rather than put up with a school that was not providing the kind of education they wanted. The wealthy will always find a way to escape bad schools, whether by buying into the postal zone of a high reputation school or opting for private schools. Choice gives low-income families and the middle class the same options. That ability to choose, to pick what they consider the best for their child/children, introduces competition. Competition imposes its own disciplines, improving overall performance and changing the incentives for schools, principals and teachers. In response to falling rolls, schools would have to lift their performance to survive. Private and alternative schools would be able to compete on an equal basis with State schools. Parents and students with particular needs would be more likely to have those needs met. They could 'shop around' for the best school for their children.

Choice would improve the present system of public education, which is inefficient and often crippled by bureaucracy. Monopoly and central planning have not worked much better in State education than they did in the economies of the socialist republics. Despite huge increases in inflation-adjusted levels of expenditure, New Zealand students' achievements in comparison with other countries (according to the limited information available) are static at best and in decline in some academic disciplines. The implications of this are both social and economic. The global economy pitches us against foreign competition, especially from Asia where countries like Japan and Korea now sit at the top of the scholastic tables in some important subjects such as mathematics. There is a connection between this educational improvement and the rapid increase in their national average incomes and standards of living. With choice, performance would matter. Good schools would prosper and expand; badly performing schools would shrink and die if they didn't change. Poor educational practice would be weeded out and good practices exposed.

THE PROPOSED SYSTEM

What follows is an outline of my proposed education system. In order for it to be implemented, parents and students and schools would have to make some changes.

The bases of the proposed system would be:

1. Individual choice, made by the parent or student.
2. Money will follow the student. Parents and students will become consumers of educational services in an open market-place.
3. The revenue/money for education will come from parents or students, who will buy the education services they want directly.
4. There would be tax reductions or cash grants (vouchers) for pre-school, primary and secondary schools.

(i) Certain levels of family income (dependent on family size and the number of children at school) will become tax-free in any one year:

1 child	$32,000
2 children	$42,000
3 children	$52,000
4 children	$62,000

For instance, the amount of taxation a person on $32,000 a year with one child at school will pay under existing tax rates during the year 1993/94 is $8040. The saving of that amount under the new system would enable the family to:

(a) Save towards retirement needs for both super-annuation and health (see Chapters 6 and 7)	$2240
(b) Take out a catastrophic health care insurance policy for the family (see Chapter 6)	$1200
(c) Pay expected extra health care costs currently paid for by government (see Chapter 6)	$ 400
(d) Meet the costs of the child's education	$4000
	$7840

(ii) The tax-free income level for any one year will be higher for parents with children who require more expensive educational care, e.g., those with impaired sight or hearing.

(iii) For those families whose income is less than the tax-free level allowed, a cash grant (voucher) would be available, equivalent to one dollar for every three dollar shortfall in their income. This would ensure that low-income families were generally made better off by the changes, notably in terms of the choices available to them, but also in dollars in the pocket.

(iv) Universities and other tertiary institutions: The government would guarantee loans taken out by students only if the parents had been in the low-income category during their child's years at school and had had to use government cash grants (vouchers). In those cases, parents would have been unable to save in order to help their child through tertiary education and would be unlikely to act as guarantors on bank loans taken out by their child. A transition period from the present position to the new approach would be needed.

Introducing the New System

1. In early May of the year prior to the introduction of the new system, parents would apply to the school at which they would like to enrol their child/children the next year.

2. Schools would be responsible for advising a parent, at the earliest possible date, whether an enrolment is accepted or not. Parents would immediately have to indicate whether they wish to proceed with their application. Where acceptance was conditional, schools would have to advise the parent of the circumstances under which it would become unconditional. For example, students from Invercargill who applied to be enrolled at an Auckland-based school might be told by the Auckland school that it would establish a school in Invercargill, but only if it received 200 applications for enrolment from Invercargill.

3. Parents could accept entry for their child at one school only. However, they would be free to change the place at which they enrol their child at any time up to the end of August. Obviously if a family moves to a new town between then and the start of the school year, they would be able to enrol their child at a school in the new area.

4. After the start of the school year, parents would be free to move students at any time to any school willing to accept the child. Schools accepting new students would be responsible for advising the Ministry of Education and the Inland Revenue Department (IRD) of any changes.

5. Those schools that had accepted more enrolments than the number of places available would, on 1 September, apply to the Education Property Trust (EPT) for more accommodation, indicating where they wanted it and for how many students.

6. Schools with fewer enrolments than the number of current places available would advise the EPT of their

situation and indicate what accommodation they would still require.

7. Schools would advise the IRD and the Ministry of Education of all enrolments.

Parents and Students

1. Parents and/or students, including those who receive tax relief or assistance through the cash grant (voucher) scheme, would be able to spend their additional income at any registered school they wished, public or private.

2. Parents/students would not necessarily have to spend all their money at one school. This would allow schools within schools or other alternatives to develop more easily, for example, music or sports schools run by specialists in those areas.

Schools

1. For the first two years, management of government-owned schools would be in the hands of a board, half of whose members would be appointed by government through the Ministry of Education and half elected by parents who have children enrolled at the school.

2. The board would be fully responsible for all school activities, including the appointment of all staff, the negotiation of the individual salaries of all staff (which could vary according to a teacher's ability and performance) and all organisational matters. Undoubtedly many of these matters would be delegated to the principal.

3. The board, if it wishes, could sub-let part of the school on a for-profit or other basis, for specialist activities — sport, music, dance, art, cultural activities, etc.

4. The board could decide on individual contracts of employment with some teachers who may or may not have responsibility for employing other staff. For example, pre-school and the first two years of primary school could be contracted to one teacher who would run his or her own business and be responsible for employing all the staff in that area.

5. Schools would have the right to decide whether or not to

accept applications for enrolment.

6. A school which has accepted more enrolments than it can cope with in its existing facilities would be able to apply to the EPT for additional facilities which the EPT would be bound to provide. This should cause no problem as existing student demand matches the facilities available.

7. At the end of Year 2, public schools would be formed into companies with boards appointed by the shareholders and with an appropriate debt/equity ratio.

8. Each school would set its own fees according to the services offered.

Universities and Tertiary Institutions
Changes are needed in tertiary education to improve performance levels there too. The changes would also bring better class scheduling, better degree structuring (three years instead of four, etc), year-round use of very expensive facilities and much greater emphasis on the performance of the academic staff.

1. Universities and tertiary institutions are to be financed entirely by fees from students. This reflects the fact that most people with tertiary qualifications earn considerably more than those without them.

2. Government assistance would be limited to guaranteeing the loans of students from low-income families.

3. A phase-in period of five years would be required before reaching the financing position outlined in 1 and 2 above.

4. Each government-owned institution would be run by a board, 75 per cent of its members appointed by government and 25 per cent by the students. The board would be fully responsible for all activities, as set out above for schools. Undoubtedly many of those matters would be delegated to the chancellor/chief executive.

Property
The proposed system is about matching parents' and students' choices with the facilities available. It starts with X number of students and X number of classroom places.

What I am advocating would mean there would be small schools, large schools, schools within schools. Unless there were someone to facilitate that match, the system would not work.

1. All government education property would be transferred to an Education Property Trust (EPT).

2. The EPT would be responsible for the sale (transferring the ownership) to others, on commercial terms, of all school and university property within seven years.

3. The EPT would establish the rent for each school and each component of that school in the interim. This would also apply to universities.

4. The EPT would have the right to sell property in any way it sees fit, but would have to consult the owners or management of the school or university renting the property prior to any sale.

5. The EPT could retain the right until a property is sold to let the property to more than one person, company, school or university. For example, a school might be set up to cater only for ages 2 to 6, another could be a one-teacher one-class school for 30 post-primer children who started at age 7 and went through as a group until they were 12. It would allow variety.

6. The EPT would automatically make accommodation available to a new user if that school were registered and had enrolments from parents/students. In any given area there are X number of students and a certain amount of accommodation. The EPT would have the task of ensuring there was accommodation to meet the demand (number of enrolments). (See 5 above.)

7. Where an application for accommodation was made by a 'for profit organisation', then the sale of the school should be made without delay. How the school is sold would be up to the EPT to decide, but it might well be negotiated as part of the arrangement for making classrooms or a school available. (See 6 above.)

8. The EPT would be responsible for ensuring policies did not impede competition. In fact, the bias should be towards

encouraging competition, even if that means a school was let to more than one operator.

9. At the end of the second year, government-owned schools and universities would be formed into companies with an appropriate debt equity/ratio along the lines carried out for State Owned Enterprises.

Government

The government's role in the proposed system would be kept to a minimum. It would be strictly administrative and the responsibility of the Ministry of Education. The Ministry's two primary functions would be to provide information and to monitor the overall system.

1. Information — A small group would be charged with the responsibility of providing up-to-date information to schools on New Zealand educational research and what is happening overseas.

2. School/Technical Institute/University Registration — A small group, limited to around 20 people. Its tasks would be:

(i) To register schools/technical institutes/universities; that should be as automatic as possible. The following factors would be seen as favourable:

❐ Established school at the time the new system is introduced.

❐ Parental/student support for the school, technical institute, university or teacher college demonstrated by the number of enrolments.

❐ Ownership in whole or part by a partnership of the teaching staff.

❐ Ownership by an education trust.

❐ Business ability of school owners.

❐ Specialist school.

❐ Experienced teaching staff.

(ii) To provide applicants with reasons for the group's decision where registration is denied or withdrawn and therefore the school has to cease to operate.

3. Monitoring — Government would provide a declining grant during the first five years of the new system to set up a competitive private sector monitoring and information system covering the performance of individual schools (an educational equivalent of Standard & Poors). The aim would be to provide parents and students with maximum information on which to base choices.

4. Teachers — Individual schools would advise the Ministry of Education each year of the names and addresses of all staff employed during the year and their qualifications.

5. Examinations — Schools would advise the Ministry of Education of any external examinations undertaken by their pupils and the results of those examinations. The Ministry would have the right to request schools to undertake tests from time to time if the Ministry thought it appropriate, for example, a school receiving a low grading from private sector monitoring groups.

6. Curriculum — Schools would be free to design their own curriculum and to choose their own method of instruction, provided it involved certain subjects to certain levels, for example, English and maths.

THE EFFECTS

Once free of the inflexible and restricting system which operates now, parents, students and teachers would be more creative in going about getting what they wanted from education. Some, but by no means all, of the possible advantages would be:

1. Teachers would become true professionals and operate in the same way as lawyers, accountants or engineers currently do. Teachers' status would rise within the community to the very high levels seen in countries with high educational standards. For example, in Germany, France and Japan teachers are regarded extremely highly. Teachers would have the same options available to them as those working in the other professions — direct employment, ownership (of schools) through a partnership,

or part-ownership through shareholding. They would be rewarded in the same way, either with a salary from their employer, with a share of the profits from a partnership, or as owner of the business.

2. Teachers electing not to remain within the education system or those unsuccessful in obtaining a position under the new set-up would be entitled to normal public sector redundancy.

3. For teacher superannuation there would be arrangements similar to those made when Telecom, New Zealand Post, Forest Corp, etc were formed into state-owned enterprises.

4. Existing public or private schools, popular with parents because they teach what parents want and in a manner parents like, would seek to expand their franchise by opening elsewhere if they could attract students in sufficient numbers.

5. Existing public schools with the same approach to education might decide to amalgamate and establish their own 'brand', either throughout New Zealand or in one particular area.

6. Some teachers would seek to form partnerships in order to purchase schools and establish their own school 'brands' (along the lines that lawyers and accountants do, for example, Chapman Tripp and Price Waterhouse).

7. Entrepreneurs and companies from overseas with an interest in education would seize the opportunity to start up in the business in New Zealand. We already have other alternative education systems such as the Montessori, Waldorf and Rudolph Steiner schools operating privately. An additional possibility, for example, might be Robert Kiyosaki, co-founder of the Excellerated Learning Institute and author of *If You Want to be Rich and Happy, Don't Go to School*. Kiyosaki is highly critical of education systems that demand that some students fail. The traditional system in the US failed him when he was growing up and he now provides the kind of learning and material he wished the system had given him.

8. Existing New Zealand businesses, often in conjunction

with educators, would establish their own school or a chain of schools, or a university or chain of universities.

9. Ownership of educational institutes by local communities would be likely to occur in more remote areas of the country.

10. Competition to attract students and provide them with what they need in preparation for life would become the name of the game.

I have listed 10 things that might happen under the new system. I am not saying that they are the only things or that they would definitely occur. They are simply ideas. Under what I have proposed, every educator and entrepreneur would be searching for better and better ways of educating the country's children and re-educating many of its adults.

Competition

Competition, an essential factor in the system, would take a variety of forms. It would ensure diversity as schools sought to provide what parents and students wanted — excellence for all according to ability. Desmond Nuttall, director of research during the late 1980s for the now defunct Inner London Education Authority, says, 'Parents take choice very seriously and research shows great consistency in what they tend to be looking for: they want order and discipline, academic achievement, and proximity.' In other words, parents tend to want the best school possible close to home. However, the new system would also enable parents to bring the school of their choice to them. They might well live in the southernmost part of New Zealand but if they wanted a style of education popular in Auckland they could approach the school concerned to enquire about the possibility of that school trying to find the numbers to justify establishing a similar school in the parents' area. Teachers and those wishing to enter the education business will be asking, 'How can I satisfy the consumer?' What the parents want could result in some of the following — very different from what we are used to now:

1. Schools could be set up to operate for a varying number of hours a day and a different number of weeks during the year. New Zealand, with 190 school days a year, is one of a number of countries (USA, 180 days; England/Wales, 192 days; Australia — NSW, 200 days) whose children put in markedly less time at school than a number of nations with very successful economies and/or reputations for academic excellence. Top of that list are Japan (243 days), West Germany (226–240), South Korea (220) and Israel (216). Some schools might operate as much as 50 weeks a year; though that does not mean individual teachers would work all that time. For example, parents who need to have their children cared for after school because they are working would possibly look for a school which was open between 8 am and 5 pm. The teaching programme could vary beyond 3 o'clock — it might concentrate on activities such as sports, homework, music, film and video-making and art. Or the school day might be constructed in a completely different way, perhaps on the lines of the longer school day in many Asian countries, where academic learning periods are interspersed with far more recreation breaks than in Western schools in order to increase children's capacity to concentrate and learn. It also broadens the relationship between teacher and student and makes school a place of both play and work. During holiday periods the schools could run special programmes. Whatever they did would be done to cater for the needs of the parents and the students. It could also mean that parts of the school programme would be optional — some parents may only want their children at school for the traditional time. Other parents who needed to have their children cared for because they are working could pay for the longer tuition and specialist assistance.

2. Schools and universities would vary dramatically in size. You could have a school with a student roll as small as 10 or 12, or possibly even less (home schooling, for example) all the way through to schools as large or larger than the

present ones.

3. You would see chains of schools, offering the same approach to educating children at each school, no matter where it was located. This has happened in New Zealand with some church schools, especially those run by the same religious order. There are still integrated Catholic schools that retain their own 'ethos' which is an important factor in parents choosing to send their child to one Catholic school rather than another.

4. The age of students covered in schools would vary. You might have schools that admitted children from shortly after birth through to the end of secondary education, while others might specialise in pre-school, or pre-school and early primary years. There would not be the arbitrary breaks in a child's school life with he or she being forced to change school. There would be no barriers to children entering or staying on at a school that suits them and their family just because of their class year. The needs of the disadvantaged would be taken seriously and their circumstances taken into account.

5. Specialist schools would develop to meet the needs of people with special interests or special requirements, such as those with impaired sight or hearing or with talents and ambitions in dance or music.

6. Specialist schools could be established within schools. Schools might franchise out the teaching of music, art or sport, or the teaching of the severely handicapped.

7. Schools would develop that were known for their concentration on particular subjects, as is already happening with Maori schools; for example, where Maori would be the main language but students would still be taught all the other subjects such as maths, history, English, geography and science.

8. The quality of the education being provided, the service to the parents and students, and the cost would become the main motivating factors driving schools. They would be competing to ensure students achieved their full potential. There would be more emphasis on success. Schools would aim to ensure every child felt self-confident, rather than

feeling they were failures, as happens to so many now. Schools would look at each child, see what motivated him or her. They would find what the child was good at, and ensure that he or she was successful.

There are already examples of this diversity within a few public school systems, although only on a limited scale. They are exceptions because they still operate within top-down systems. They have to rely on an exceptional administrator to allow the diversity to develop. Unsatisfactory schools are still rewarded with funds and students they don't deserve. Other schools are closed, or merged, or changed in character, and choices are therefore eliminated. Choice and diversity are always going to be the exception in a public system (whether funded at district, city, or national level) because of the disincentives to take risks and to innovate. Bureaucrats and politicians seek to reduce risks by regulating, which means extending their empires.

One of the best examples of diversity and choice is in New York City's East Harlem District 4. In 1973, District 4 had the lowest reading scores among the city's 32 community school districts and only 7 per cent of the students entering Benjamin Franklin High School ever graduated. With little to lose, the district's new school superintendent, Sy Fliegel, began experimenting. He let individual teachers create whole new curricula centred upon the performing arts, bilingual education or environmental studies. With parents' permission, students could choose among teachers and curricula. Soon the district had a dozen little competing 'schools within schools', all operating outside the system's traditional framework. This also introduced market principles — if kids didn't sign up for a programme, it was closed down. One teacher tried to set up a curriculum around sports. It was one of the few programmes to fold. The most popular academies included the Isaac Newton School for Math and Science, the Harbor Performing Arts School, the Central Park East schools — a group of progressive schools, and the Children's Workshop. This last is the smallest of the alternative schools, a one-room second-through-fourth-grade class for children with behavioural problems.

By 1982 there were 22 alternative schools in District 4. A small number were elementary schools and the rest junior highs. Even though competition for the most popular meant that not all could get in, half of East Harlem's junior high students were attending one of the alternative schools. Between 1978 and 1989 District 4's reading scores rose by 14.2 per cent compared with 2.3 per cent for the city as a whole. In 1974 only 15.3 per cent of the students had been able to read at or above grade level. In 1991, 43 per cent of East Harlem students were doing grade-level work; the city average was 49 per cent. The District now regularly sends students to New York's élite high schools and on to colleges and universities. In 1974, such results were considered impossible.

Britain's Education Reform Act 1988 has also tried to introduce a form of parent choice by limiting the local education authorities' (LEAs) power to control where students can go to school. Open enrolment has worked quite well within strict confines. The Act restricts parents' choices to existing schools, the one exception being the city technology colleges (CTCs), built especially for children in the poorer urban areas — the ones who most need help and whose existing schools are failing them. There are only 15 CTCs up and running, and the concentrated criticism of the education establishment and the Labour opposition, shortage of private funding and excess capacity in the existing system, mean more CTCs are unlikely to be built. While they are only a minuscule addition to the system, they do demonstrate some of the principles we should be adopting. Student/parent response is another gauge of the success of what they are offering — all CTCs are over-subscribed, with three times more applications than places on average.

John Chubb and Terry Moe defined their attractions:

The CTCs' programme combines academic and vocational training, is closely linked with industry, and gives special

107

emphasis to maths, science and technology, including the most recent developments in computers and information processing. This is also the kind of curriculum that has special appeal to urban children, many of whom are turned off by pure academics, and are especially interested in gaining technical proficiency and work-related skills of value in a modern economy . . .

A standard line from critics is that the CTCs are selective, that they 'skim the cream' by taking the best students. But this is not true in any meaningful sense. The CTCs want students who are motivated to learn, who have a special interest in what the CTCs have to offer, and whose parents are committed to being involved and supportive. This has nothing to do with class, ethnicity, or other bases of social stratification. The CTC ethos is one of hard work and high expectations — for everyone. Indeed, they keep their children in class more hours per week and more days per year than the State-maintained schools . . .

As organisations the CTCs are free of LEA control, and the whole idea is for them to use their autonomy to develop the programmes, staffing, curricula and relationships most conducive to effective schooling. School heads are expected to take the lead — not just manage — and they have every opportunity to strike out in imaginative new directions. Not surprisingly, teachers are flocking to the CTCs. According to Cyril Taylor, chair of the CTC Fund, they recently had some 2000 applicants for 50 advertised jobs. This, while the establishment talks of teacher 'shortages'.

The 1988 Act also allowed schools to 'opt out' of the system, freeing themselves from LEA control and becoming subordinate only to the Department of Education and Science whose present stance is hands-off. All sorts of schools are trying to opt out, in half the LEAs in Britain and in rich and poor areas alike. By November 1992, 350 schools had completed the process of opting out, and two-thirds were operating with their new autonomy. If current projections remain on target, 1500 schools are expected to have opted out of LEA control by April 1994. Meanwhile, in March 1993, it was announced that 500 further education colleges were leaving local council control at the start of a drive to catch up with Germany's higher retention rates in its education system among 15- to 18-year-olds and its superior standard of technical training.

Finally, there is learning itself. Learning is the end point of everything I have discussed here. The fact that students are not learning what they need in order to have satisfying, successful, creative and financially rewarding lives is what has inspired this reappraisal of our present system. Many people around the world have criticised the current state of education, and the failure to provide what is needed.

One of the most pungent is Thomas Sowell of the Hoover Institute in the United States. His book, *Inside American Education,* includes a blistering indictment of the education élites. Education in this country has not reached the state Sowell is fulminating against, but anyone who is prepared to look honestly at our system today can see local equivalents and in some cases the same corruption he is criticising:

> They have taken our money, betrayed our trust, failed our children, and then lied about the failure with inflated grades and pretty words. They have used our children as guinea pigs for experiments, targets for propaganda, and warm bodies to be moved here and there to mix and match for racial balance, to pad enrolments in foreign language programmes mislabelled 'bilingual', or just to be warehoused until labor unions are willing to let them enter the job market. They have proclaimed their special concern for minority students, while placing those students into those colleges where they are most likely to fail. They have proclaimed their dedication to freedom of ideas and the quest for truth, while turning educational institutions into bastions of dogma and the most intolerant institutions in American society. They have presumed to be the conscience of society and to teach ethics to others, while shamelessly exploiting college athletes, overcharging the government, organising price-fixing cartels, and leaving the teaching of undergraduates to graduate student assistants and junior and part-time faculty, while the tenured faculty pursue research and its rewards.

Thomas Sowell is calling for nothing less than a revolution in schools. I also think a revolution is needed.

Fiscal Impact

The adoption of the education system I have outlined in

this chapter would have a significant impact on government spending. It would immediately remove $5000 million of educational expenditure from the government budget and replace it with $1200 million of targeted low-income cash-grant payments for education.

This reduction in financial commitments would enable the government to immediately reduce income taxation to nil for families with children at school, up to the following levels of family income:

1 child at school	$32,000
2 children at school	$42,000
3 children at school	$52,000
4 children at school	$62,000

Where any family fell short of the above income levels, the family would qualify for an education cash grant (voucher) of one dollar for every three dollars that their income was short of the prescribed income level.

The cost of the cash grant (voucher) scheme would fall as employment increased, partly as a result of dramatically lower taxes and partly because of the better incentives for business that would exist. The cost to government of university and technical institution education would decline over five years as a result of moving the cost on to the individual student or family. The government would have a contingent liability to the extent that it guaranteed student loans.

6 Health Care by Choice

*People want doctors to take responsibility for making them
well, and they want someone else to assume responsibility for
paying for it. Medical statistics indicate that many people
place a very low price on good health. They treat their bodies
as something to be abused instead of maintained. The result
is that about 70 per cent of all health problems are self-
induced . . . I do not question the right of people to abuse
their health because the individual's ownership of his own
body is the most basic property right of each person. But the
people who work to maintain good health have the right not
to pay for the consequences of an involuntary health
programme that will do nothing but encourage bad health
while encouraging lax medical treatment.*

John Galt, *Dreams Come Due: Government and
Economics As If Freedom Mattered*

In New Zealand, nearly 80 per cent of the money spent on
health comes from government and most of that
expenditure is made through the Department of Health. Of
the remaining 20 per cent, about 15 per cent is from
private patients whose contributions make up the greater
part of spending on geriatric, paramedical, dental and
specialist care; just over 2 per cent is from insurance
refunds, which go mainly to pay for short stays in hospital
and general practitioner (GP) visits; and a similar amount
is from payments by the Accident Compensation
Corporation (ACC) towards short stays in hospital and
paramedical, GP, specialist and diagnostic services.

According to the 1991 statement of government health
policy, *Your Health and the Public Health,* in the preceding
10 years the Department of Health's budget expanded from
$1.1 billion in 1980 to $3.8 billion, a 27 per cent increase
over and above the increase in consumer prices during that
period. Despite this, in health service terms, the 1980s

were marked as a decade of growing disquiet from health professionals and the public about falling standards of health care. A series of government reports gave official recognition to the system's multitude of inadequacies but engendered little change. By 1990 there was a general feeling that health care was in crisis. Two years earlier, the Hospital Taskforce observed that:

> . . . most New Zealanders have come to believe that a wide range of health services will be available, as of right, when they want them. In reality the system falls well short of this . . . [But] government cannot do everything for everyone. All the technological possibilities of modern medicine cannot be made available . . . Nor can people avoid responsibility for their own health in the expectation that outside agencies will protect them or [automatically and for little or no cost] repair the effects of their neglect.

There are a number of pressures on the health system that did not exist in 1938. Changes in family structures, the growing number of households with both parents at work and the increased tendency for families and individuals to move away from home towns have reduced traditional family care of the elderly and disabled. Various groups in society have come to feel badly and inappropriately treated by the existing system. An increasingly educated society wants more information, more say and more control over their health care. And a rapidly ageing population will begin to put greater and greater strain on resources. This situation is being repeated all over the world. At present, 18 of the 24 countries in the OECD are either planning or enacting health reform. In the 1992 election in the United States, health reform was one of the main campaign planks of presidential winner, Bill Clinton.

The change of government in New Zealand at the end of 1990 was also expected to bring changes to the health system. Revisions in funding, provision and management structures came into force in 1992/93. Unfortunately for the people who work in the health sector, and who are thoroughly demoralised by the endless tinkering of the past few years, and equally unfortunately for the people they serve, the latest changes still will not solve the continuing problems of cost, efficiency, equity and morale.

The present problems have been a long time in the making, appearing slowly as the State health system grew haphazardly. In *Healthy Competition,* authors John Logan, David Green and Alan Woodfield listed some of the results, including the following:

> Since 1938 no political party in power has fundamentally changed the structure of medical care delivery, and the poor have been major losers. The reason is that the GMS [General Medical Services] benefit has fallen to a very small proportion of the cost of visiting a GP, who is the gatekeeper to medication, specialist referral, and hospitalisation. The uninsured poor have considerable financial difficulty getting access to medical care, and some have attempted to bypass the GP in favour of care in outpatient departments of public hospitals, to which they are not 'properly' entitled. The uninsured poor are also most likely to be found on long waiting lists for elective surgery in public hospitals. Over time, the poor have been getting a smaller proportion of health expenditure. The system designed mainly to protect them has ended up enriching the middle classes.

Many of the issues and arguments canvassed in the previous chapter on education are just as applicable to the health system — competition, choice, ownership, access for the disadvantaged and the transitional costs encountered in moving from one system to another. But perhaps the most important from the point of view of the person looking for medical treatment or advice is access. As Logan et al record, the irony of the present situation is that the very people the system was designed to help have become the ones it gives least assistance to.

Access at primary (GP/specialist) and secondary (hospital) levels is in each case beset with its own set of problems. In the primary sector, they can be traced right back to the fight between government and the medical profession at the time of the Social Security Act 1938. To quote Logan again:

> The government believed it had received a mandate to introduce a free and universal health service. Unfortunately

for the government, the medical profession refused to play its prescribed role. Virtually all members of the New Zealand branch of the British Medical Association refused to join a state-funded capitation scheme or become salaried rural or hospital medical staff, and insisted on maintaining a fee-for-service payment structure. Moreover, the government's approved fees were not accepted as full payment . . . and what emerged was the so-called 'dual system' of public and private health care delivery.

When this dual system began, the GMS benefit covered about 75 per cent of the standard fee for a visit to a GP. By 1988 it covered less than 10 per cent of the normal adult fee although there were more generous arrangements for some groups such as the elderly, children, social welfare beneficiaries and the chronically ill. Despite the fact that it has been increased substantially since then, the fees the public are asked to pay have not decreased to any noticeable extent. Strict controls on the number of doctors practising in this country through the limited number of places at medical schools and through immigration policy, mean there is virtually no pressure on doctors to lower prices. And, despite the 1986 reform of the Commerce Act which prohibits collective pricing agreements and set minimum fees, primary sector doctors are remarkably consistent in their prices.

Primary care is funded through what one government report called 'a bizarre mixture of subsidies . . . set at widely varying levels, between zero and 100 per cent'. There is no rationale for the differences — some services such as laboratory tests are virtually 100 per cent subsidised whereas X-rays have a much lower subsidy. As a result, a patient can miss out on the most appropriate treatment. It also encourages over-use of the more heavily subsidised services which still have to be paid for by the government (i.e., the taxpayer). There are no limits on the use of services which are subsidised, so spending is uncontrolled. In 1990/91 the government paid approximately $945 million in primary care benefits but had no way of finding out how effectively the funding was used and no way of making sure it went to those who needed it most. The user part-charges in primary care are limited to a small range of services and are not related to people's ability to pay.

Access can also be limited by a person's locality. The distribution of GPs across the country is very uneven with rural areas and small towns often inadequately serviced while the affluent areas in large cities are frequently relatively over-serviced.

ACC payments allow immediate access and more favourable treatment for people injured in accidents, while those incapacitated through illness receive no comparable help. Beneficiaries receive more generous subsidies than people on low wages whose after-tax income is the same or in some cases less than that of beneficiaries.

Access by the general public to hospital care is equally arbitrary and is regarded as the greatest failure of the hospital system. Unless a person is injured in an accident or suffers a medical emergency such as appendicitis or a heart attack, he or she can wait for up to four years for elective surgery in a public hospital. How long the patient waits depends on where he or she lives and what kind of operation is needed. GPs and specialists can give endless examples of people whose lives have been radically changed because of the length of time spent on a waiting list — further deterioration of their condition, severe pain, loss of mobility, loss of employment, loss of independence, financial hardship and reliance on a sickness benefit (which is an additional cost to another part of the State welfare system).

Between 1981 and 1991 the number of people waiting for surgery rose from about 38,000 to around 62,000, an increase of just over 60 per cent. Those numbers would not be so important if the time spent waiting was relatively brief. The problem arises when, on average, 55 per cent have to wait more than six months and 15 per cent more than two years for their operation (1988 figures). These figures do not take into account the people waiting to get on to the waiting lists. A person must first get an out-patients appointment to determine whether or not he or she needs treatment. In 1991, waiting times for a general surgery out-patients appointment were between one week and six months; for ear, nose and throat patients they were up to 12 months. However, a person who has insurance or who can afford to pay for an initial appointment with a private specialist operating in the public system, can go directly on to a waiting list for surgery, avoiding out-patients completely. According to the Hospital and Related Services Taskforce (1988):

> *Hospitals have great difficulty in determining patients'*
> *priorities. They tend to respond to plaintive pressure from*
> *patients, general practitioners, politicians or the media. The*
> *uncomplaining, less articulate and poorer members of society*
> *tend to gravitate to the end of the queues. Every waiting list*
> *accumulates a number of people at the end who have been*
> *waiting a very long time . . . The middle class have much*
> *more ability to work the system. They are also more likely to*
> *be insured, which allows them to opt for private treatment if*
> *faced by too long a wait.*

However, even people with insurance are restricted in the treatment they can have in private hospitals. For instance, many private insurance companies will not cover high-cost intensive treatment.

The Regional Health Authorities (RHAs) which fund public hospitals have their budget allocated by the government, basically on a per capita basis. When the authorities have to make cuts, they usually find the easiest way is to reduce services. In fact, the public hospital system in New Zealand, like the NHS in Britain and the Canadian national health system, uses waiting lists as one of the ways to ration services and thereby limit the total amount spent on health care. A few years ago, *The New England Journal of Medicine,* in analysing the costs of health care in Canada and the United States, concluded that Canada had found a way to produce health care at less cost that the US and that the reason was the former's socialised health system. In fact, Canada spent less of its GDP on health care (just under 9 per cent in 1992 compared to 12 per cent in the US) not because its government had found a way to produce health care at lower prices but because it limits the total supply of services made available. Just as in New Zealand, this rationing of supply denies treatment to some and makes others wait.

However, there are problems in just looking at GDP/GNP type figures. John C. Goodman and Gerald L. Musgrove pointed out in their book *Patient Power* that:

> ... over the 20 year period, 1967 to 1987, Canada's real GNP per capita grew 74 per cent while that of the USA grew only 38 per cent. If you look at health care spending alone, rather than its relationship with GNP, we discover that before Canada implemented its system of national health insurance, the country was spending 75 per cent of what the United States spent in health care per person and in 1987, Canada continued to spend 75 per cent of the US level.

Real health care cost increases over the 20-year period have been virtually the same in both countries.

Because of the limits imposed on expenditure and resources and the elasticity of demand, there is a great need to make the most efficient use of the resources that are available in order to provide as much health care as possible. But the way the health system has been structured has made this unlikely. There is very little awareness of the cost of services and procedures and of the relative benefits of different treatments according to cost. In some cases, even heads of hospital departments have virtually no idea how much each procedure costs. In both primary and secondary sectors uneven levels of subsidies obscure the real price from professionals and consumers.

Inefficiency, lack of cost controls and poor management in the secondary sector are important not just because the sector consumes more than two-thirds of health expenditure but because of its size. Hospitals form the largest industry in New Zealand and are the biggest and most complex of the State businesses. In most towns that have one, the hospital is the largest employer. How they perform has a significant impact on the economy.

In 1987, the American firm Arthur Andersen and

117

Company were commissioned by the Hospital Taskforce to report on the relative efficiency of the hospital sector. The major part of their work was comparing costs and work practices between hospitals within New Zealand. Despite quibbles about some aspects of their methodology, commentators inside and outside the system agreed with the overall findings: that there were massive inefficiencies and huge gains to be made in better use and reallocation of resources in the secondary sector. The gains were between 24 per cent and 32 per cent of operating expenditure, approximately $450 million to $600 million in 1986/87 values. The first was the equivalent of the government grant to the Auckland Hospital Board for operating expenses that same year; the second was almost as much as the combined operating grant for the two largest hospital boards in the country, Auckland and Canterbury. A major part of the gains came from reducing the length of hospital stays, reducing hospital facilities, greater efficiency in hospital departments and more efficient support departments. There were also substantial gains in improving incentives within the system.

According to the Andersen report, although there was little attention paid to good management, there were places where efficiency levels were good. They reflected the excellence of individual managers, and in nearly all cases the service had a good or very good reputation, disproving the concern that greater efficiency causes a drop in quality. However, the perverse incentives of the system to date give no reinforcement to good management but instead reward poor performance, inefficiency and cost overruns with continued funding and in some cases, where services are in jeopardy, extra funding. One of the most graphic examples of cost variation and therefore potential gains is in geriatric care. In 1987 the *lowest* cost for a geriatric patient in an acute hospital ranged between $64 to $199 per day in a small hospital and $99 to $657 per day in the largest hospitals.

At the time Arthur Andersen were reviewing the secondary sector, taxation-funded spending by the government had increased over the previous two years by 50 per cent in money terms and almost 20 per cent in real terms. Despite this, there was only an insignificant increase in the services provided by the public hospital system.

For some years now, medical researcher Dr Max Gammon has been comparing input and output in British hospitals. He has labelled his findings 'the theory of bureaucratic displacement' and says that in 'a bureaucratic system . . . increase in expenditure will be matched by fall in production'. Such systems, he says, act 'rather like "black holes" in the economic universe, simultaneously sucking in resources and shrinking in terms of "emitted" production'.

A couple of years ago American economist Milton Friedman tested Gammon's law on the US hospital system. Although the health system in the United States is regularly referred to as a market-driven system, this is very far from the case. In the last 25 years the government has become a major player. Since 1966 and the introduction of Medicare and Medicaid, the government's role in the health system has burgeoned, especially at Federal level, both in spending and in tax and regulatory intervention. The US Government's share of total health spending went from 15 per cent during the 1920s to 25 per cent in 1965 and then surged to 42 per cent in the next two decades, roughly the same level as today. At the same time, private spending on health, which had remained fairly constant between 1922 and 1958, also rose, at first slowly and then rapidly.

But as government and private expenditure grew, Friedman found that hospitals' output fell. After taking into account a number of factors such as the advances in medical science and technology that allowed more procedures to be performed outside hospital and quicker recovery time for those in hospital, he concluded that Gammon's law was at work in the US system.

One of the factors that has driven up costs in the US and that holds up costs and wastes resources in New Zealand

and in countries such as Britain and Canada is restrictive practices in the supply of medical care. A true free market in health care would mean an end to the medical monopoly, to the enforced licensing of health-care providers, to mandatory insurance cover, even to the distinction between prescription and non-prescription drugs. Although the argument for licensing in all occupations has been to protect consumers from the incompetent and unscrupulous, it does not stop consumers from being hurt, as a variety of cases in the past few years have shown. At the same time the consumers' choice is reduced, prices rise and the rewards go to a select few at the expense of many. As Arthur Caplan, director of the Centre for Biomedical Ethics at the University of Minnesota, says, 'Health care is a very labour-inefficient enterprise. You have highly trained people doing things that could be done by others.'

Two of the best examples in the medical world at present are nurse practitioners and midwives. Doctors also resist competition from physician assistants, osteopaths, podiatrists, chiropractors, optometrists, acupuncturists and pharmacists, all of whom earn less, on average, than physicians. Arthur Caplan describes nurse practitioners (registered nurses with additional training) as 'an underutilised, untapped resource that could help reduce the cost of health care significantly'. In particular, he suggests that nurse practitioners could serve rural and inner-city areas where doctors prefer not to practise, and do an 'excellent job at primary care'. The only obstacle — 'doctors want to exercise their monopoly power'.

The medical profession and the health system combine forces to shut out independent practice nurses in this country. The 1991 government health report, *Your Health and the Public Health,* cited just one case:

> When the tiny township of Matata in the Bay of Plenty set up a community health committee, it had no visiting doctor, no Plunket or public health nurse, and restricted access to the district nurse. A doctor now holds a once-weekly clinic there, but the Matata Community Health Committee feels that the community's needs would best be met by a community clinic

staffed by an independent community practice nurse . . .
[with] no tie to a particular doctor.

Unfortunately for the community, subsidies are paid for
practice nurses only when they are employed by a doctor.
By making RHAs the purchasers of health services, the
latest health reforms may allow Matata to get their
community practice nurse; but restrictions, such as not
being allowed to prescribe, will still limit a practice nurse's
effectiveness.

The midwives' story is a similar one. As normal
pregnancy and birth has become increasingly medicalised,
more and more women have started asking for a service
which treats the process as a natural one and not an illness
which needs heavy medical intervention. Midwives offer
this service, keep closer contact with the mother before and
after the birth than the great majority of doctors, and
generally cost less. However, allowing them to work
without a supervising GP or obstetrician has been
strenuously fought by doctors in many countries including
America and New Zealand.

The argument used repeatedly is that babies and
mothers are put at greater risk, especially if the birth is
difficult. However, studies do not bear this out. In 1960 in
Madera County, California, neonatal mortality dropped
from 24 to 10 per 1000 births when nurse-midwives were
introduced into a poor agricultural area. After pressure
from the State medical association ended the programme in
1963, midwives were replaced by obstetricians and the
neonatal mortality rate rose to 32 per 1000 births while the
number of women receiving no prenatal care doubled. In
Holland the national health-care system deliberately
reversed a trend towards hospital-style births a decade ago.
A study of all births in 1986 found that, at all risk levels
after 32 weeks' gestation, perinatal mortality was 'much
lower under the noninterventionist care of midwives than
under the interventionist management of obstetricians'.

The reason always given for intervention is protection of
a group or society which would otherwise be exposed to

unacceptable risk. Government intervention in health care (and intervention/regulation by the medical profession) is usually explained as being the result of market failure. Health care is considered different, like education, and a number of reasons are commonly given to justify government becoming involved.

The first is that private insurers are not as willing as a State insurer would be to cover people on low incomes or with serious health problems. Logan et al point out that:

> *It may be true that the poor cannot afford health insurance premiums, but it does not follow that the state must be a monopoly funder, less still that the state must directly supply health care. We have already shown that the New Zealand welfare state has* not *effectively insured those on low incomes. Instead, the state covers large hospital expenditures for low and high income patients alike.*

On the argument that private insurers in a competitive market try to 'shed high-risk applicants', the authors point out that competitive insurers have incentives to offer low premiums to all risk classes but they also differentiate between risk groups so that the more risky pay higher premiums.

Government regulation and subsidy are said to be necessary when a market is heavily regulated and there is only slight chance of real competition. The obvious answer here is not more regulation (and distortion) but less. By breaking down the barriers to entry into the health market and expanding the number and variety of suppliers of medical care, the costs to consumers can and will be reduced.

Those in favour of State intervention also argue that when third parties pay for medical expenses in a free market, it can lead to the over-supply and over-use of medical services. However, one of the great strengths of the private insurance market is that it relieves people of large and unanticipated medical bills. Certainly it is not easy for insurers to monitor the actions of providers and consumers which partly determine the demand for medical care. The question is: Does the State handle this any better, given that the same problem occurs in government insurance schemes? Some researchers have suggested that the government possibly might improve on market arrangements by taxing commodities which encourage poor health and subsidising those that promote good health.

The former argument on the over-use of medical services, often referred to as 'moral hazard', has a sister, 'merit goods'. Whereas with the first the concern is that too many health services will be provided and consumed, with merit goods the fear is that not enough health services will be used. The same élite or governing group that decides when enough becomes too much are also the ones who judge that people have not used enough health care. Education is another merit good where ordinary people, apparently, are not capable of choosing the 'right' amount for themselves.

Attached to the merit good argument is a concern about consumers' lack of information in a free market. People cannot know everything about everything. Instead they hire experts to act as agent and consultant, be it a doctor, lawyer, real estate agent or car mechanic. Logan et al point out that 'to say that doctors or other professionals exploit the ignorance of their clients is like saying that teachers exploit the ignorance of their pupils or road-map sellers exploit the ignorance of tourists'. This exchange of expertise for payment works most efficiently in a free market as long as there are strong laws against fraud and misrepresentation. What is not clear is how government intervention can correct this consumer 'disadvantage'. Patients know no more under a government-run medical system.

The one place where most people agree that it is worthwhile for government to become involved is in the general area of public health. When the actions of individuals have negative effects or impose a cost on those around them, for example, pollution, and the polluter can escape the full cost of his or her actions, then the level of pollution is likely to rise. Conversely, if a person does something that benefits many people but can get no reward for it, then too few positives will be produced. In public health, the two major areas where there can be negative effects from people's actions are in infectious diseases and sanitation. On the positive side, it is possible that private industry would be unlikely to support pure research or research that has no immediate marketable results, and therefore a case could be made for some government subsidy. In New Zealand, government expenditure on public health and medical research is about 2.3 per cent, a negligible amount of the total expenditure on health and health-related services.

Because there are always going to be constraints on the quantity of health services available, no matter what system is chosen to organise health care, the most fundamental question is how to provide care to the poor or those overwhelmed by severe illness. Obviously the more efficient the system, the more people will be able to afford it and the easier it will be to provide for those who cannot, through public assistance. The government can help people pay for health care without taking over the medical business just as it can help them pay for food and clothing without nationalising supermarkets and clothes stores. In order to gain that efficiency and maintain it, we need a health system where choice and competition can operate freely and where regulation of all kinds is kept to a minimum.

What follows is an outline of the proposed health care system, its key objectives, how the system would function, and the principles to be followed in its design, along with some comments on how the health market-place in New Zealand differs from other product markets.

PROPOSED HEALTH CARE SYSTEM

Health Market
Consumers in New Zealand have no opportunity to reduce waste, inefficiency or high prices by searching for good, attractively priced health services. Producers are not rewarded for finding better ways to meet consumer needs.

The reason for this is that in the health-care sector, normal market procedures have been replaced by government institutions and rule making. For example:

❏ Consumers are not spending their money but someone else's money. New Zealand's cost-plus system could never exist if patients were essentially spending their own money.

❏ Producers' incomes depend less on service to patients than on meeting the policies of third parties' (government, ACC and private insurance) reimbursement formulas.

❏ Individuals mainly have to take what is provided. Choice is limited.

❏ Innovation and technological change are often seen as negative.

❏ Normal advertising is off limits, so information is at a premium.

❏ Virtually no negotiations take place over price.

❏ Self-interest is often serviced by withholding information in the medical market-place.

Key Objectives

❏ To ensure the system is fiscally sound, that is, sustainable.

❏ To provide assistance to meet the needs of the most disadvantaged.

❏ To ensure that any income transfers are made efficiently.

❏ To create a structure of incentives that encourages self-sufficiency.

❏ To transfer power from large hospital institutions and government bureaucracies to individuals.

❏ To ensure patients become principal buyers of health care.

❏ To remove health care as much as possible from the political arena, where well-organised special interest groups cause so much damage.

❏ To introduce competition via market-based institutions.

Roles

In a health-care system that meets the objectives just mentioned, the roles of patients, doctors, hospitals, insurance companies and government will be very different. The main differences will be as follows:

❐ *Patients* rather than third-party payers (for example, a Regional Health Authority) will become the main buyers of health care with the opportunity to compare insurance plans and prices and to make decisions.

❐ *Doctors* will no longer serve third parties but instead will help the patient make informed decisions.

❐ *Hospitals* will no longer serve third parties or physicians, but will compete in the business of health-care delivery by improving quality and lowering prices.

❐ *Insurance companies* will tend to specialise in the business of insurance and reimburse policy-holders in cases of unforeseen health care treatment.

❐ *Government* in its role of insurer will no longer serve as a buyer of health care but will, in effect, pay the insurance premiums of low-income people. In its policy-making role it will promote the objectives of the proposed system on the demand side by encouraging private payment of small medical fees and ensuring people have private health insurance for large items of expenditure, and life-long savings for medical needs in retirement. On the supply side it will encourage free and open competition in the marketplace for hospital services, doctors, specialists and private health insurance.

Principles

Why is it that although we all know that free markets work while bureaucracies like communism do not, in the area of health care this message falls on deaf ears? Despite the fact that we cannot dismantle the present health care system overnight, we can start to move rapidly in that direction if we are prepared to adopt the right policies. There are some specific principles that need to be followed:

❐ Ensure that all New Zealanders have the means to

purchase a no-frills catastrophic insurance policy at a reasonable price.

❐ Ensure that people can choose among competing health-insurance policies in order to select the type of coverage best suited to their individual and family needs.

❐ Allow individuals the opportunity to choose between self-insurance and private third-party insurance for minor medical expenditure.

❐ Ensure that all New Zealanders build sufficient savings to look after their medical expenses in retirement.

❐ Ensure that people have the opportunity to compare prices in the market-place.

❐ Provide suppliers of medical services with new opportunities and rewards for finding cost-reducing ways of delivering medical care.

❐ Ensure that those people who are retired at 30 June 1993 are adequately provided for in the new system.

The System

The proposed system that follows is based on the concept of everyone being responsible for buying insurance to cover themselves against major and unexpected medical costs, and the costs of any additional services they might choose, in return for a reduction in taxes. Where beneficiaries or those on low incomes have difficulty covering the cost of the insurance premiums, the government will provide subsidies but the choice of the insurer will still belong to the individual.

Contract I

1. A compulsory insurance policy will cover annual health costs in excess of 5 per cent of the family income. Compulsory insurance is designed to cover low-probability but high-cost events such as hospitalisation. This is when insurance cover is likely to be of most value to people. Moreover, experience shows that people tend to insure against the more serious and expensive incidents and not for the routine, such as a visit to the doctor; just as motor insurance is not taken out to cover regular servicing costs.

Permanent residents and citizens of other countries who have work permits or who are studying in New Zealand will be included in the scheme. Tourists and other short-term visitors will not.

The proposal includes a significant deductible (the amount paid by the insured person before insurance cover begins — like the 'excess' payment in car insurance). This is intended to encourage the consumer to keep a check on the health supplier, particularly in low-cost treatments. It is also intended to stop numerous low-value claims. The level of the deductible will limit any efficiency cost imposed by compulsory insurance, as most families could be expected to voluntarily buy such insurance even without a compulsory scheme. Its level varies according to family income. This means that families on high incomes will be required to fund a larger proportion of their health care expenditure from income, savings or voluntary insurance.

For a family with an income (male and female combined) equal to $30,000 a year, the maximum annual health-care costs they will have to pay for, other than the cost of their compulsory insurance premium, will be around $1500. Income is to be determined on the taxable income of the whole family. A family includes members up to the age of 18; anyone over 18 will be classed as a separate family.

2. The policy is to be non-cancellable and is to be renewed annually by the policy-holder. This allows people to change insurers, who must face competitive pressures. At the same time, insurers will not be permitted to cancel or refuse to renew a policy. This will help prevent their skimming off low-risk individuals and leaving high-risk people without cover. This rule will be backed by a requirement that all members of a family have to be covered. In this way, a child born with serious health problems will automatically be covered by the parents' insurer. The existing family insurer will also be required, if requested, to insure an existing member setting up a separate family (for example, people aged 18 and over). In this way the establishment of new families will not lead to a loss of cover.

3. Premiums will be set in the market on an actuarial basis

taking account of broad risk factors. Generally insurers will be permitted to offer insurance contracts at rates which they choose. A competitive market, with low barriers to entry into and exit from the industry, will ensure that rates reflect actual costs. Insurers will be free to establish broad risk categories — for instance age, occupation, location, gender, smoker or non-smoker — and to charge different premiums based on these factors. These will act as incentives to a healthy lifestyle. Premiums will also differ depending on the size of the family.

Insurers will not, however, be allowed to take account of a particular family's medical status or claims history in setting premiums. This will prevent insurers from using the premium price to push high-risk families into cancelling their policies. In effect, premiums will be set on a group insurance basis.

4. The insurer can set up lists of approved health providers and has the right to seek second opinions before approving treatment. Once health spending exceeds the deductible of 5 per cent, the consumer has little incentive to contain health costs for the rest of that year. To help address this problem, insurers will be allowed to approve health providers and to require members wanting treatment to be examined by health professionals appointed by them. These techniques for improving the incentives to economise on health spending already apply to some private health-insurance policies.

5. Another way of controlling the problems of escalating costs referred to above is to permit insurers to own and operate providers of health services. Some insurers already own hospitals (for example, Southern Cross). In a competitive market for health care and health insurance, other health services might be provided by insurers. They should have the opportunity to organise services in the most efficient way.

6. The contract will include mental illness, geriatric care and ACC-related health care. It is intended to provide comprehensive cover for health-care costs, regardless of the cause of ill health. This will avoid artificial boundaries

between accident and sickness and enable health care to be integrated. Geriatric care can be expected to be assessed according to the degree of support that the patient requires. I believe a much greater diversity of treatment will emerge with better use of the full range of health professionals and greater emphasis on non-institutional care.

7. The policy is to cover health treatment in New Zealand only. People travelling overseas on business or holiday will not be covered. Similarly, travel overseas for treatment will be covered only to the extent of the equivalent cost of the treatment in New Zealand. These measures are necessary to add an element of certainty to the potential cost of treatment.

8. Experimental treatment and procedures are excluded. Their potential high costs suggest that insurers should be allowed to exclude them from their policies.

9. The maximum annual cost of treating a person for a single illness will be limited to $1 million. Exclusions for particular health conditions, for example, AIDS, are not proposed. An upper limit on the insurer's exposure for a single illness or accident will, however, add an element of certainty to the maximum possible cost of claims. The costs in excess of this amount will be covered by reinsurance.

10. Insurers can offer separate policies to cover health-care costs other than those covered under the compulsory contract. Such supplementary contracts will not be subject to any special terms and conditions. Insurers will obviously take into account the incentive implications of offering insurance for part or all of the deductible element of the compulsory contract. They might, for example, charge higher premiums than otherwise under the compulsory contract, the voluntary contract, or both.

11. The cost of collecting insurance premiums can be reduced by providing for a direct credit to the insurer's account with direct debits in the insured's bank account, or by deductions from pay or benefits. The knowledge that policies are non-cancellable weakens the incentive for the insured to pay his or her premium. Government regulation

will be necessary to ensure payment, and assistance in policing non-payment and non-participation will be necessary.

Contract II

The second compulsory contract is designed to ensure that when people reach retirement age (65 by the year 2001) they have saved sufficient funds to meet their health-care premiums until the end of their lives. The aim of this policy is to have comprehensive coverage of people aged 65 and over, without recourse to the State. Uncertainty about being able to afford health costs in old age is a key concern of people approaching retirement. Health-care costs for the elderly can be substantial. This proposal will give them security.

The details of the proposed contract are as follows:

1. The policy becomes compulsory from age 18. The point at which people should have to start saving involves a trade-off between the annual amount which must be saved and the period over which saving takes place. The suggested starting point of 18, although not recognising the high costs involved in job training and establishing families, which younger people incur, is offset by the tax reductions proposed as part of the wider reform measures contained in this book. A person will be allowed to save more than the compulsory amount. Voluntary contributions can be withdrawn at any time or used to reduce the level of compulsory savings that need to be made in subsequent years.
2. The annual savings will be set to fund the estimated cost of health insurance premiums from 65 until death. The compulsory deduction of income has been set at 2 per cent for the first five years and at 2.5 per cent thereafter until the age of retirement is reached or a person's fund reaches the estimated cost of health insurance premiums from 65 until death. Any shortfall in the amount saved at retirement will be made up in the same way as in the case of pensions payable in retirement (see Chapter 7).

3. Each person's savings will be accounted for separately. The scheme will operate on an individual basis. Savings will be accumulated in each person's name. Savings sharing between couples will be the same as in providing for retirement pensions.

4. People over the age of 65 will personally be required to pay for annual health costs up to a limit of 5 per cent of their post-retirement income. The provisions of Contract I would apply.

5. The insurer will be required to cover the contributor for his or her health costs, beyond the 5 per cent threshold, from age 65.

6. Savings will be locked in. A contributor will be able to access his or her savings only on taking up permanent residence in another country. Immigrants will generally be required to contribute a lump sum appropriate to their age. The estate of people who die before reaching age 65 will receive the balance (including interest) in the contributor's account. There would be no refund when people aged 65 and over die. Contributors will not be allowed to borrow against their accumulated savings.

7. Policy-holders will be permitted to take out additional insurance.

Regulatory Issues
❐ The government will have to legislate for compulsory coverage, the deduction of contributions from wages, salaries and the self-employed, and the collection of contributions by the Inland Revenue Department.

❐ Low barriers to entry into and exit from the insurance industry are necessary to encourage insurers to be efficient. For this reason, industry-specific regulation of insurers should be avoided as far as possible. The primary responsibility for evaluating the financial stability of insurers should rest with consumers. They would be permitted to take their business to another insurer.

In the case of Contract I, the cost to the consumer of non-performance by the insurer is limited, as the contract is renewable on an annual basis. The maximum loss is the premium paid for the balance of the year, the cost of taking out a new policy, and the cost of treatment for those who are ill or become ill prior to buying another policy. These costs are likely to be small. Therefore, industry-specific regulation is not justified.

However, a consumer could suffer a greater loss in the case of Contract II, as savings from age 18 and insurance cover from age 65 are at stake. In the event of such a loss, the government would be likely to have to make a higher top-up on retirement than otherwise would have been expected. In those circumstances, there is a stronger case for some prudential controls on suppliers of Contract II than there is for Contract I. Such suppliers might have to be rated on their claims-paying ability, at least annually, by a recognised international insurance-rating agency. The government should approve rating agencies for the purpose, and ratings should be public and disclosed to all consumers. Since insurers that offer Contract II are also likely to offer Contract I and voluntary contracts, this provision will have some spill-over benefits to consumers of other contracts and is likely to become the industry norm.

Implications for Core Health Services

Under the government's proposed health reforms (1993), core health services are to be defined. This has not been done yet. Core health services are those services to which everyone should have access on affordable terms and without unreasonable waiting times. The present definition of a core service has become a matter of argument, especially in certain areas. One example is ear, nose and throat surgery where long waiting lists include substantial numbers of people waiting to have their noses straightened.

In the system being proposed by government, the list of core health services is to be based on an evaluation of whether the value people place on a health service justifies its cost. I see considerable difficulties with this approach. A central agency does not have the information or resources to determine the costs and benefits of the full range of possible health-care services. These depend on the nature of the patient's condition and the value he or she puts on its alleviation compared to the benefits of buying other goods and services. It involves factors such as pain and suffering which are difficult to evaluate. In addition, a specific list of qualifying services will inevitably lead to fuzzy borders and the gradual lengthening of the list of core services. The ACC scheme provides a good example of this problem. It now covers, and at great cost, conditions and events which were never envisaged or which it was not intended to cover at its conception.

Another difficulty is that if core health services are provided free or at modest cost to consumers, the total cost of health care to the government (and therefore the taxpayer) will be excessive. Therefore the government will be forced to rely on non-price rationing methods, such as waiting lists and poor quality service, to contain costs. These are problems that the definition of core health services is supposed to help alleviate, but which it has proved unable to do.

The scheme proposed here, in contrast to the government's approach, avoids the problem of defining specific core health services. I envisage few exclusions under the system, as competition is likely to promote a range of policies which are attractive to consumers. The best course is to enable consumers to show their preferences directly by their spending decisions. This can be done by private provision of health care, compulsory health insurance for large medical expenses and voluntary arrangements for other health costs.

Implications for Taxes and Benefits

Under the proposed scheme, funding of health care (other than programmes with significant 'public good' attributes, regulation and public health administration) is transferred from the public sector to the private sector. The government will be able to reduce its tax take as public expenditure on health falls, in the process helping people to meet higher private expenditure on health care. In addition, low-income families and beneficiaries will be assisted by government grants. Total public health spending, other than on teaching and research, amounted to $4.15 billion in 1990/91, or $1220 for every New Zealander. Most of this money can eventually be re-directed through the tax and benefit system. If, for example, three-quarters of the 1990/91 expenditure on public health had been returned to people via the tax system, direct taxes on individuals could have been reduced by about 24 per cent on average. This would also have brought additional desirable effects. The efficiency improvements referred to earlier and lower debt from the privatisation of Crown Health Enterprises (CHEs) such as hospitals would enable the deficit to be reduced over time.

Taxes on Alcohol and Tobacco
Taxes on drinks containing alcohol and on tobacco and products containing tobacco, which exceed $1 billion a year, have been justified partly on the basis that they balance the cost which the consumption of these substances imposes on society. The provision of free health services implies that consumers of these products do not directly bear the full cost that their use of alcohol or tobacco imposes on the rest of the community. If health costs are charged to individuals as proposed, directly or through the insurance premiums they pay, there would be a strong case to reduce such taxes to reflect the shifting of a major part of the cost which currently falls on taxpayers.

The Accident Compensation Scheme
The basic goal is to ensure that, in the event of incapacity, everyone is eligible for an acceptable level of income support and has access to health-care services on fair terms. But before considering what needs to be done about accident compensation, we need to consider how to deal with the unfunded liabilities of the present system.

Ongoing liabilities arising from the existing scheme have been assessed at $4 billion on an undiscounted basis, or

$2.5 billion net in present-value terms. If the Accident, Rehabilitation and Compensation Insurance Corporation (ARCIC) is to be opened up to competition, or the private sector is left to take over completely, this issue has to be dealt with.

Recommendation: Decide how accident compensation costs will be recovered in future under a competitive model and then apply a percentage to all annual premiums to cover the continuing cash expenditure for current liabilities. In other words, future policy-owners will pay for today's unfunded liability on an equitable basis. This would include self-insurance on a full cost basis.

Policy Proposals

Work-Related Injuries
1. Providing compulsory insurance cover for work-related injuries should be the responsibility of the employer, including self-cover for the self-employed.
2. The compulsory scheme will continue to be earnings-related with an upper limit on any payout of $600 per week gross, or 80 per cent of previous earnings if this is lower than $600, up to retirement age.
3. Companies or individuals will be entitled, if they so choose, to take out insurance for:
   (i) Payments beyond those specified in 2 above.
   (ii) Lump sum payments.
   (iii) Disability payments.
4. The cost of the compulsory health-care cover as it relates to accident compensation should be kept separate from income protection. In other words, the premiums should have two distinct parts: (i) the cost of earnings-related cover, and (ii) health-care cover.
5. The compulsory health-care cover should involve an acceptable minimum level of disability, vocational and social rehabilitation programmes.
6. Each person will be able to put his or her share of the costs of providing work-related health-care cover for accident compensation towards the purchase of a

comprehensive health-care insurance package for themselves and their family.

7. Self-insurance will be an acceptable practice for large firms where the employers, instead of paying premiums to an insurance company, cover the risk themselves. The definition of 'large' should depend on risk classification.

8. Experience-rating (where premiums reflect the claims record) will automatically develop in a competitive market and should be encouraged.

9. The cost to the employer of providing insurance cover for work injury and health-care costs will be left to the market and competition between insurers.

10. Private-sector insurers will be allowed to operate in the area of injury compensation.

11. Any regulatory issues and reporting requirements of insurance companies will need to be laid down before the introduction of the new schemes. One requirement that may be almost sufficient on its own is to get each company rated annually according to their claims-paying ability.

12. Whether a new State-owned enterprise is necessary to replace the existing ARCIC, whose only task will be to pay out existing liabilities, needs to be determined in light of the response of the private sector to the new opportunities created by opening up the market.

13. Employers will continue to be responsible for the first week of compensation. However, they should be able to fund a longer stand-down period if they have the financial ability to do so, and thereby reduce their premium payments.

Motor-Vehicle and Other Injuries

1. Providing compulsory cover for motor vehicle and non-work-related injuries will be the responsibility of the individual. For these purposes, individual cover is defined as family cover where appropriate (for example, a family of four has one policy cover).

2. The compulsory scheme will continue to be earnings-related with a minimum level of payout being the appropriate invalid's benefit for the family unit.

3. Individuals will be entitled to take out more cover if they wish for:

  (i) Payments beyond those specified in 2 above, including the earning potential of students, people temporarily out of the workforce and children.

  (ii) Lump sum payments.

  (iii) Disability payments.

4. The cost of the compulsory health-care cover as it relates to motor-vehicle and non-work-related accidents should be kept separate from income protection. In other words, the premiums should have two separate parts — the cost of earnings-related cover, and health-care cover costs.

5. The compulsory health-care cover costs will involve an acceptable minimum level of disability, vocational and social rehabilitation programmes.

6. Each person will be able to use the health-care cost of his/her cost of vehicle- and non-work-related insurance cover to purchase a comprehensive health-care insurance package for him/herself and the family.

7. An open enrolment regulatory approach for individual (family) policies will be required so that everyone can get cover along with broad risk-rating categories and individual experience-rating within broad bands.

8. The cost of cover to the individual (family) will be based on market-related premiums and competition between insurers.

9. Private-sector insurers will be allowed to operate in the area of motor-vehicle and non-work-related injuries.

10. Any regulations and/or reporting requirements placed on insurance companies will be the same as those required for work-related coverage by private insurance companies.

11. Whether a State-owned enterprise is required in this area will depend on the response of the private sector.

12. Employees will need to provide evidence to their employers, including government when the main source of income is social welfare, that they have taken out the minimum level of cover for vehicle- and other non-work-related accidents. If they have not, then a deduction (for example, 2 cents in the dollar) towards future cover will be

made from all income.

13. Any government assistance toward helping an individual (family) with the cost of non-work-related cover will be targeted and paid directly to the insurance company of the insured's choice.

TRANSITIONAL ISSUES

The transition from the present health system to the proposed system raises a number of issues which will have to be addressed. The main ones are:

❒ Privatisation of Crown Health Enterprises (CHEs): I cannot see any difficulties in making the transition from Area Health Boards (AHBs) to Regional Health Authorities (RHAs) and CHEs (public hospitals and other health-related institutions) and then to privatisation. The process is similar to that followed in other privatisation exercises.

❒ Property: Under the present system, CHEs are owned by the State. The capital costs of maintaining these properties are substantial and in the budget squeeze of recent years, one of the areas where health and hospital boards have chosen to save money has been in maintenance. The 1991 Health Services Taskforce was told of one hospital that required over $1 million of maintenance work because no funds for maintenance had been set aside. Under the proposed system, hospital and health-services property should be sold within an agreed period of time. The mechanisms for managing this would be the same as those used to change the ownership of schools and other education property.

❒ Development of a private insurance market: The existing health insurance market is small and heavily distorted by the current structure of the health system and the way health services are funded. Provided that the government adopts a credible reform programme with a transparent end point, and an appropriate regulatory regime is introduced, private-sector health insurers will respond. The decision of AMP to offer health insurance in anticipation of the National Government's health reforms illustrates the willingness of private-sector firms to enter the market.

❏ Initial insurance coverage: If there is a concern that existing high-risk consumers, such as those in poor health, will not be offered insurance, it may be necessary to require insurers to provide coverage to everyone who applies to be covered during an initial period. If this is done, an insurer should have the right to decline to provide a policy if it could demonstrate that its risk was clearly unrepresentative of the population; for example, if a disproportionate number of diabetics sought cover with one insurer.

This new system provides for 'grandfathering' of coverage (an insurance policy is non-cancellable) once the scheme is under way. An alternative would be for the government to undertake to cover people who cannot obtain insurance when the scheme is introduced. However, this would result in the government continuing to underwrite health risks for some time and should be avoided.

❏ Special consideration for the retired: Not only will people retiring in future enjoy a higher level of certainty but the proposed system does away with any economic requirements for the present system to cut existing services further. The government would recognise the contingent liability existing for those in retirement at 30 June 1993 by issuing retirement bonds for the full extent of this liability. This would be done to make it clear what their accrual claims were. The status of the bonds would be the same as that of any recognised indebtedness of the government. Each person, in return for their share of the bonds issued, would be provided with a health-care policy on terms provided for under Contract II, as already described.

EFFECTS AND BENEFITS OF THE SYSTEM

Under the present health system government laws and regulations restrict who may provide which health-care services or products to whom and under what circumstances. As a result, New Zealanders are not free to get the health care they want from the providers they choose. The policy described here will bring benefits to those involved in the health-care industry and to those who use their services.

The benefits for the government will be:

❐ The de-politicising of decisions on the provision and funding of health care.

❐ The elimination of non-price rationing of health services and therefore the virtual elimination of waiting times for elective treatment.

❐ The provision of security against large and unpredictable health costs.

❐ The transfer of management of health risks to private sector specialists.

❐ The freeing up of the government to allow it to focus on its key responsibilities: setting and enforcing the rules, the provision of public goods, and supporting those in need.

❐ Fiscally sustainable savings from greater efficiency in the health-care market.

❐ The reduction of public debt from the privatisation of CHEs.

❐ A credible and politically sustainable health policy.

The benefits for users of health-care services will be:

❐ The ability to exercise their preferences directly.

❐ More responsive health-care providers and an improved quality of service.

❐ Secure health care for the elderly.

❐ Lower taxes.

The efficiency benefits are numerous. They will bring:

❐ Increased competition in the provision of health care which will reduce prices and improve the quality of services.

❐ Innovation, with greater flexibility and diversity of services.

❐ Greater consumer choice.

❐ Optimal insurance arrangements that will help contain costs, and at the same time insurers and consumers will monitor health providers.

❑ The production of relevant information on health services (including advertising).

❑ The integration of health-related expenditures — between primary and secondary care and between sickness and accidents.

❑ Better allocation of resources within the health sector, including better decisions on new technology and other labour and capital trade-offs.

❑ The best regulation of health and insurance markets.

Some of the benefits and effects of implementing the system are expanded below.

1. Security will be improved:

(i) Those who are retired will realise that their position has been made secure because the cost of government health care has been reduced by more than 50 per cent and will rapidly reduce further; and the issuing of health bonds will be a guarantee of health coverage.

(ii) Those over 45 and within 20 years of retirement will know that while they will have to contribute yearly towards their own health care in retirement, it will certainly be affordable to them, whereas at the moment it might not be.

(iii) People under 45 with more than 20 years to go to retirement will be assured that their contributions will bring them adequate, affordable health care in retirement. They will benefit from lower personal taxation rates for a major part of their working lives. Also, it will dramatically improve their incentives to earn income and save.

(iv) Low-income earners, beneficiaries and non-earners will all find that their access to health care is secure as a result of the changes.

2. Economic benefits:

(i) The system will provide a major source of funds for long-term capital markets which would, in turn, have a positive effect on growth.

(ii) It will help solve the fiscal problem caused by increased health expenditure.

(iii) It will enable a quick phase-in period from the present system to the new system of health support.

3. Improvements in structure:

(i) Doctors, nurses and other participants in the health system will form partnerships to run their own hospitals and establish their own brand of care.

(ii) New Zealand and overseas individuals and companies with an interest in health care will take the opportunities offered here to start their own hospitals.

(iii) Competition to provide services at an acceptable price and of an acceptable quality will become the main motivating factors of those involved in health care.

Professor Patricia Danzon from the University of Pennsylvania has said that 'there is no free lunch in health insurance, public or private: consumers cannot have unrestricted choice, total financial protection and low cost'. In fact there is no free education, free health care, free pensions or free welfare benefits. Everything costs; everything has to be paid for. The difference between systems is whether the cost is visible or hidden. Even if you never work a day in your life and contribute nothing to the taxation pool of government revenue, you can still lose under the present State-controlled social welfare system because what benefits you do receive from the State may be smaller and certainly will be less reliable over time than they might be.

Under the system proposed here, both the costs and benefits are visible for all to see.

FISCAL IMPLICATIONS

The adoption of the health system I have outlined in this chapter will have a significant impact on government spending. It will remove around $2400 million of health expenditure from the government budget immediately.

This reduction in financial commitments will enable the government to immediately reduce income tax. The 15 cent income tax bracket will be increased from $9500 to $12,000, a saving of $325 a year for a taxpayer classed as single. Along with the reduction in education expenditure, it will enable the government to immediately reduce income taxation to nil for a family with one child at school earning up to $32,000, with an additional tax-free income allowance of $10,000 for each additional child at school.

7　Security and Fairness

*The modern welfare state which [the Labour Government]
erected was a cunning construct, though this was neither
obvious at the time nor simply the result of deliberate
calculation. In particular, the new state placed few demands
upon the public's fragile trust in the powers and intentions of
government. It offered immediate benefits at little obvious
cost to large and powerful sections of the community. It
promised everyone that they would be major beneficiaries
within a relatively short space of time. Its welfare
programmes were to expand slowly, so that their true costs
and implications across the lifetime of the individual should
not be at once apparent.*

David Thomson, *Selfish Generations?*

Ninety-five years ago New Zealand introduced its first
social welfare measure, the Old-Age Pensions Act 1898, a
fully means-tested pension that was unfunded and non-
contributory. Its terms of qualification were extremely
stringent. Fewer than one in three people over the age of
65 fulfilled the criteria, and payments were less generous
than those of early pension schemes in many other
countries. Although the pension was increased during the
next two decades, by the end of the 1920s old age pensions
accounted for only 0.7 per cent of GDP. Total social welfare
spending, including widows and war pensions, public
health and education expenditure and government loans to
buy homes, amounted to around 6 per cent of GDP. At this
time most New Zealanders paid no income tax, so social
spending came from indirect taxes, such as customs duties.

The turning point in New Zealand policy on social
welfare was the Social Security Act 1938 — a system of
monetary benefits on a contributory basis, the contributions being fixed according to income. However, there

was also a non-contributory superannuation scheme which eventually replaced the age benefit with a non-means-tested payment to everyone.

Events in the 1930s, especially the Great Depression, had focused attention in the industrialised world on the inability of large segments of the elderly population to make adequate provision for themselves in later life. The percentage of elderly doubled in the lifetime of people who turned 65 during the 1930s. Employer-sponsored retirement schemes had proved to be inadequate. The transition from an agricultural to an industrial society was also well on its way, with all the attendant repercussions. Agricultural employment had been less sensitive to recessions and the elderly could choose to go on working until death or to hand over their enterprise gradually, while retirement by degrees was more difficult in industry. In addition, industrialisation and mechanisation favoured younger workers.

The national retirement programmes, developed as a result of all these factors, were seen as mechanisms for saving on the part of the worker and his or her employer to provide security in old age, with government controlling the investment of the worker's savings. In accumulating these savings, each generation of workers would provide for its own financial needs when people could no longer support themselves through work. What the framers of these programmes did not understand or anticipate was that most of the programmes would never create real savings for their economies, as most would be run largely on a 'pay-as-you-go' basis, i.e., the money from those paying into the scheme would go straight out again in payments to people receiving pensions. Time, the changing economic situation and ageing populations eventually exposed this system as unsustainable. Over the past 10 years a number of countries have modified their retirement schemes and others are considering changes.

Throughout the 1950s and 1960s, direct government spending in New Zealand on those over the age of 60 was about 3.5 per cent of GDP. By the 1970s, the cost of superannuation was causing growing concern. At the beginning of the 1970s, Labour was in opposition, and I was set the task of designing a new scheme that would remove some of the concerns about private superannuation schemes then in operation and put the brakes on the cost of any public scheme. Norman Kirk, Leader of the Opposition, was also interested in exploring the possibility of a universal 'super' scheme which paid people in retirement according to what they had earned while in work.

The New Zealand Superannuation Act 1974 was the Labour Government's answer to all these concerns. On 1 April 1975, employees between the ages of 17 and 65 and their employers began compulsory contributions to either the New Zealand Superannuation Fund or another approved scheme. The worker's contribution was to be 1 per cent of his or her total taxable income; the employer's contribution was to at least equal that amount. Contributions were to increase gradually until they reached 4 per cent of taxable income. The resulting fund would pay a pension worth about 60 per cent of the contributor's regular income. Age benefit and superannuation pensions already existing at the time were not affected. The Labour scheme ended 22 months later, after a change in government, when national super-annuation was introduced.

The fund created by the 1974 Act had been seen as a major source of development finance. Retirement savings are traditionally the primary reservoir of funds for long-term capital markets. In 1991, Ord Minnett Securities did some calculations to see what would have happened if the funded scheme had not been abolished, and found:

On the basis that the savings [between 1975 and 1991] were invested in 40% government stock, 30% in domestic shares and 30% in world shares, the fund would have had a capital base of just below $40 billion at the end of 1991. That is almost two times the size of the government's overseas debt, more than two times its domestic debt, or more than two times the current sharemarket capitalisation. New Zealand would have no current account deficit, would have had much lower inflation throughout the eighties, and a significantly *better performance. That would have given the fund a much better performance. It is not unlikely that the current size of the fund would have been large enough to finance the current GRI out of its income stream.[1]*

Instead of that situation, national superannuation now consumes 6.5 per cent of the GDP. That figure will grow over the next 50 to 60 years as the number of people in retirement increases in comparison to the number of those in work. In 1991/92, the estimated cost of national superannuation (excluding the 1991 reforms of the scheme, some of which were not implemented) was $5.5 billion, or $4.3 billion if allowance is made for the tax surcharge and normal income tax on superannuation. According to government sources, the average person is contributing over 8 per cent of their income in tax to pay for this. Put another way, the cost of GRI in 1991/92 was 50 per cent more than the total net corporate tax collection forecast for that year.

In New Zealand, as in other developed countries where similar cost problems are occurring, a rapidly ageing population will make it extremely difficult to maintain the current level of retirement income, unless steps are taken now to ensure that those in the workforce start to save for their own retirement whenever possible. Without change, the shift in demographics will continue to create problems for fiscal policy. The number of people retiring each year for the next eight years is around 13,000. This number is set to increase to 27,000 in the year 2001 when the retirement age becomes 65. From then on, the number climbs steadily until it reaches more than 50,000 in the year beginning July 2023. According to the Statistics Department, by 2031 there will be 31.7 people over the age of 65 for every 100 aged 15 to 64. The present ratio is 18 to every 100. Therefore, while there are only 13,000 people retiring annually, this country has an eight-year opportunity to do something about its deep-seated

---

[1]Ord Minnett Securities NZ, Saving and Superannuation: The Reduction of Government Involvement, 1991.

superannuation problem without putting too much strain on the existing workforce.

In New Zealand, everyone has looked to government for two things — prosperity and security — and government has been failing them on both. Social welfare measures such as national superannuation have been able to carry on for a long time without any visible signs of strain because the nation has been living off human capital (people didn't take their social welfare benefits out of turn) and economic capital (the government was not hugely in debt).

All that has changed. Now a third of the population is receiving some form of State benefit or assistance while government has such a huge debt it no longer has room to move. The size of our national debt is one of the major reasons why people feel threatened and no longer believe they can trust government to provide prosperity and security. They would like the country's debt to be dealt with but their fear is that fixing it will hurt them. They want to feel more secure, but, unfortunately we have reached the point where if something is not done to permanently reduce the debt, and eliminate the reason it continues to climb, then nobody will be secure.

However, before looking at what can be done about income in retirement, perhaps it is advisable to ask why government should become involved at all. After all, some high-income nations such as those in Asia do not have State superannuation schemes as we know them. None the less, I do not believe that there are any governments in the OECD that would allow people in retirement who are unable to work to go without an adequate income to buy the necessities of life or to go without health care. I certainly do not want to live in a country that lets that happen. It would be turning our backs on more than 60 years of caring, as well as the philosophy that is at the base of New Zealand society — that we look after those unable to look after themselves.

Once government is committed to providing that kind of care, public attitudes and logic more or less insist that any pension scheme is universal. For example, two men, Smith and Brown, are born at the same time. They get the same educational qualifications, work alongside each other in the same butcher's shop, marry and have the same number of children. They live in the same neighbourhood and their income and expenses are the same. If Smith saves enough throughout his working life to support himself in his retirement and Brown saves nothing at all, it is impossible, politically, to sustain a system where the taxpayer supports Brown and not Smith.

Nevertheless, there are problems with universality. As we know, systems like New Zealand's 'pay-as-you-go' retirement scheme inevitably help drive the government account into deficit. At the same time, for those in real need, the size of a universal pension is never enough, simply because it must be paid to everyone. For those totally reliant on it, it is a pretty meagre living; and for the well-off, it amounts to pocket money.

The only fair way to manage a universal scheme, in terms of cost and equity, is for everyone to provide for their own retirement to the extent that they are able. That means government has to put in place a clear dividing line between helping those who are unable to save sufficient capital for their own retirement (low-income earners) — the welfare function — and those who do earn sufficient income during their working life to be able to save and provide for themselves. Any shortfall in capital savings by low-income earners during their working lives needs to be made up in the year of their retirement by the government. During the transition period from a cash-flow system to a savings system, even high-income earners might have a substantial shortfall because of the limited number of years of saving they have available to them.

The change, therefore, from a pay-as-you-go welfare system to a savings system is not without cost. In the early years, the current workforce not only has to start saving in order to provide for itself, but must also continue to pay taxes so that those now on a pension can continue to be paid.

This demands that:

❒ The transition is made as short as possible so that the costs are not unnecessarily prolonged and the benefits are brought forward as much as possible. This can best be done by a package of measures of which superannuation is an important part, but by no means the whole.

❒ There is strong government involvement in the early years of transition to ensure certainty and see that all elements of the package are put in place and are adhered to. Confidence that the government will see the whole programme through to a conclusion will be vital if some people are required to pay more in the short term on the understanding they will be rewarded later on with lower taxation.

A change from an unfunded welfare pay-as-you-go scheme to a funded savings scheme will not only reintroduce a sense of security but will also bring with it a number of economic benefits, including long-term capital markets, higher growth and a reduction in the cost of investment in areas demanding long-time horizons. It would help reverse New Zealand households' recent low savings ratios as well. This country's households currently have one of the lowest savings ratios in the developed world. It declined from about 10 per cent of disposable income during the 1970s to a slightly negative position at the end of the 1980s.

People have to realise that what is currently called a superannuation scheme is not one at all, as it involves no savings element. It is, in fact, a welfare income transfer system, paid to all, virtually, no matter what income they have enjoyed during their working lives. It does, however, create the feeling that people will be looked after in retirement, irrespective of whether they save or not. The problem today is that many people regard the taxes they pay now as a down payment on the pension they will receive. They see the taxes as equivalent to savings, which leads them to save less personally. This dilemma was highlighted in David Thomson's book *Selfish Generations?* Yet savings are important. It is savings that make possible investment and the accumulation of capital — plant, machinery, trucks and so forth. Increasing the capital stock makes us more productive and raises our standard of living. A worker can shift more gravel with a truck than a wheelbarrow. The truck is an investment made possible by savings. Lower savings mean a lower capital stock and that equals lower productivity and output. The pay-as-you-go scheme, by undermining savings, undermines growth.

The cost of the present system to the taxpayer is also considerable. The loss of income in taxes during his or her working life far exceeds any benefits that might be received from taxation. Today the current superannuation scheme costs the taxpayer the equivalent of 33 cents in every dollar they pay in personal taxation. When you add health costs at 30 cents in the dollar to this, that means that 63 cents from each dollar of personal taxation goes to pay for those two items. Add to that 30 cents in the dollar for debt, partly incurred as a result of not funding superannuation and health costs in the year they occurred, and more than 90 cents of every dollar of personal taxation goes on those three items alone.

A pay-as-you-go system where the number of people retiring each year will more than double over the next 30 years, where the percentage of retired people to those in the workforce will climb dramatically, means either benefit levels will have to be reduced substantially or the contributions (taxes) of the workforce will have to increase. Both options are politically unsustainable.

A compulsory savings scheme, by comparison, is inherently more stable. Those who oppose it on philosophical grounds should be aware that we already have compulsion now — in the form of taxes to pay for superannuation. In fact, the tax the average person on $30,000 is required to pay to meet the current pay-as-you-go scheme is twice as much as that person would have to put aside under a savings scheme to provide themselves with a pension equivalent to that paid by the government today (assuming a 3 per cent real rate of return on savings and 3 per cent inflation).

What I am proposing only requires a person to save until

their funds have reached a level which will provide them with a pension equivalent to what the government would pay them if they had no income. Once the minimum level of savings, and thereby pension level, has been reached, savings then become optional. Inevitably, under a pay-as-you-go scheme, people who have paid taxes all their lives will demand that they also receive a pension from the State, irrespective of any other income they might have in retirement. The logic of this, from their point of view, is that they have paid more taxes than those on low incomes who will get a pension without question. The fact that politicians collectively find these demands impossible to withstand is because there are always some politicians who will promise more — witness the Alliance promise to lower the entitlement age back to 60 and to get rid of the tax surcharge.

Government policy should not create groups of 'haves' and 'have nots' through the arbitrary distribution of income from one group in society to another. In order to be successful, changes in the system of contributing to retirement income will have to take into account the inability of the elderly to adjust easily and give adequate time to younger workers to adapt. The situation of those more than half way through their working lives also has to be taken into account.

Any discussion of retirement income needs to consider economic life-cycles. For most people, earnings are accumulated through a major part of their lives starting from the early twenties and going through to the late fifties or early sixties. People then expect 20 or more years in retirement. Because the period of retirement is so long (and with medical advances may well extend further) a substantial period of time is required to accumulate sufficient resources. The young worker is likely to oppose any immediate changes which jeopardise the position of those in retirement or close to retirement, just as the latter would oppose them, because the young also expect to retire one day and would not like to think they could find their security similarly put at risk. The young must feel that public policies are treating them equitably and that the policies will last, both politically and financially. As one report on superannuation said, 'A retirement programme that cannot be sustained is not a retirement programme.'

All these concerns are very real and unless they are dealt with openly and satisfactorily then any new pension scheme will fail. The essential elements of any successful scheme are:

❐ First, those who are already retired and receiving a pension must be placed in one group with their retirement income continuing to be funded from taxation. However, the number of retired people who are unfunded should be capped where it is today so that the burden on tax revenue reduces over time.

❐ Secondly, those close to retirement need to contribute up to their retirement and then have the capital savings they have put aside topped up from (a) employer contributions, and (b) savings in government expenditure.

❐ Thirdly, young workers also need to start saving for retirement. However, they will be able to offset their current savings against their compulsory savings if they wish to. They need to be able to see clearly when tax reductions are due and therefore see the trade-offs involved and how and when they will benefit. Eventually a savings scheme will correct the imbalance in the redistribution of income currently taking place between the young and old that has been highlighted by David Thomson. It is a redistribution that currently favours those 60 years and over with the 'ageing' of welfare systems here and all round the world. As a result, this older group can expect to receive more from the scheme than they contributed; while, under present circumstances, the young (born after 1955) can expect to pay in more and get back only a percentage of their contribution, which decreases the later they were born.

If we deal with these three issues, and the current 'ageing' of the welfare system, the concerns of those at all stages of life are recognised. There is protection and security for those who are retired or close to retirement; and the young will see the viability and sustainability of the policy because it is fully funded, as well as recognise the incentive features of lower taxation.

THE COMPULSORY SAVINGS SCHEME

What follows is an outline of the proposed pension scheme, its key objectives, my evaluation of the reasons for compulsion, and the parameters on which my model is based.

Key Objectives

❏ To broaden coverage to include all New Zealanders of working age.

❏ To ensure that all New Zealanders can enjoy a level of income in retirement greater than the current living-alone superannuation benefit; in other words, to provide a reasonable minimum income.

❏ To provide assistance to meet the needs of the most disadvantaged.

❏ To improve incentives for employment, assist and reward effort and, in a broader sense, self-help, participation and dignity.

❏ To ensure that income transfers are made efficiently so that any welfare losses are minimised, economic growth is improved, not inhibited, and the changes contribute to jobs.

❏ To ensure the system is fiscally sound, that is, sustainable.

❏ To ensure that income distribution between generations is fair and equitable.

❏ To help create a structure of incentives that encourages self-sufficiency.

❏ To minimise transitional costs as much as possible.

Principles

1. Economic Efficiency:

Any superannuation programme should be actuarially sound and should, in the majority of cases, result in a one-on-one link between future contributions and the actuarial value of benefits earned by contributors.

Consequences:

(i) The retirement test will be eliminated (super-annuation tax surcharge).

(ii) The system will move as close as possible to market solutions. New market-related superannuation schemes will completely replace today's pay-as-you-go scheme.

(iii) Contributions will not be tax deductible, nor will benefits be taxed.

(iv) Contributions will earn interest.

2. Past Cost: The new superannuation programme should recognise the current position of those retired or close to retirement and not try to reverse past redistributions of income. In other words, they should be treated as sunk costs.

Consequences:

(i) The contingent liabilities of the old pay-as-you-go system will need to be acknowledged for both current retirees and those currently in the work force.

3. De-politicisation: The system should be designed in a way that makes it impossible for politicians to use it for short-term political gain.

Consequences:

(i) The new benefit formula will need to be guaranteed by issuing either government bonds as future benefits are earned or a private sector equivalent.

(ii) The system will need to be set up in a way that will make it impossible to use it for short-term political purposes by altering the benefit formula.

(iii) Market prices will need to be used.

4. Communications: The new system should be as simple as is humanly possible, understood by the electorate, and nothing should be hidden.

Consequences:

(i) Transparency: Any non-insurance part of the scheme will be dealt with separately in government accounts.

(ii) Contributors will need to be kept up-to-date on the position of their investment in the new scheme.

(iii) The size of existing liabilities under the present pay-as-you-go scheme will need to be highlighted in the Budget and New Zealand's yearly set of accounts.

(iv) The scheme should not discriminate between individuals in similar circumstances.

Parameters of the Model Option

There are many options available. The answers to some key questions will determine a few important parameters and limit the range of options.

1. Should the regime aim to replace or 'top up' public provision?

The estimated net tax cost of retirement pensions for 1992/93 is around $4500 million. This represents 33 cents in every dollar of personal income tax. If employers' contributions to a new savings scheme were used only to meet the needs of retirees with a lifetime of low earning, rather than being credited to individual employee accounts, in a very short period of time the system could ensure that all retirees receive a minimum level of benefit superior to that paid today. In effect, this will mean that for all future retirees, compulsory private provision would replace compulsory public provision through taxation.

Because this would allow the current rates of personal and company taxation to be reduced dramatically, the transitional costs of moving to a compulsory savings superannuation system could be minimised, especially for those on low incomes with families.

Conclusion: A compulsory superannuation savings scheme should aim to completely replace the existing compulsory tax-paid cash-flow retirement system, with a top-up only for lifetime low-income earners.

2. What kind of compulsory scheme is best?

The nature of the scheme I propose is a basic minimum one. The aim is to ensure that as many New Zealanders as possible save enough during their working lives to pay for a basic cost-of-living adjusted pension in retirement. The best way to achieve this would be through a defined contribution scheme with a top-up for those unable to save the minimum capital value necessary. People in existing benefit schemes should be able to have their membership credited towards the compulsory scheme provided adequate safeguards are imposed.

3. Who should be covered by compulsory contributions?

All employees, the self-employed and social welfare beneficiaries should be covered. The cost of increasing income-tested benefits by 5 per cent will be $220 million net a year and should be done for all but young, single beneficiaries under 16 years of age. A compulsory contribution should not be required from non-earners, such as non-income-earning spouses. However, half the earning spouse's contributions should be transferred each year to the non-earner's account.

Conclusion: All employees, the self-employed and beneficiaries should be directly covered by contributions, with non-earners being indirectly covered, as they will have half their earning spouse's contributions credited to their account.

4. Who should pay the contributions?

While international experience varies — in Australia the employer pays, in Chile the employee — New Zealand should decide who pays on the basis of what works for New Zealand.

Conclusion: As employees get the benefit from the contributions, they should be asked to pay a percentage of their income for the purpose of providing a pension in retirement.

Any employer's contribution should be confined each year to help top up the accounts of those people who retire during that year and have not saved the required minimum capital amount. This means that employers' contributions will be higher during the early years of the scheme — 3 per cent for 7 years, 2 per cent for another 10 years and then nil. After that, any shortfall will be made good direct from other government revenue.

5. How much should be contributed?

The problems caused by small contributions should be avoided. By including all means-tested beneficiaries and their benefit income (excluding income earned by primary and secondary students) and by ensuring that the contributions of couples are shared 50/50, the problem of small contributions to anyone's account is largely overcome. To the extent that any problem remains, money saved could be transferred to various superannuation schemes on a once-a-year basis by the Inland Revenue Department (IRD), and the money invested on the short-term money market until distributed.

There is no good justification for excluding contributions by low-income earners from high-income families (for example, the wife of a high-income earner), who make up a large part of those on low incomes (excluding beneficiaries and students). The exemption of the first $5000 of income per year, for example, as suggested by the Todd Committee on Superannuation, is not only not justified for the above reason, but also because it only raises the marginal contribution rate to achieve the same level of savings. For example, take someone on $20,000: to raise the same level of contribution it takes an 8 per cent contribution if a $5000 exemption is provided, against a 6 per cent contribution if there is no exemption.

6. What is an appropriate ceiling to set?

A ceiling (target capital value) should be set which enables a pension to be purchased that is approximately equivalent in value to the current pension level. There are alternative benchmarks against which to set the ceiling. I favour setting the ceiling at a capital value of $122,500 in 1993 dollars which would provide a non-taxable pension of $10,000 a year. A non-taxable pension of $10,000 is equivalent to a taxable pension of $12,300 a year, or around $400 above the current living-alone rate, which is the highest rate of payment available.

7. What is the appropriate tax treatment for compulsory contributions?

There is no need for tax concessions in a compulsory environment. In any case, it would only delay the reductions in personal tax that will be available as a result of the introduction of a compulsory saving scheme.

8. Should end benefits be gender-rated or gender-neutral?

Given that the scheme will be compulsory, there are good grounds for gender-neutral annuities. The option of requiring higher contribution rates from women because of their longer life-expectancy is simply not necessary. Many would see it as unfair and, given the nature of pooling being required from couples, it would not make much sense for many anyway.

9. What should the contribution rate be?

In calculating the percentage of gross income which would be required to replace the pay-as-you-go compulsory tax-paid pension with a $10,000 a year annuity, I have assumed:

❐ A real tax-paid earnings rate of 3 per cent per annum on the money saved.

❐ That it would be based on total assessable income.

❐ A 5 per cent contribution rate for the employee for the first five years.

❐ That this rate would be increased to around 6.5 per cent thereafter; that is, once personal income-tax rates had started to be reduced dramatically.

Table 1: Means of fully funding a pension of $10,000 p.a. in retirement

Age at start of contributions	No. of years of contributions	Annual contributions	Income needed at 5%	Income needed at 6.5%
18	47	$1202	24,000	18,500
20	45	$1302	26,040	20,050
30	35	$1990	39,900	30,650

Table 1 shows that most people who enjoy continuous employment will save the greater part, if not all the capital sum required, to pay for their retirement benefits at a rate of 6.5 per cent. This is especially so if one remembers that those with qualifications earn more than those without but are likely to spend less years in the workforce, while those on lower incomes are likely to enter the workforce at a younger age, thereby saving over a longer period of time.

Once the required minimum level of savings has been achieved, an exclusion certificate would be issued by the fund manager if requested, provided the member's partner's account is also fully funded. If not, the member's contributions would be used for this purpose until the partner's account was fully funded.

Most superannuation schemes could be made to qualify with minor changes. Past contributions could be used to limit further contributions if the taxpayer chose, but this may not be in his or her interests. It will depend largely on the taxpayer's age. If he or she is unlikely to save the total capital contribution required between the introduction of the scheme and retirement, thus requiring a top-up from employer/government, it would not be in his or her interest to use past contributions without safeguards.

Couples should share their contribution. This would avoid the situation where a non-income-earning partner of a high-income earner could receive a lump sum subsidy payment towards the pension on retirement, which two low-income-earning partners could not. Administrative problems in this situation can be overstated; all that would be required is a yearly reconciliation.

The longer it takes to change from one scheme to the other, the longer it will take to see the benefits that would come from a compulsory scheme, and the more likelihood of it being overturned by a politician who is prepared to sacrifice future generations for his or her political ambitions of today. I therefore favour a one-hit approach to contributions, using a package of measures to ensure that the tax savings available as a result are targeted to guarantee that low-income families in particular are no worse off as a consequence of their contributions. In order to bring forward the benefits of a compulsory superannuation scheme to its very beginning, an employer-contribution rate of 3 per cent of the company payroll should be set for the first 7 years, then 2 per cent for 10 years and nil thereafter. The amount collected each year would go to offset the shortfall in contributions of those people retiring during that year. In this way a person who retires the day after the scheme is introduced is fully funded.

Conclusion: I favour an initial 5 per cent contribution rate for individuals in the first five years of the scheme and 6.5 per cent thereafter, with compensating tax reductions for low-income families. (When the compulsory contributions for health insurance are taken into account, contributions total 7 and 9 per cent of assessable income.) Employer contributions of 3 per cent for 7 years and 2 per cent for 10 years would go to meet any shortfall in employee lifetime contributions. As individual employees' capital savings rise and the yearly rate of contributions increases, the rate of the employers' contribution would fall to nil in Year 18.

10. What is the basis of contributions?

In order to keep the contribution rate to the lowest possible level and to ensure comprehensive cover with minimum leakage, I favour assessable income for wage and salary earners, the self-employed and beneficiaries, including their respective share of any profits of companies in which they have shares. In the case of employer contributions, I recommend that it be based on the total salary bill of the company or employer.

The issue of individuals who prefer payment in fringe benefits over income would largely be overcome if, as tax rates drop dramatically, the government gave some preference to wage and salary payments over fringe-benefit payments.

11. Who should manage the funds invested?

The funds should be privately managed by pension funds approved by the Reserve Bank and subject to a number of rules and conditions:

❐ A half-yearly, full public disclosure of performance in comparison with other funds.

❐ Regular updates of information to members.

❐ Full portability for members to change to another scheme.

❐ Fund managers would need to meet a number of

prudential, capital and regulatory requirements. These rules and conditions should be laid down and overseen by the Reserve Bank of New Zealand in much the same way as they do for trading banks. Rules may include capital adequacy, fund separation and valuation methods.

❐ Each fund would be subject to audit each year.

❐ Each fund would be required to be graded by a rating agency on a regular basis.

❐ The value of units would need to be quoted regularly so that contributors can make informed decisions.

12. Should there be a government guarantee?

No, but the fact that employers' contributions each year along with government contributions go to make up any shortfall in a retiree's savings fund, in effect provides an informal guarantee.

13. What is the best collection process?

With employees and beneficiaries all covered in practical terms, someone must collect the contributions and pass them on to the qualifying fund manager. I prefer using the revenue authorities to collect contributions (as for PAYE) and to have them pass on the payments to the nominated fund manager. The revenue authorities will need to check whether payments are being made in any case, which is far more difficult if they are being paid directly to a number of fund managers by hundreds of employees. The audit task involved under those conditions would be horrendous for IRD and should be avoided.

Conclusion: Contributions would be paid monthly to IRD. Whether they were dispersed monthly by IRD or three-monthly would be a matter of negotiation between fund managers and IRD. Fund managers would have to decide between the cost of monthly distributions and any shortfall in investment returns. However, the IRD could authorise client payments to go direct to fund managers where they consider this is in order. This authority should not be unreasonably withheld.

14. Can a contributor change funds?

Members, at their option, should be able to transfer from

one fund to another for a small administrative fee. Members should also be able to belong to more than one fund at a time, provided that they do not join a second fund until they have invested with the first fund at least 20 per cent of the required capital value needed to buy the minimum pension.

15. When can funds be accessed?

Compulsory contributions should be preserved until the age of eligibility for the retirement pension, gradually raised to 65 in 2001 as planned at present. The only exception to this would be short-term residents who leave the country permanently. Immigrants to New Zealand should be asked to pay a higher contribution rate, according to their age, or a lump sum on arrival, to help ensure they will have sufficient funds available on retirement to buy their pension.

16. Should there be restrictions on the type of investment?

On the basis that funds will have to meet prudential, capital adequacy and regulatory requirements laid down by the Reserve Bank to be registered as an approved fund, as well as being subject to an audit each year and a regular grading by a rating agency, no restrictions on the type of investment are required.

17. What type of end benefit would be best?

Members would be able to elect to withdraw from the qualifying fund at any time after reaching the State pension age, whether or not they continued to work. The withdrawal benefit would be the total amount standing to the member's credit and could be used in the following way, depending on the size of the fund:

❑ To buy the minimum annuity required by law, i.e., $10,000 p.a. in 1993 terms, with any balance being taken in a capital lump sum or used to buy additional annuity.

❑ To put towards buying the minimum annuity with the balance of that annuity being met from a government contribution for that year.

❑ To leave the amount standing on reaching retirement age to the person's credit, to accumulate further interest until called upon. If it is not called upon before the person dies, then the amount standing to that person's credit at the time of death goes to that person's estate. If called upon at an age later than retirement, the procedures outlined above apply.

❑ The minimum pension would be inflation-linked, with the government undertaking responsibility in this area if no private-sector party is prepared to.

❑ Early retirement would be an option for those with more than the required amount of capital. However, retirement could not be taken before the age at which the retiree could buy a $10,000 cost-of-living adjusted pension.

Funds established for the purpose of providing annuities would be subject to the same rules and regulations as those outlined for qualifying savings funds, along with a yearly actuarial report.

18. Death before State pension age.

The balance standing to the credit of a member who dies before State pension age would be transferred to the surviving spouse's pension fund (*de facto* or *de jure*) up to the capital value required to purchase that person's pension. The remaining funds could be used in any way the surviving spouse chooses. If there is no spouse, the standing balance would go to the estate.

19. Tax treatment of people in retirement.

As superannuation schemes move to maturity, there will be no need for any tax surcharge to be imposed on income earned in retirement. I have allowed for the surcharge to be phased out over 10 years. In addition, for those retiring during that time, the amount of the pension subject to the surcharge will be limited to the government or employer contribution towards their pension and not the individual's compulsory contributions. In other words, if the capital value saved by the retiree equals 40 per cent of the pension payable, then the surcharge will apply only to the remaining 60 per cent.

20. Pension Levels.

The level of pension payable to those retiring after the

scheme is introduced will be slowly increased each year from the existing levels until the stage where those retiring in Year 11 will be entitled to a full non-taxable annual pension of $10,000 in 1993 dollar terms, irrespective of what contributions they have made over that 10-year period.

Table 2: Current level of superannuation compared to proposed structure after 10 years

	Current level of superannuation	Proposed level after 10 years	Increased pension level
Married couple	Net $15,178	$20,000	+ $4822
Single person	Net $ 9,107	$10,000	+ $ 893
Single person, living alone	Net $ 9,865	$10,000	+ $ 135

Anyone already in a retirement income scheme at the time the compulsory scheme is introduced would have their existing retirement contributions held in a separate account for them to use on retirement. Any contributions beyond the minimum level are to be available to the contributor at any time and for any purpose and without penalty.

21. What happens if this policy is put in place?

A. Security will be improved.

(i) Those retired now will realise that their position has been made more secure because of the rapidly reducing cost of superannuation in terms of the government's budget. The yearly reduction in the rate of surcharge will improve the financial position of many people now in retirement, or soon to retire.

(ii) Those over 45 years of age, within 20 years of retirement, will realise that, while they will have to contribute yearly towards their own retirement pension as a result of the new policy, it will now certainly be available; whereas they may currently have doubts about what, if anything, they are going to receive in their old age under the present scheme. Their pension will be at a higher level than now available; and they are also likely to benefit from lower taxation for a number of years.

(iii) Those under 45 years of age, more than 20 years from retirement, will know that their own contributions will buy them an adequate pension at age 65 or, in cases where this does not occur, that any shortfall in the capital amount will be topped up by a government contribution. They will benefit from lower taxation rates for a major part of their working lives.

(iv) Low-income earners, beneficiaries and non-earners will all know that their position will be secure as a result of the change, despite their low- or non-earning situation.

(v) The scheme accepts 65 as the age of normal retirement but provides for both later and earlier retirement, provided a pension of $10,000, cost-of-living adjusted, is available. It also retains the plan to gradually phase in 65 as retirement age, as is currently contemplated.

B. Incentives will be improved dramatically on a number of fronts.

(i) As the tax surcharge on retirement income falls over 10 years and is then reduced to zero in Year 11, the incentive to save and invest in order to earn taxable income in retirement increases.

(ii) Lower personal and company taxes increase the rewards in earning income and then saving a portion of it.

(iii) Household saving ratios will increase.

(iv) The increase in savings will be reflected in an improved current account for New Zealand.

(v) The inter-generational issues involved in welfare provision, especially retirement provisions, will largely be solved.

C. The government's and country's economic situation will be improved.

(i) The pension funds will provide a major source of funds for long-term capital markets which, in turn, will have a positive impact on growth.

(ii) The fiscal problem which would have been created by a rapidly ageing population will be largely avoided.

(iii) The costs of superannuation will be reduced gradually to very low levels as the compulsory scheme totally replaces the present pay-as-you-go scheme.

(iv) By ensuring a steady income stream in retirement which everyone can see is financially sustainable, political interference from then on will be kept to a minimum.

(v) The distortions in investment decisions which are characteristic of the current system (for example, investment in housing rather than investment that provides a regular income) will be minimised.

(vi) The policy makes the most of targeting of public expenditure by ensuring that only those people with insufficient lifetime income receive assistance from the government towards retirement.

(vii) It avoids the political problems that would go with reducing the level of the benefit further, as some people advocate, or implementing some form of means test (asset test).

(viii) It enables a quick phase-in from one system to another which no other system would allow, thereby ensuring political sustainability.

(ix) The new system will encourage individual initiative by not penalising savings and taxing future retirement income.

(x) It will increase competition between savings institutions.

(xi) It will highlight the costs of inflation for everyone to see.

(xii) Government expenditure will be reduced by a massive $23 billion or 70 per cent over 35 years.

(xiii) Personal tax rates are reduced over time to zero and government relies more and more on consumption tax for revenue.

FISCAL IMPLICATIONS

Long Term

The proposed compulsory savings scheme reduces the government's annual superannuation expenditure to the sum required to top up any shortfall in the savings of individuals retiring in any financial year. Given that someone earning $20,000 annually (in 1993 terms) for 45 years would save the right amount (assuming a 3 per cent real rate of return and inflation at 3 per cent), it will be readily seen that most New Zealanders would have little difficulty in doing so. Even those who spend long periods on benefits during their working life could make major contributions towards their pension in retirement. Thus the burden of superannuation 30 to 45 years from now would only be a fraction of what it is today.

On the other hand, if action is not taken immediately to remedy the situation we now face, 25 to 40 years from today the burden of superannuation, already equal to $1 in $3 of personal taxation, will climb to more than $1 in $2, given current tax rates. If we do change in the way that I have suggested, then on a comparable basis, the burden would fall to the equivalent of around $1 in $20 of the present tax level, one-tenth of where it would be without change.

Transition — Short-Term Situation

Given the fact that only 13,000 people a year will retire in each of the next eight years, we have a period of grace which we should not ignore. To wait until the number of people retiring reaches 35,000 in the year beginning 1 July 2009 would be disastrous; to put off real change until the year 1 July 2023 when the number reaches 50,000 plus would be criminal.

Consider the costs alone. In 1993 dollar-of-the-day terms, it will cost around $1500 million a year to fund the retirement income of those retiring over the next eight years. This will climb to an average cost of around $3600 million a year for the following 10 years. After that, the average would increase to more than $5000 million a year and would reach $6000 million a year in the year 2025 before settling around that figure. In other words, it will be four times what it will cost for the next eight years under the present system. To ensure that the burden of superannuation does not rise in the future, pension rates will have to be cut dramatically unless other methods are adopted along the lines I have described here.

Although there will be up-front costs for current taxpayers in transferring to a compulsory superannuation scheme, those costs will be much lower today than they would be in the future; and subsequently will become less than if we stay as we are. The following transitional costs can be isolated:

❏ Working families with children attending school — Generally protected from any adverse cash-flow impacts arising from the introduction of a compulsory superannuation scheme because of the introduction of a tax-free income level for families in these circumstances.

❏ Higher-income families — Those earning in excess of the tax-free income levels may find themselves worse off in cash terms if they currently make no annual savings, an unlikely situation. If they do save, they will be able to decide for themselves if they are to be worse off in cash terms.

❏ Single taxpayers (i.e., taxpayers with no children at school) — Will generally find that despite the tax reductions proposed they will be worse off in net cash terms for 6 to 10 years, unless they are currently saving each year. In this case, they will be able to switch savings if they want to in order to ensure they are no worse off.

❏ Companies — Will find that their profits are subject to a tax rate of 28 cents in Year 1 but will have to pay a 3 per cent superannuation contribution on the company's net payroll in that year. Whether they are better off in Year 1 or worse off will depend on the ratio of wages the company pays to tax-paid profits. The required ratio to break even will decline as company tax rates decline and the company's pension contribution is reduced. Over time, companies making profits and paying taxes will all be better off.

At the end of Year 17, even those companies who have never paid tax will be better off. Companies paying tax will increase in value as tax rates decline and tax-paid returns improve.

Although there are transition costs, other measures outlined in this book have, of course, enabled these to be minimised. And it needs to be said once again that the transitional costs pale into insignificance alongside the costs that will have to be met if we do nothing. Politicians who suggest that the problem will be solved by getting together and coming up with a solution they say they will stand by are missing the point, and deluding the public. In the unlikely event that they do work together (unlikely because of the difficulty they all have in letting go of the vote-buying potential of superannuation), the result will inevitably be a compromise and the problem still not solved. It will never be solved unless the real problem is recognised and the right solution chosen. Politicians who pretend otherwise are not doing anyone a favour.

8 SOEs – A Half-way House

One of my most engaging memories of Canada is of an interview with a journalist. I said my every visit had been just after a postal strike, during a postal strike, or with a postal strike threatened. I said sooner or later, someone would have to get around to privatising the whole thing and have done with it. The journalist said, 'Are you mad, how could we guarantee the services?'

. . . Privatisation takes power out of political parties. They can no longer use national industries to buy votes. The most infamous case in Britain was a state railway branch line. Someone calculated it cost so much to run and had so few passengers, that buying a Rolls Royce for every single person using the line would be cheaper than carrying the cost of the service.

It came before Cabinet for closure. The chief whip — it was then the Labour Party in power — said: 'There are four marginal electoral districts served by that line.' End of discussion. Governments ruthlessly use the political power they have as a result of controlling state enterprises, and they use it to make political gains rather than economic ones.

Marsden Pirie, *Principles and Techniques of Privatisation*[1]

Fifteen or so years ago, vast differences existed in the levels of State ownership throughout the world. At one extreme, in the Communist economies of the USSR and Eastern Europe, the State owned almost everything. At the other extreme, in the United States, government business accounted for 0.5 per cent of total enterprise. Even within the OECD, there were huge variations. In Britain, when the Thatcher Government came to power, 10 per cent of GDP and 15 per cent of investment came from State

[1] 1990 International Privatization Congress, Canada: paper by the President, Adam Smith Institute, London.

businesses. In France, the public sector was responsible for one-third of total investment, although only 18 per cent of value-added investment. Three thousand French State businesses employed 2.5 million people — 9 per cent of the working population, twice as high as Germany and three times higher than Sweden. By 1980, however, governments worldwide, regardless of their political colour, were moving into an era of public-sector reform.

During the previous 20 years, the average government share of the economy (expenditure) throughout the OECD had increased from less than 30 per cent of GNP to 40 per cent. In the earlier part of that period, public-sector expansion coincided with rising living standards. It came to be regarded as an essential contributor to economic growth and stability. Later, in the 1970s, as productivity growth declined and inflation accelerated, views about the role of the public sector began to change. Public-sector productivity gains rose more slowly than gains in the private sector. Across the OECD as a whole, from 1968 to 1979, the price of government goods and services rose 1.75 per cent faster than private sector prices. Government budgets were increasingly unable to sustain those rising costs.

The 1980s, therefore, were characterised by the pursuit of a smaller, more efficient State sector, greater public choice, more coherent tax structures, and better control over government borrowing. One common component of that reform programme worldwide, was a major effort to extract greater efficiency from State-owned business enterprises. Throughout the decade, governments of both the left and right increasingly used privatisation to bring efficiency gains to State-owned enterprises and to ensure those gains would last well into the future.

Britain's Thatcher Government privatised 29 major State enterprises between 1979 and 1989. It sold all of its interests in water, gas and steel and most of its transport and telecommunications business. By then, the privatisation of electricity was also under way. Ninety per cent of the workers in privatised enterprises took advantage of their opportunity to buy shares. During the privatisation of State-owned housing, discounted offers helped 1.3 million people buy their own homes. The sales revenue for the 50 per cent of the State sector that was transferred to private ownership between 1979 and 1989 totalled £27.5 billion. An annual deficit of £3 billion was transformed into net profits and repayments of £400 million, with significant real price savings for consumers.

In Chile, the Allende Government's nationalisation programme had boosted the State-owned sector's share of total business from 14 per cent to 39 per cent. After the fall of Allende, the privatisation of 500 enterprises, between 1974 and 1990, moved that ratio back to 12 per cent. This reversal has played a significant part in providing Chile with a relatively stable open market economy.

Meanwhile, programmes were launched in France in 1986 to de-nationalise all government businesses in the competitive sector of the French economy, including banks, insurance companies, industrial and audio-visual activities. By January 1988, 66 competitive enterprises had been sold for 120 billion francs. More than 50 per cent of their employees opted to become shareholders in the new companies and the widest possible public participation was encouraged. The sales created 4 million new shareholders: 20 per cent of the adult population became, and remain, shareholders. There was a spectacular rebound in investment and the financial results of the privatised businesses, bringing increased economic growth, lower inflation and the stabilisation of employment.

On 1 April 1987, Japan National Railways became six private companies. Within 18 months, the growth rates of passenger traffic had improved six-fold. JNR had lost money for 23 consecutive years, accumulating long-term liabilities worth 25 billion yen. Under the new companies, with no increase in fares, the rail system moved into overall profit.

In Canada, by the late 1980s, 13 Crown corporations across the economy, including Air Canada, Canadair and Petro-Canada, had been privatised. In Mexico, the State had owned more than 1150 companies, which accounted for 18.2 per cent of GDP. Since 1983, more than 680 of them have been removed from State ownership. By the end of the 1980s, mass privatisation programmes were under way throughout Eastern Europe and the Soviet Union. Even in China, the private sector is now expected to be responsible for 25 per cent of the country's economic output by the year 2000. The trend could fairly be said to have become worldwide.

When Labour was voted back into power in New Zealand in July 1984, State-owned business accounted for 12.5 per cent of GDP and 20 per cent of total investment. In the finance sector alone, the government was the outright owner of the nation's largest commercial and savings banks, its largest motor-vehicle insurer, largest farm mortgage lender and largest residential accommodation lender. It was also owner of one of the largest merchant banks and controlled the boards of the four biggest insurance and superannuation companies. In energy and utilities, government owned the total telecommunications industry, all wholesale electricity distribution and nearly all generating capacity. It dominated wholesale gas, had major interests in oil and natural gas and owned the major coal producer. Moreover, locally elected, public-sector boards controlled retail electricity distribution, and most retail gas.

In transport, elected local authorities controlled all the ports. The government owned the rail system, a major bus network, the sole national airline, a national shipping line, the inter-island ferry service, and had a significant shareholding in all three international airports. The government also owned the postal system, more than half the commercial forests, large tracts of farmland, large quantities of non-residential property as well as substantial residential housing, the only two television channels, all nation-wide radio, a major tourist hotel chain, and most of the likely mineral resources through its ownership of extensive national parks.

New Zealanders were proud of that system: popular mythology says that State property is owned by the people. Back in the early 1950s, the country had enjoyed the third-highest living standard in the world. Voters associated high levels of State ownership with the past success of their economy. The Labour Party had traditionally endorsed and encouraged that view. State-owned enterprises operated under the direct control of ministers of the Crown, acting as elected representatives of the people. If those enterprises failed to deliver what the public wanted, then anyone could write to the minister, seeking political assistance — to get a telephone, for example. What could be more open or more democratic? People wrote to MPs in their thousands, for help to get telephones. They also believed that the system gave them better control over the prices charged by State-owned enterprises. Interest groups offended by suggested price rises could lobby the minister successfully to prevent or defer the increase.

This interaction between the public and its politicians fostered the myth that the system was uniquely responsive to the needs of the public. It also flattered the politicians. Every year, Cabinet sat down solemnly and decided how much money to vote to government businesses. They approved or vetoed all capital expenditure. Their ability to match prices to their own political priorities was very convenient. If unemployment became a problem in a particular part of the country, ministers could absorb those people into the State workforce.

It took decades for the down-side of that system to become apparent. As inflation, fiscal deficits and public-sector debt increased, ministers proved unwilling or unable to reduce the large annual losses incurred by many of the enterprises under their control. State enterprises became an ever-increasing drain on the funds of the taxpayer. The bureaucrats managing State-owned enterprises also had mixed incentives. Status and personal advancement were directly dependent on the number of employees working under them in their departments. Moreover, the prevailing management structures made it impossible for managers or ministers to measure the efficiency of a department's performance. Information systems were designed to help government ration the annual resources voted to State-owned enterprises, not measure the value of what they produced. The departments running State businesses had been given a plethora of conflicting goals. No one knew which of those goals should be given priority. Departments simultaneously advised on policy and regulation, operated as dominant or monopoly commercial players in their industries, policed their competitors to ensure they complied with regulations, and performed any social function allocated to them, cross-subsidising as necessary to fund it.

Over the years, they had often been required to hold prices below cost for favoured political constituencies, or forced to contain them across the board to hide rising interest rates or inflation. Successive governments had targeted capital expenditure to politically sensitive regions. Resource allocation was increasingly distorted. State pay and conditions were set through political deals with powerful public-sector unions. Personnel responsibility rested with central authorities. The authority delegated to the managers of State businesses was therefore extremely limited. They were quite fairly able to evade all responsibility for the success or failure of the enterprises they were supposed to be running.

In the two decades to 1985/86, the New Zealand government had invested $5 billion in just six of these enterprises — airways, State forests, the Post Office, State Coal, electricity and Lands and Survey. The net return on their assets, worth $20 billion, was zero. State Coal had lost money for 20 of the previous 22 years. The nation was not getting value for money. By the time Labour took office in 1984, interest on public-sector debt made up 18 per cent of all government expenditure. The fiscal deficit inherited from the previous government was 9 per cent of GDP. For me, as Minister of Finance, value for money was increasingly important. Inevitably, State businesses were among the many areas that underwent intensive evaluation and restructuring. But privatisation had never been part of the Labour Party's plans for improving public-sector business efficiency.

My first attempt to obtain agreement on a comprehensive approach to State-owned enterprise reform was in May 1985. I wanted to transform them into competitive State-owned businesses by removing their monopoly status wherever possible, and transferring any of their non-commercial obligations to other government agencies. Managers could then become personally accountable for SOE performance. Despite a Cabinet instruction to the government departments involved to report back within three weeks, months went by as bureaucrats battled each other and their ministers for control of the policy process. Every imaginable excuse was raised to delay, defer or re-litigate the approach taken by Cabinet. The first break-through came with help from two totally unexpected quarters.

Environmental pressure groups had been unhappy that advice on forestry conservation policy came from a department with major responsibilities for commercial cutting. They demanded the transfer of cutting operations to a separate 'commercial agency'. The head of the State Services Commission, a die-hard traditional bureaucrat, took fright under the mistaken impression that the term might imply privatisation. He demanded that they be transferred instead to a commercial State corporation. Nothing could have suited me better. The crucial precedent had been successfully established. In December 1985, the government announced the principles to be applied to SOEs in future:

❏ Non-commercial functions would be moved from major trading SOEs to other State agencies.
❏ Ministers would set strictly commercial goals for SOEs, then hold managers responsible for achieving them.
❏ SOEs would trade competitively, without advantage or disadvantage, with business rivals and potential rivals.
❏ Each SOE would be restructured for this purpose under

new directors appointed from the private sector.

Early in 1986, it became clear to me that government spending had to be cut by $1 billion to keep the 1986/87 fiscal deficit within acceptable bounds. It became equally clear that our new SOE principles could reduce the deficit by a further $1 billion in the years to come. New Zealand desperately needed to achieve that benefit as soon as possible. In May, we announced that electricity generation and wholesaling, State Coal, the Post Office and Civil Aviation would all be moved into new corporate SOE structures. The postal, telecommunications and savings bank activities of the Post Office, bracketed together for purely historical rather than rational reasons, were transformed into three separate business corporations.

Each corporatised SOE was required to fund its own activity by borrowing in the market-place. Henceforth, each would pay taxes and dividends like any other commercial company. Nothing in the new arrangements prevented the government from using SOEs as a vehicle to deliver social services; but from now on, instead of hiding the costs inside cross-subsidised SOE prices, the government would be required to budget on a separate and therefore transparent basis, and contract SOEs to deliver such services. Geoffrey Palmer, Attorney General and Deputy Prime Minister, developed an umbrella Statute to streamline the reform process. Effective from 1 April 1987, it provided a consistent framework which avoided the need for time-consuming case-by-case legislation.

By mid-1992, the corporatisation of State-owned business enterprises had been further extended to include electricity generation and wholesaling, forestry, railways, works and development, television, radio, computing services, property services, Lands Corporation, meteorological services and airport holdings. The locally elected harbour boards controlling the major ports had also been transformed on the same principles into competitive profit-making businesses.

The gains in efficiency brought about by these structural

changes dumbfounded even the most sceptical opponents of State-owned enterprise reform. The old Post Office Savings Bank, in its first year as a commercial State-owned corporation, cut staff by 30 per cent, reduced its retail outlets by 40 per cent and turned an expected loss of $50 million into a $31 million profit. In six months the new Forestry Corporation achieved a $59 million turnaround. It returned a cash surplus of $24 million, compared with the cash deficit of $35 million recorded during the last six months before its transformation. Within 12 months, the number of employees, including contractors, had been reduced from 7000 to 2600 without loss of output. The cash surplus rose steadily to reach $150 million during the year to March 1990.

The new Coal Corporation, in its first three years, boosted output per employee by nearly 60 per cent. The workforce was halved, but production increased. One mine expanded production by 20 per cent, using one-third of its previous workforce. Real prices per tonne fell by 30 per cent during that period. New Zealand Post reduced its staff by 30 per cent in four years, held the price of standard letters throughout that period, which included the introduction of GST, and increased on-time deliveries from 80 per cent to 98 per cent. Since corporatisation, NZ Post has put $190 million back into the public purse through tax and dividend payments to government.

The Electricity Corporation of New Zealand, established in 1987, reduced real unit costs by 28 per cent by 1990/91 and real average wholesale prices by 13 per cent. Staff numbers were cut from 6100 in 1986 to 3400 in 1991. Productivity, measured as gigawatt hours per employee, increased by 71 per cent. Sales rose and ECNZ increased its share of the energy market from 43 per cent to 50 per cent. After-tax profits grew by 187 per cent to $404 million. Telecom Corporation of New Zealand reduced its staff from 26,500 in 1986 to 14,000 in April 1990. Productivity, measured on the number of lines per employee, rose by nearly 85 per cent. The real price of telephone services was slashed by 20 per cent in the year to September 1989. A technologically inadequate network system was transformed. The number of customers served by digital lines has, for example, been increased from 30 per cent to 93 per cent. By April 1990, profits had risen by 300 per cent.

The transformation brought about by corporatising ports was equally dramatic. The number of waterside workers employed nationwide was reduced virtually overnight in 1989 from 3300 to 1800, without loss in the national tonnage being handled. Vessel turnaround times improved enormously — for example, by 56 per cent at the Port of Tauranga between 1989 and 1991.

Moreover, the gains in all those areas enhanced each other in many cases. Improved efficiency in ports, transport and electricity, for example, added 20 per cent to the value of the government's plantation forests, very big users of all three. Obviously the down-side of all this adjustment was a significant increase in short- to medium-term unemployment. It was a penalty that had to be faced right at the start of the process. Tens of thousands of totally unproductive jobs in the State sector had been adding costs to the rest of the economy for decades. If the country wanted to lay a sound foundation for economic growth, those costs had to be removed to allow for improved international competitiveness. In general, staff adjustments took place without dismissals or significant industrial disruption by public-sector unions. Generous redundancy payments encouraged people to take the money voluntarily and try their chances. However, corporatisation and the loss of monopoly rights in certain sectors have actually increased the total number of jobs. For instance, since the telecommunications industry was opened up to competition and operators like Clear Communications entered the market, the number of people employed in the industry is up by 3000 on the pre-corporatisation workforce.

New Zealand Institute of Economic Research studies show that, across seven of the larger SOEs between 1988 and 1992, revenue rose by 15.5 per cent to $5.9 billion, after-tax profits quadrupled from $262 million to $1023 billion and staff numbers fell from 67,600 in 1987 to 31,500 in 1992. By 1991/92, the dividend contribution to the State from SOEs and other government businesses was $700 million, equivalent to one-third of the tax paid in the same period by private-sector companies. If one adds to the $700 million the tax paid by the SOE corporations, SOE reform had achieved the $1 billion in savings which in 1985 I had calculated was possible in years to come. The efficiency gains won in the process played a crucial role in restoring the international competitiveness of the economy.

At the same time, senior Ministers in the Labour Government had been aware from the beginning that corporatisation was a system with fundamental shortcomings in the longer term. The weaknesses of the SOE model arise from inherent limitations in government ownership. Because State ownership is not contestable, SOEs are not subjected to the discipline exerted in the threat of takeover. Because they have no shares on the market, variations in performance are not reflected in visible share-price movements. Investment analysts have no interest in continuously monitoring their performance. Instead, bureaucratic monitoring systems have to be imposed through independent State agencies such as the Treasury, in an effort to provide a surrogate for market supervision. Those agencies report directly to the government, creating continuous temptations for ministers to intervene in the detailed decision-making of SOE boards and managers. But when ministers make crucial operating decisions, management can no longer be held accountable for the SOE's performance.

Theoretically, under the SOE model, State-owned enterprises are in no way guaranteed by the State. If they get into trouble, the government can sack the board, restructure the organisation or, if it chooses, let the business go bankrupt. But lenders know that any of those actions tend to be extraordinarily embarrassing, politically. Politicians will avoid them, if possible. Lenders therefore perceive that in practice an element of implied guarantee continues to operate. As a result, creditors may subject

SOEs to a less-intense scrutiny than they would give private-sector firms.

For all these reasons, SOEs' lack of tradeable equity means that they are under significantly less pressure than private-sector companies to maintain competitive levels of performance. The success of SOEs to date relates more to the excellence of their boards of directors, and the CEOs chosen by those boards, than to factors arising from ownership. Because SOE reform was so radical, wide ranging and crucial to economic efficiency, the best business talent in the country could be attracted on to the boards. On the other hand, skilled and imaginative directors naturally want to make the best they can of the business on a long-term basis. In a dynamic market, that often means continuing technological improvement and, as necessary, diversification into new areas, to match the pace of competitive developments in the private sector. Both of those trends cause problems for the Crown.

First, development and diversification require capital investment. Governments are inevitably hard-pressed to find capital. The major interest of Cabinet and Caucus may not be the development of the business; it often may be in using SOEs as a 'cash cow' to help fund social services, particularly at times when the government is under fiscal pressure or finds itself lagging in the polls as an election approaches. Secondly, the Crown is inherently a risk-averse owner — it may not wish to increase its exposure in a particular industry. Yet, the medium-term future of the business may require that new risks be taken. Telecommunications developments, such as telephone, facsimile and electronic data interchange are already major threats to New Zealand Post's earnings in the traditional market for delivering physical communications. To meet that competition, NZ Post must move a proportion of its business into the electronic age. In fast-changing markets, a risk-averse strategy may prove high risk in the long run.

In addition, skilled and imaginative managers who took their positions on the understanding that they would be granted autonomy within a framework of ministerial goals, are likely to resent subsequent interference in day-to-day management. If politicians attempt to interfere, the managers tend to fight, protest, or even resign on the grounds that the State has broken the contract it made with them. Conversely, ministers tempted to intervene in day-to-day management are unlikely to place a priority on independence of mind in making appointments. If that ministerial inclination is obvious, then the best managers are unlikely to apply.

The architects of corporatisation therefore anticipated from the beginning that if reform was allowed to stop at that point, its achievements were likely to be degraded as time passed. Moreover, in the period following corporatisation, other profound economic forces were also at work. Excessive public debt and the continuous propensity of ministers to increase social spending were still creating serious pressures on the government's budget.

Even Labour, a political party historically dedicated to public ownership, was ultimately forced to start asking itself some fundamental questions: Why did the government own so many enterprises in New Zealand? The answer, in most cases, was a matter of historical accident. What disasters might occur if some of those enterprises were sold to fund reductions in the public debt and to reduce the country's exposure to future exchange-rate risks? It took case-by-case analysis to answer that question, but frequently the analyses projected significant net benefits to the public if the enterprise was sold. The Labour Cabinet was compelled to recognise that the rising interest bill on public-sector debt threatened its ability to budget for what it regarded as desirable social service goals. It also left those services at serious and avoidable risk of disruption in the event of any major economic shock. Notwithstanding its traditional opposition to privatisation, the Government finally decided it was time for the hard decisions.

In December 1987, with public debt standing at 75 per cent of GDP, I announced the government's intention to repay one-third of the debt, about $14 billion, by 1992, through a programme of asset sales. During the next two years, under Labour, major privatisations included the Bank of New Zealand (47 per cent), Petrocorp (100 per cent), New Zealand Steel (100 per cent), Development Finance Corporation (100 per cent), Postbank (100 per cent), New Zealand Shipping Corporation (100 per cent), Rural Bank (100 per cent), State Insurance (100 per cent), the government's 75 per cent interest in the Synfuels gas-to-gasoline plant, Government Printing Office (100 per cent), 40 per cent of the cutting rights to State exotic plantation forests, Tourist Hotel Corporation (100 per cent) and Telecom (100 per cent).

From the outset, public attitudes to the asset sales programme proved more favourable overall than anyone expected. The 1987 corporatisation of Air New Zealand, which abolished the airline's domestic monopoly, created almost instant recognition that public ownership is not necessarily the issue of most concern to the general public in their role as consumers.

Throughout its history as a State-owned monopoly in the domestic market, Air New Zealand had provided minimal facilities for its customers. The airline's capital city terminal was a prefabricated building of World War II vintage. Passengers trudged through the rain across windswept tarmacs to board planes. In-flight refreshments were limited to tea or coffee served with two dry biscuits and a small piece of cheddar cheese. On arrival, passengers had to wait up to 20 minutes to retrieve their luggage. The loss of Air New Zealand's privilege as a monopoly and the entry of Ansett into the domestic market transformed that situation virtually overnight. Both airlines worked 24 hours a day, seven days a week, to build quality terminals and covered access to planes. Customers got more flights, cheaper flights, better food, friendlier service and a virtual end to the wait for luggage. In 40 days, the new competitive system delivered highly visible benefits to the travelling public which State ownership had failed to provide in 40 years.

Such an obvious example of improved service enabled

consumer attention to focus on regulatory reform, which introduced competition as a means to improving efficiency and offering better customer service. The removal of State monopolies, a primary driving force behind corporatisation, was equally central to Labour's privatisation programme. It took priority over all other objectives. In every case, prior to sale, the regulatory framework surrounding the business was reviewed, to allow maximum competition and contestability. Where choices existed between heavy-handed regulation and competition as a means of preventing abuse of the consumer by dominant players, competition was systematically preferred. To the maximum extent possible, the government avoided setting up industry-specific regulatory bodies. In our view, such bodies were eventually likely to become growing bureaucratic empires imposing avoidable costs on the community and prone to capture by the industries they were set up to regulate.

Wherever possible, therefore, reliance was placed on the general laws of the land which legislated against abuse of dominant market position, via the Commerce Act and Commerce Commission. Where strategic interests were involved, or natural monopolies could not be eliminated, or where the removal of cross-subsidies was judged politically impracticable, the Kiwi Share mechanism or Deeds of Understanding were used to impose appropriate limitations on SOEs and private bidders.

Privatisation policies can be undertaken for many reasons. In Britain and France, for example, wider shareholdings by the public was one of the main objectives. In New Zealand, efficiency and then debt reduction were regarded as the primary objectives. Ministers were fully aware of and motivated by the question of efficiency, but it did not suit Labour Party philosophy to give it priority in the government's public rationale. Whatever the principal goal of privatisation, it inevitably affects the selection of a nation's privatisation strategy. In New Zealand, the aim was always to obtain the best possible price, subject only to the regulatory goals already mentioned. Competitive bidding by tender was the preferred sale mechanism. It enabled the government to extract full benefit for the taxpayer from the value potential owners were prepared to put on strategic control.

However, by the end of 1988, the left wing of the Labour Party was already seeking to reassert its traditional dominance. The government's capacity to maintain the pace of reform dwindled. The sale of Telecom was successfully completed for $4.25 billion, but the left wing of Caucus succeeded in forcing the rejection of a fully commercial bid for the remainder of the Bank of New Zealand. It claimed the timing was wrong and the price was inadequate. NewLabour's Jim Anderton, now leader of the Alliance Party, said it was an outrage even to consider selling BNZ, a 'jewel in the Crown' of State ownership. The extent of the bank's bad debts and inadequate performance was rapidly demonstrated soon afterwards. Rejecting the offer ultimately cost taxpayers more than $500 million.

The increasing dominance of Labour by the left saw National returned to government by a landslide in November 1990. But that victory, theoretically of a free-enterprise party, brought highly ambivalent attitudes to the Treasury benches. Many National MPs had no real understanding of SOE reforms. Some of them, including some ministers, still saw hands-on control of SOEs as a means of delivering politically valuable rewards to favoured interest groups. Further reform, even reform proposed by government ministers, and in some cases endorsed by Cabinet, was therefore continuously and publicly opposed by government backbenchers. The government itself became one of the most significant forces in the community in generating a backlash against further reform.

In the two and a half years following National's election, the remainder of the BNZ was finally sold. Other privatisation has been limited to a further 16 per cent of exotic plantation cutting rights, Housing Corporation prime rate mortgages, Government Supply Brokerage and minor oil holdings. By late 1992, asset sales revenue had reached only $12 billion, still $2 billion short of Labour's original $14 billion target. Moreover, the SOE model had already come under increasing attack by Government MPs, not just backbenchers but all the way up to the Prime Minister himself. The opportunity for this political conflict arose out of compromises which Labour had made during the original process of corporatisation. In crucial cases, massively inefficient cross-subsidies had been carried over into the SOE system and then further carried into privatisation itself through the special Deeds of Understanding or the Kiwi Share mechanism.

Major loss-making operations were thereby lodged, like foreign bodies, inside organisations required in every other respect to face open market competition from rival suppliers. A structural Catch-22 situation was created for those SOEs: to fund cross-subsidy losses, they had to overcharge other customers in the profitable areas of their business; but those profitable areas were now subject to competition. The situation of SOEs placed in that position was not commercially sustainable in the long run. But their efforts to find a viable solution inevitably galvanised all the vested interests who benefited by those cross-subsidies. The interest groups knew they could not win as long as the battle had to be fought on a commercial basis. What they needed was a return to the old policies of political intervention which gave them their privileges in the first place. They had built-in incentives to discredit the whole commercialisation process, past as well as future.

The Deed of Understanding setting up NZ Post was a typical example of these problems. It required continuing cross-subsidies for loss-making rural mail. But 70 per cent of the company's business had been deregulated completely. In those areas, NZ Post faced unfettered market competition. It was therefore funding its cross-subsidies by charging $40 million a year over and above fair market rates on standard business letters — the profitable part of its residual area of monopoly protection. However, the level of that protection had been reduced over five years from $2.25 an item to 80 cents, to encourage efficiency. Moreover, nothing prevented fax and electronic data interchange from competing head-on with business mail. Faced with a situation which was not ultimately sustainable, NZ Post increased its rural delivery fee by $40 a year (77 cents a week). All hell broke loose within the government, which was trailing in the polls and had a large rump of rural MPs. They saw the increase as a heaven-sent opportunity to win electoral credit by attacking the avarice of the company. A special Parliamentary Select Committee was set up to inquire into the increase. In the wake of that inquiry, the government considered including a pledge to remove rural delivery fees entirely in its 1993 election manifesto.

Telecom, despite privatisation, faces even larger problems. Its Kiwi Share requires that residential rentals rise no faster than the rate of inflation, unless its operating profits are unreasonably affected. The company is simultaneously locked into a commitment to maintain the existing nationwide telephone service. According to company estimates last year, its loss on local calls was consuming toll profits at the rate of $250 million a year. The tolls market, however, is fully deregulated and intensely competitive. The cross-subsidy has permitted Telecom's major competitor, Clear Communications, to win market share four times faster than originally predicted by independent reports to the Labour Government, and twice as fast as Telecom's own estimates.

Recognising that the government was in no mood to consider renegotiating the Kiwi Share, Telecom therefore planned to hack into its own costs in the most aggressive way possible. In 1993, having already reduced staff from 24,500 in 1987 to 13,600 in 1992, the company announced further reductions of 5000 people during the next five years. That may postpone rebalancing, but it does not remove the pricing anomalies which continue to limit performance in the tolls market.

The Electricity Corporation faced even more difficult problems after corporatisation in its relations with vested interests and politicians. Several interlocking steps were still required to ensure that the electricity industry achieved maximum efficiency in the interests of every New Zealander. The national grid, as a monopoly, had to be separated from generation and placed under appropriate regulation. The proposal was that it should be owned by a club consisting of the retail supply authorities, major users and ECNZ. It could then become the common carrier for a competitive electricity-generation industry. Parallel with those developments, retail supply would be opened to competition wherever practicable, then corporatised and/or privatised with a significant gifting of shares to consumers.

However, the retail electricity market was riddled with anomalous cross-subsidies. Prices to consumers varied from area to area as much as four-fold, purely as a result of differences in local cross-subsidy policy. Retail supply authorities differed enormously in their levels of efficiency. But the traditional, locally elected boards were in a strong strategic position to pose as the custodians of parochial interest. Moreover, the proposed club ownership of the national grid was dependent on a price set by negotiation and political pressure, rather than commercial bidding. No means existed to reach agreement.

In the end, the government was forced to opt for setting up the grid as a new Crown company. Retail supply companies then had built-in incentives to blacken the reputation of ECNZ, regardless of performance, and discredit the whole of the reform process. As a mere half-way house in electricity reform, ECNZ was vulnerable to that pressure. Under the SOE model, competition is the primary discipline which aligns the interests of State-owned corporations with those of the consumer. ECNZ, though subject to intense competition from other forms of energy, remained the dominant supplier of electricity. It had, at that stage, no defence against self-interested opponents who, fearful of losing their own status and power, chose to portray the corporation as bent on unfettered abuse of monopoly power.

In due course, ECNZ sought price increases closer to the long-run marginal cost of future power stations. Opponents portrayed this as rapacious profit-maximising by an irresponsible monopoly unconstrained by either market or ministerial discipline. The government, which as owner sets ECNZ's profit requirement, opted to court popularity by siding with the vested interests. The Prime Minister intervened personally, telling the public that 'the SOE model inherited from the previous government is not working'. SOE heads who did not toe the line might have to be sacked, he said.

Detailed new plans were developed to 'monitor' SOEs more intensively, including, in some cases, the establishment of advisory committees representing vested interests. State corporations were subjected to annual investigation by parliamentary select committees with the power to ask questions about any detail of operations, well beyond the limits allowed in a private-sector company's AGM. MPs did not hesitate to abuse that privilege by extracting information aimed at giving them purely political advantage. Information was sought with the sole intention of turning it to discredit the SOE. An atmosphere of confrontation was deliberately fomented by the government to deter SOEs from taking politically difficult decisions designed to benefit the consumer and the national interest in the longer run. NZ Post chairman, Michael Morris, summarised the dismal consequence of this inadequate leadership at a two-day SOE summit in November 1992:

> Until now, management and government shared a belief that privatisation is the only viable solution to these dilemmas. Interest groups, however, have been unusually successful in recent years in capturing quite large sections of public opinion. Both management and government may now need to compromise their objectives by sacrificing economic efficiencies and sale proceeds which would otherwise have been available to improve the nation's competitive position.

Other signs of damage became apparent soon afterwards. Two of the highest-calibre chief executives, reading the direction in which events were moving, gave notice of resignation. Dr Roderick Deane, chief executive of ECNZ, moved out of SOEs to join Telecom in the private sector. Harvey Parker, CEO of NZ Post since corporatisation, joined Telecom Australia to play a constructive role in future public-sector reform on the other side of the Tasman.

In terms of the wider picture, reform of public-sector businesses in New Zealand is far from complete. The State still owns enterprises worth about $20 billion. In addition to ECNZ and NZ Post, in June 1993 they included the Coal Corporation, Railways Corporation, New Zealand Rail, Television New Zealand, Radio New Zealand, Government Computing Services, Government Property Services, Airways Corporation, Works and Development Services, the New Zealand Meteorological Service, Airport Holdings, Land Corporation, public hospitals and education facilities. The gains brought to the public by corporatisation in the last six years remain at increasing political risk. In contrast, the post-1987 improvements of privatised SOEs are impressive and much more secure in the long term. They now have the flexibility to pursue their natural opportunities. Their new owners have provided them with access to superior management, marketing and production systems.

Naturally, privatisation does not eliminate all problems. In competitive markets all companies face difficult choices. But they have much stronger incentives now to reach timely sustainable commercial decisions. Given competitive markets, those gains inevitably benefit consumers through lower prices and improved choice. The incentives and sanctions which condition their performance cannot be replicated in the public sector. Privatisation greatly reduces the possibility of direct political interference in operating decisions. It ensures that investment is based on commercial, not political criteria. It removes the problems caused by the intense cost-dominated scrutiny of public-sector remuneration. It rewards appointments made strictly on merit, without cronyism. Given a competitive environment, it orients all company activity towards the satisfaction of consumer needs.

Perhaps still more importantly, it also frees governments from the conflicts arising from their multiple roles as owner, regulator and producer. It encourages them to focus on the policy-making role of setting the best possible framework in an even-handed way for all business activity. And by increasing the creation of wealth throughout the economy, it improves the ability of government to pursue its own broad social goals.

It is for all of these reasons that I advocate the privatisation or transfer to government-owned corporations of those schools and hospitals not privatised, and all other assets, as soon as possible. Table 8 in Chapter 12 establishes an asset dollar sales programme which, along with fiscal surpluses from 1995/96 onwards, would gradually reduce government interest payments from $4600 million to zero by 2010/11, a savings in taxation of more than $100 a week for a family of four.

9   Combating Disadvantage

Imagine that you are the parent of a small child, and in some way you are able to know that tomorrow you and your spouse will die and your child will be made an orphan. You do not have the option of sending the child to live with a friend or relative. You must choose among other and far-from-perfect choices. Your first choice is to place your child with an extremely poor couple by the official definition of 'poor' . . . This couple has so little money that your child will be badly clothed and will sometimes go hungry. But you also know that the parents work hard, will make sure your child goes to school and studies, and will teach your child that integrity and responsibility are primary values. Your alternative choice is to place your child with parents who have never worked, who will be incapable of overseeing your child's education, who think that integrity and responsibility are meaningless words — but who have plenty of food and good clothes, provided by others. Which couple do you choose?

Charles Murray, 'The American Experience with the Welfare State'[1]

In posing that question, American social scientist, Charles Murray, offers a hard extreme choice, an uncomfortable decision, with no possibility of extenuating circumstances. Nevertheless, he knows where his child would go in such a situation: to the first family. There is, he says, nothing really surprising in this. Throughout history, human behaviour has shown repeatedly that the qualities parents want their children to carry into adult life include self-reliance, self-motivation and the ability to make decisions based on sound values.

In asking the question, Murray is not recommending the first family as an ideal situation, but he is challenging

[1]Michael Jones (ed.), *The Welfare State: Foundations and Alternatives.*

those who make social policy to be more honest about the aims and actual results of their programmes:

> Let us by all means have a society that is compassionate and tries to do good. But let us also think much harder about what 'compassion' and 'doing good' mean. And if we cannot expect to revolutionise policy, let us at least be intellectually honest and stop the double standard, stop applauding ourselves for doing unto others in the name of compassion what we would not do to ourselves or to those we love.

One of the common factors in current worldwide discussions on social policy and welfare is that after periods of 20 to 50 years, and unimaginable sums of money, the problems of disadvantage and poverty have not been eliminated or even noticeably decreased. The reforms of the social welfare systems in Britain, the United States, Australia and New Zealand do not reflect a desire to discontinue them but rather to make them more efficient and more successful in alleviating and improving the conditions of those they were designed to help.

Two examples of this shift in policy took place in Australia at the end of the 1980s. The first was the marked move away from universal to more targeted benefits, and the second a change from the unemployment benefit to training schemes for the long-term unemployed. In 1930, Sir Keith Hancock, describing that country's main political philosophy, wrote:

> Australian democracy has come to look upon the State as a vast public utility whose duty it is to provide the greatest happiness for the greatest number.

A similar expectation has been true on this side of the Tasman. Whether you agree that this is a rightful (and righteous) role of the State, or not, the unassailable fact is that more than 50 years later the practical effects of this philosophy have not been what were expected.

In the years following the Second World War, there was general consensus on the goals of the budding welfare system. The first was the reduction of social and economic inequality; second, the fulfilling of certain basic needs, as of right; and third, the demonstration and encouragement of kinder and more communal relations between citizens. On all three counts the present system could be said to have failed: socio-economic inequality still exists and is possibly increasing; some people continue to live impoverished and disadvantaged lives because certain basic needs go unattended; and people's relationships with one another are not noticeably more harmonious or filled with neighbourly concern. In addition, we have seen the development of two totally unexpected side effects — dependency, through the creation of incentives that encourage people to change their behaviour and circumstances so as to qualify for benefits; and political capture, where influential lobbies manipulate the redistribution process to their own advantage.

We have found that people have not behaved as the designers of the welfare system expected and needed them to in order to fulfil the system's stated purpose. Instead of fostering altruism and a sense of mutual obligation, we have ended up with middle-class welfare capture and welfare dependency. One of the principal purposes behind the policies outlined in this book is to change the system's incentives (and, as a result, make those original goals achievable), to wean the middle class away from benefits they don't need and, in the words of President John F. Kennedy, to give the disadvantaged a hand, not a hand-out. The last is perhaps the most important as it affects us all when it is successfully achieved. Delivering real gains to people who are disadvantaged is crucial because it automatically delivers something of value to everyone.

The gains we should be aiming for are not just economic. Income is obviously important to the disadvantaged, but it is not enough to remedy their situation. They have an even greater need for encouragement and the opportunity to make some real progress for themselves by themselves. In helping them to win independence and contribute more to society, instead of always being on the receiving end, their future is transformed and everyone else's improved. Those gains also have an important role to play in creating a dynamic economy that provides higher incomes for everyone and therefore builds a fairer society. The alternative is a country with a permanent underclass of alienated people with no stake in prosperity and no social harmony.

The key issues which affect the disadvantaged include unemployment, race, crime, health, education, housing, welfare and the economy. None of the pressures these issues place on people can be solved with short-term, quick-fix answers from government. All of them need to be placed within a medium-term approach to policy if they are to be solved. And, because the issues are linked, and the public know it, none can be solved in isolation. Inadequate parenting, lack of motivation, insufficient skills, alienation, unemployment and delinquency reinforce each other. Low income, inadequate housing, poor health, lack of opportunity and lack of economic growth are all part of the same syndrome.

The personal goals of underprivileged people are essentially the same as those of the rest of the community. They want the opportunity, security and dignity which come from fair treatment, productive employment, rising living standards and personal choice. At present they are worse off than others in society because they lack skills, information, motivation and the spur to achieve. Their condition makes them vulnerable to social and economic pressure. They find it hard to survive without help. However, if the help we provide locks them into the role of passive recipients, all the State and society does is turn their vulnerability and dependency into a permanent condition.

It becomes a vicious cycle. The disadvantaged need access to education, health care, housing and benefits that will act as a guard against emergency, adversity or disability. Education where they learn nothing, life on a benefit, or unproductive dead-end jobs simply perpetuate their problems. Scope for constructive personal choice is basic to the dignity of human beings. A central feature of life for the disadvantaged is not just lack of money or housing. It is the total lack of choice. Equity matters not just to them personally but it is also the means to ensure a better life in the future for their children and grandchildren. The motivation-sapping effects of their situation mean they have a greater need than other people for the kind of incentives that will lift their morale and help put them back on their feet so they are able to contribute to society and make progress themselves in doing so.

Any programme of reform has to be about goals, objectives, dreams and practical commonsense delivery. It needs to unite society by appealing to the majority of voters. People have to be encouraged to think about where New Zealand can be in the future and where they would like to be during the next 5 to 20 years. The community as a whole is desperate to see improved growth and the investment needed to develop future growth. The social costs of very low growth over the past few decades have damaged the security and well-being of people at every level of society. While the costs hit the disadvantaged harder than anyone else, their reaction to their situation has an impact on everyone.

Many barriers stand in the way of meeting the broad objectives laid down at the inception of the welfare system, but none of them prevents our making a major advance in their direction, provided that we deal with them systematically. The objectives and how we gain them need to be carefully explained to the public so they understand what is happening and what is intended. People know that growth is the only way to avoid the erosion of living standards, to recapture that sense of national well-being and to get jobs that last. That necessarily involves a reduction of waste, inefficiency and avoidable burdens on those who create and contribute to growth.

In any economy, resources are limited and scarce. The challenge is to make the best use of them. That was part of the reason for turning many government businesses into State-owned enterprises. But there are all kinds of factors mitigating against using resources really well. Institutions frequently have a vested interest in maintaining the existing distribution of wealth and traditional programmes. Some of the sound and fury surrounding the recent health reforms, in fact any discussion of reform, has been from and about vested interests. In other cases, such as the excessive protection of some industries at the expense of others, the privileged classes get more than their fair share at the expense of the less privileged. Attitudes and understanding can be so conditioned by the past that people find it hard to see the benefits of change. The result is intervention to benefit special-interest groups. We need to keep reminding ourselves that one person's privilege is another person's disadvantage. If we protect past privilege, we entrench that disadvantage.

When this wasteful and uncompetitive approach is spread across the economy, it holds back the economic growth needed to create employment and sustain a healthy welfare system. Much-needed investment money is forced off-shore to buy into economies that will give good returns while the local economy suffers from low rates of investment.

In these circumstances, consistency is essential to credibility and public confidence whenever government programmes have a medium-term goal. Without goals and priorities, strong leadership and good communication, all these problems can reduce public confidence. Unwavering leadership is necessary to help the public through the time lag between promise and final delivery. Without it, both the waiting period and increase in interim costs destroy the consensus for change. For instance, valuable efficiency gains and new ways of delivering services look like nothing more than cuts in service.

New Zealanders, as a whole, have fallen into a trap over the past four years of looking at the country's problems in isolation and only in terms of today. They need to widen and lengthen their perspective. Some of our main difficulties are short-term consequences of actions taken to achieve real economic and social gains. The most obvious example, and the hardest for those caught up in it, is

199

unemployment. Some key problems of the past, such as high inflation, have been solved as a result of reforms already in place. The problems that remain cannot be remedied by shortening our focus and trying to avoid them with *ad hoc* short-term solutions. With that kind of approach the long-term gain is lost and the palliative solution is, in any case, merely temporary. The only true remedy, and the only way we can make sure the situation of the disadvantaged is dealt with constructively, is to focus on long-term gains and pursue them.

There are a number of key principles which underpin policies that deliver positive results for the under-privileged. The first is economic growth. Jobs are the foundation of personal and family security. Growth is what safeguards the whole system of social provision. Policies that foster growth and share the rewards fairly — for example, low tax rates, the GMFI and education cash grants — are the biggest contribution we can make to help disadvantaged people. Policies that sacrifice future growth prospects to provide immediate comfort, such as higher budget deficits and a softer approach to monetary policy (i.e., higher inflation), hurt the disadvantaged severely in the longer term. If we try to 'buy prosperity' with high deficits, debt and inflation, the world market will pass its own judgement on our prospects. The disadvantaged will suffer more than anyone else in society if that happens. Society needs to understand this in order to prevent it. It cannot be argued with any credibility whatever that the recipes of the 1930s or 1960s have anything much to offer in the modern world.

Important though growth is, growth alone is not enough to win back high employment. There are other factors at play. The process of improving the allocation of resources has put heavy pressure on employment everywhere as the privileged sectors have had to adjust. The subsequent improvement in economic growth, which we are only just beginning to see, will not necessarily bring with it a recovery in employment. Whether improved growth brings jobs or not depends to a large extent on the flexibility or rigidity of a country's labour market. Countries with inflexible labour markets experience higher job losses over longer periods in response to changes in the international economic environment. Privileged rigidities in sectors like education and health have an adverse impact on employment and inflation. A more flexible system, such as the one I have been discussing, would open major new opportunities for those without work and boost national incomes. This system could include:

❏ GMFI encouraging people to take work.
❏ A minimum wage set at the invalid benefit rate.
❏ Lower taxation.
❏ Competitive education and more choice.
❏ Competitive health care and more choice.
❏ Security in superannuation and post-retirement health care.

Undue rigidities and the wrong regulatory system have increased unemployment and hurt the disadvantaged disproportionately. The avoidable costs imposed by rigid work practices and welfare programmes fall most heavily on part-time workers, families and racial minorities, the most vulnerable people in the job market. For example, where the expected productivity of a worker is lower than the required statutory minimum wage, the worker cannot get a job. The intention of the minimum wage legislation was to benefit and protect the lower paid. However, one result in an economy under pressure which is expanding only slowly, is that many of those people have been locked out of employment for so long they are now finding it almost impossible to get a job. Despite this, the opportunity is there to give the disadvantaged person job experience and start them climbing the employment ladder. If the minimum wage was lowered to the level of the invalid benefit and then supplemented by a GMFI related to each individual's circumstances, there would be two beneficiaries. It would be less costly to the State and of more human benefit to the worker to let him or her into work and then top up the wages.

There is another reason for reconsidering minimum wage levels. As the labour market increasingly dispenses with national borders, relative wage rates become international. What an employer can and will pay will no longer reflect just a worker's productivity but the productivity and wage rates of workers in other parts of the world. This is particularly true for unskilled labour. The ability of New Zealand and other OECD countries to hold the wage for unskilled work so far above Asian, Chinese and Indian wage rates is progressively diminishing. High unemployment in the OECD partly reflects an oversupply of unskilled labour, yet the unskilled wage is still being held well above international market levels. This will put heavy pressures on welfare systems and national economies.

The relationship between benefit levels and take-home pay plays an important role in incentives to work and to learn work skills. If the difference between employment and unemployment is insignificant or negative, there is no reason or stimulus to find a job. At the same time, employers will not hire where the total cost to them exceeds the level of productivity they can expect to get from a worker. When long-term unemployment erodes skill, confidence and motivation, it can be expected that what an employer will pay will fall below the level of the minimum wage.

While various government job schemes have had some degree of success, good on-the-job training does much more for a worker's dignity, security, confidence and work skills. That is why I have advocated the introduction of a GMFI so strongly in this book. It would deliver $70 to $80 a week more to an unskilled worker who took a job rather than remain on the benefit with no other income. It is also why I have advocated taxing the additional earnings of those on benefits from the first dollar but allowing them to earn much more before it places them in a situation where it is no longer worth increasing their earnings. The result of these measures would be that margins between workers and those on benefits would be widened without having an adverse effect on those who are unable to take advantage of the new opportunities to work. It is a chance to make a dramatic and positive difference to the lives of low-income families, and therefore one that should be seized.

The principles of caring and efficiency also have a considerable impact on policies designed to help the disadvantaged. Without efficiency, improved equity is impossible. Even the existing level of care comes under increasing threat. Waste consumes resources, as in health and education funding, which would otherwise be available to improve fairness throughout the community. Certainly everyone involved in wasting resources collects a 'rent' — a larger dividend or pay packet — but at the expense of the whole community. The elimination of waste inevitably reduces the employment and pay packets of those who were involved in producing it. People as well as money and physical resources are forced to relocate to activities which produce a greater benefit to the community in the long term through growth and jobs. It is nonsense to pretend, as some are doing today in the health area for instance, that a change in the status quo for them is a reduction in equity overall. The interest groups who make that argument are stating a case for their own gain at the expense of everyone else's well-being.

The benefits of privilege are concentrated in the hands of well-organised groups. Those who enjoy privileges have a greater chance to make gains and naturally object loudly and violently if anyone threatens their 'economic rent'. Moreover, it is a mistake to think that those who benefit from State privilege are all wealthy capitalists or owners of companies. Workers and unions in privileged sectors also pick up their share of the rent paid by the rest of society; yet society receives no benefit from it.

The costs of privilege are dispersed widely across a community of consumers and taxpayers who are not well organised and have no single unified voice. In addition, it is difficult for the general community to identify the price it pays for the privilege of others. While the cost of any one privilege, per consumer or taxpayer, is unlikely to be great as an annual payment, the hidden costs of the total privilege system can be very large and damaging to the economy. At every stage, the burden falls heaviest on the employment chances and incomes of the most vulnerable and least privileged groups. They tend to be even less articulate and less organised than others, and in general incapable of defending themselves. The challenge, therefore, is to act on their behalf in a way that will bring positive changes, unlike some of the well-meaning demands of the churches, recognising that many (e.g., the health groups and teachers' unions) will oppose moves to improve the disadvantaged person's position. All the actions taken by the Labour Government between 1984 and 1988 could be defined as eliminating privilege.

It is worth looking at one of the most fought-over social welfare areas in recent years — the public health system. The present National Government has, to a degree, played into the hands of the interest groups in the recent controversies. They have allowed it to appear that the changes in the health system (which do not go far enough) are being driven purely by fiscal and efficiency considerations. The government is not seen as asking the vital questions: Who should the public health system be benefiting most; and what should it deliver?

The fact of the matter is that the whole public health system should exist to serve the purpose of improving equity across the community. Its supposed objective is to ensure that groups who could not otherwise afford health care have access to the best services, a task it is failing to do (and in which it will continue to fail unless a policy such as that outlined in Chapter 6 is implemented). Changes in staffing and resource allocations are not evil but essential in the health sector, not for negative reasons but rather to achieve improvements in care for all, particularly for the underprivileged who are too often the ones on the waiting lists. The issue needs to be turned around. It should be seen for what it is by the public — a positive programme, not a negative one.

New Zealanders have created rods for their own backs in

areas such as health care and education by worshipping sacred cows that do not exist. It serves nobody well if we pretend that we have a totally public system in health or education — we don't — and therefore that is what we must have. It is illogical to promote policies designed just for a public system when we have a private one as well working in tandem. This is simply an attempt by the vested interest groups to lock the rest of us into a position where we are unable to review other options on their merits to provide the best benefits to the disadvantaged and the rest of the general community. They have made the system more important than the people it is serving.

Similar confusion exists about the supposed advantages of provision in kind over provision of the means to afford services, which would free people from the monopoly suppliers they face today. If New Zealanders are given the opportunity to consider with open minds the question — What method delivers the best opportunities to the greatest number of the disadvantaged? — there is little doubt about their answer. A recent public survey found that most people thought the best medical care was provided in private hospitals but the trouble was they didn't have access to it. That is why the monopoly suppliers are so active at the moment. They cannot afford to lose control of the terms of the debate.

Income support policies have as their objective the redistribution of income fairly and efficiently. This means that:

❐ Assistance should meet the needs of the most disadvantaged.
❐ Benefit provisions should avoid creating severe disincentives for employment; instead they should assist and reward effort and, in a broader sense, self-help, participation and dignity.
❐ Benefit levels should provide reasonable minimum incomes.
❐ Income transfers should be effected efficiently and, in particular, should as much as possible minimise welfare

losses, not inhibit economic growth, and contribute to jobs.
❏ Tax collection and benefit payments should be such as to minimise interference with people's lives and choices.
❏ Transfers should be fair to taxpayers, people in paid work and beneficiaries.
❏ The system should be fiscally sound, that is, sustainable.

Despite increased expenditure, the present system of income support has failed to meet all these key objectives.

Any action to reduce the deficit will affect income distribution, either through tax or spending changes. The implication is that the government must decide which groups it really wants to help, and focus decisions about income support on those groups. Decisions should be made based on the evidence of inequities, inadequacies and disincentive effects in the current assistance structures. The key areas of choice in the field of tax/benefit reform are:

1. The distributional effects of funding the deficit by expenditure costs or increased tax. In this case the trade-offs are between:

❏ Applying increases to all benefits, which increases revenue requirements and worsens benefit/wage margins, and means higher effective marginal tax rates for all taxpayers.
❏ Holding overall levels of assistance, or allowing revenue-neutral changes in benefit relativities to address existing inequities, which avoids increasing the tax burden.
❏ Reducing levels of assistance for selected beneficiary groups, or across the board, which reduces revenue requirements.

2. Universality versus targeting, a choice which impacts on two key principles in income maintenance — focusing assistance on the most disadvantaged, and creating incentives for employment. The trade-offs here are between:

❏ Universality, with average and lower levels of assistance

for all who qualify, irrespective of need, which is fiscally expensive and likely to leave the most disadvantaged inadequately protected.

❒ Targeting, with varying levels of assistance according to need with a better chance of ensuring adequate support for the most disadvantaged.

❒ In each case, a compromise between higher/lower levels of assistance and higher/lower disincentive effects.

3. Adequacy versus incentives, where a basic value judgement must be made between the extent of income support and the preservation of income and saving incentives. It is impossible to fully satisfy both of these objectives. There is a strong element of trade-off between the adequacy of benefit levels and the structure of work incentives that can be provided. There are two concerns that arise in relation to the incentive issue:

❒ The poverty traps that occur where there is little or no increase in disposable income when there is an increase in hours worked; and

❒ The welfare traps which occur if the level of benefits are such that a person is better off (or close to better off) out of the workforce altogether and receiving benefits rather than working.

Virtually all Western countries are having to face the dilemma posed by the compromise between incentives and adequacy. Positive incentives to work are vital to both the long-term welfare of the individual and to society.

4. Part-time and full-time work. Participation in paid work is the most reliable source of income and well being for people who are capable of it. The greatest degree of independence can be achieved by meaningful full-time work, and income support should be designed to promote it. There may be an equal case, however, for the tax-benefit system to encourage part-time work on the grounds that it is increasingly available, a more realistic or preferred choice for some groups, and a way of acquiring, maintaining or expanding work skills.

In the final analysis, all the principles, the framework of policy, are not about economic or social theories. They are about and for people. How do you give people a real chance to live successful lives that contribute to the country's economic and social progress? Every New Zealander knows we cannot succeed as a nation unless the first New Zealanders, the Maori people, are part of that success. Escalating racial conflict is an economic and social dead-end for both races. It is totally inaccurate for either Pakeha or Maori to think that something deep in the spirit of Maoridom rejects the opportunities to actively participate in the economic and social life of the nation.

In the 1840s and 1850s, Maori were among the prime movers in expanding industries such as road building, bush felling, house building, flour milling, coastal and trans-Tasman shipping and many others. An Auckland newspaper, commenting in 1853 on their energy, skill and success as farmers, graziers, ship-owners, artisans and labourers, called them 'the main props of New Zealand'. If that early period had been the pattern for the next 150 years, then today Maori would have been up with the Goodmans and Fletchers, among the captains of New Zealand commerce. However, between 1860 and 1890, the pressure from a growing European population, money, rifles and diseases bought and drove the Maori people from all those mainstream activities. They were pushed out to the rural margins of the colony.

Traditional Maori values focus on lost land and fisheries. In fact, their real loss was the far wider opportunity to participate as equals in the development of the nation in the 100 years since then. The various tribal organisations understandably want ground to stand on. They feel it is the only way to guarantee their own existence in perpetuity and ensure that their identity is maintained. This may well be a fair analysis of the situation for those tribal organisations, but I do not accept that the fate of individual Maori depends primarily on owning land. In modern societies worldwide, the vast majority of people make their way in life and contribute to the wealth of their countries through their knowledge of and skill in using information and technology.

The foundation of modern wealth is know-how. The driving forces are technology and information management. We have to match the rest of the world in those areas if we want a better future. That is the real challenge for both Maori and Pakeha in the decades ahead. The same imperative faces all nations — African, Chinese, Arab. Information and technology cannot be dismissed as alien Pakeha concepts. They are the common international currency of the globe. If the Maori people do not face this fact, they will end up driving their children and grandchildren into increasing poverty. If the whole of New Zealand society does not accept it, we will all end up sending Maori down another blind alley.

It is pointless, for example, for the government to give the ownership of a fishery to the Maori people if they become merely absentee landlords who leave the fishing to be done by someone else. In that case, they get money which has been earned by the work and skills of others. That is just a social welfare hand-out in a different form — the kind of 'assistance' that has been destroying their initiative for 50 years. It rewards the wrong kind of behaviour and makes it unnecessary for them to contribute to the economy. The real purpose should be to increase the skills, participation and contribution of Maori people in the economy they share with everyone else so that they and the rest of the community can have an improved future.

Unless it becomes a priority for Maori to participate on equal terms, they will end up with no satisfactory home in New Zealand or anywhere else in the world, whether they own land or not. By allowing the racial debate to polarise around the literal and historical provisions of a 150-year-old treaty, we enshrine the past and run the risk that Maori as a race will end up confined to it. Settling past grievances, where that can be done without damage to the future, is one part of the task. But the real gifts we have to make to the Maori people are ones we should be offering to all citizens: the opportunity, motivation, incentives and skills needed to participate as equals in the growth of the nation; and the ability to contribute to New Zealand's success in the 21st century.

The past is not the answer to any problem. It defines the problem. Forced from the mainstream last century, the Maori established a separate rural society. Although never wealthy in the economic sense, it was independent and rich in taha Maori. From that base came political leaders of national importance and scholars of international fame. But when the population overwhelmed their rural economic base in the 1950s, the children of that society were suddenly forced into a head-on confrontation with mainstream urban living, and they were unprepared.

Migration has been a normal event for rural children throughout the world in the 20th century. The countryside has been equally unable to provide jobs for tens of thousands of Pakeha children. Relatively well prepared by their parents and schools, they have moved by way of nursing school, training college, polytechnic and university into skilled occupations and well-paid jobs that hold new opportunities. That was not the fate of Maori youth, often only 15 or 16 years old, arriving in town without appropriate education, job skills or urban attitudes. Their arrival coincided with the failure in our maladjusted economy to create enough productive jobs for our growing labour force. For many young Maori, the battle was lost before it began.

The children of those young Maori faced an even worse fate. Entering school with low self-esteem, they lost heart, learned little, and a complacent Pakeha system branded them lifetime failures. The disastrous consequences of that comprehensive failure by both races to consider the future are recorded in the statistics on Maori educational failure, unemployment, welfare dependence and crime.

But none of this is the whole answer. Pacific Islanders arrive here landless and unprepared for modern life. On the whole, they are making their way better than a lot of Maori people. So are the grandchildren of the Chinese goldminers who came here with nothing a century ago and faced an even larger cultural gulf, along with discrimination of the most blatant and inexcusable kind.

About 1975, an essentially thoroughly healthy spirit of rebellion took root within Maoridom against a future of permanent poverty and alienation. But it is not enough to aim simply to fight the land wars of the 19th century all over again, either in the courts or on the battlefield. Land, forests and fisheries may have been regarded as the major treasures of the past, but our most important treasure, whatever our race, is the potential skill and talent of our people. Whatever grievances the past may have generated, the core of the racial problem in New Zealand today would not exist if a majority of young Maori were moving confidently into the future, well equipped to meet and master the challenges of urban life in the 1990s and 21st century. To be a doctor, an architect, a plumber or a nurse, to work a computer, run a thriving business or sit on the board of a corporation are all blessings as good as a plot of land or forest. One of the facts of late 20th century life is that the vast majority of New Zealanders of all races will remain more or less landless, apart from their own house and section.

The Pakeha community has the wealth to create the opportunity; but that will be useless unless Maori community leaders throw their weight behind a new message: Learning is the key to the future. They have already rightly identified that intensive work has to begin at pre-school level, particularly for disadvantaged children, so they can enter school with the best chance of success. Well run pre-school programmes which involve parents along with the children have proved able to make improvements in achievement and lasting reductions in delinquency and dependency. They provide a vehicle for transforming the parents' attitudes to education. That tackles one of the central problems faced by Maori children trying to learn. Exactly the same need exists for Pakeha children from disadvantaged backgrounds in order to open up the prospect of a better future for them.

All these children deserve something extra regardless of race, to help them achieve constructive personal lives in the adult world and to give them the ability to provide their own children with the right start in life. This does not just apply to the under-fives. An intensive effort is required throughout early childhood, up to seven or eight years of age, if they are to have a good foundation for their lives.

We must also recognise that we have misspent billions of dollars in the last 30 years putting disadvantaged Maori and Pakeha children through standard school courses that simply did not work for them. Education is ineffective unless it creates an environment which encourages and enables such children to shine and to feel themselves achieving something they personally think is worthwhile. These are lessons the young people of Otara taught me 16 or 17 years ago when I was involved for a while in their Te Puke O'Tara multicultural centre. Self-help and self-esteem are central. When minority groups achieve satisfaction in their own eyes, your opinion or mine does not really matter. But it certainly will not be enough to encourage Maori children to shine solely in Maori subjects. They have to survive in a global village founded on technology. There is no road back to the simplicities of past eras. The only road open is the road ahead of us. Those who left school without skills will have to acquire them or spend the rest of their lives on a benefit, living in relative poverty at the expense of the rest of us. Training programmes are not there just to disguise the unemployment figures. Whether or not present schemes are adequate, they are trying to tackle one of our most fundamental social problems. And if the training is not adequate, maybe the time has come to make the trainers more directly accountable to trainees by allowing the latter to choose among competing course providers.

The State has also played a key role in killing Maori initiative over the last 50 years. Maori independence has been devastated in the past by badly designed assistance programmes. Instead of putting money into providing an adequate preparation for life in today's society, the government poured resources into hand-outs, so Maori had no need to acquire new skills.

It is just a nonsense to think that Maori cannot run successful businesses. Many did exactly that in the period before 1860 and a lot are doing it in New Zealand today. But the race as a whole is behind the rest of society in economic development. They need to more than match the pace of the rest of the community to bridge the gap. The barriers to more rapid Maori economic development have been identified, not least by Maori themselves. In part, it comes back to lack of education and experience. In part, the traditional social structures which are used to manage communal Maori enterprises are not always well adapted to commercial decision-making, and may set self-defeating objectives for business operations. It may seem irresistibly attractive to make a business serve social purposes in the community and use it to create jobs, subsidise cultural projects or as a vehicle for community aspiration. In fact, diluting the commercial purpose results in a low rate of return or loss. The business is less able to pay competitive wages. Less income, not more, is generated to assist future job creation. Social purpose then becomes a reason for seeking State subsidy. The subsidy gets built into 'normal' operating costs; and the business ends up further than ever away from being able to stand on its own foot.

There is more social benefit in doing things well than we can ever get from doing them badly, no matter how good our intentions may be. That is a lesson the whole of New Zealand is still trying to learn. What we face today in our race relations is the accumulated cost of a long-term failure by the people of both races to face up to their real responsibility, which is to the future, not the past. Our descendants, 100 years from now, are going to honour or curse us on the basis of the decisions we take today and their impact on the country they inherit from us. It will be totally irrelevant to them whether or not we implemented the literal provisions of the Treaty of Waitangi. What will matter to them is whether the country we pass to them is one worth living in. Fairness to the past is important and we should not neglect it, where fairness can be achieved. But it is fairness to the future which will give our descendants something to celebrate 50 and 100 years from now. That is a truth that applies to all races and across all strata of society.

10   The Politics of Reform:
The Art of the Possible[1]

When in doubt, a political proverb ought to go, opt for the innocuous. Plenty of politicians have been damaged by taking stands on war, taxes, gun control, and free speech, but no one ever lost an election because he sent out a free calendar. Statesmanship has its rewards, but they are frequently posthumous; it's easier to expedite, to facilitate, to intervene — to be nothing more than an exalted messenger boy whom the other messenger boys call 'my distinguished colleague'.
James Bennet and Thomas DiLorenzo, *Official Lies: How Washington Misleads Us*

Politicians worldwide tend to avoid reform until it is forced upon them by some costly economic or social disaster. They close their minds to the obvious need for change because they believe that decisive action will automatically bring political calamity upon them and the government. As the country drifts closer to crisis and the problems are no longer deniable, they persuade themselves that to do anything within a relatively short time of an election would give the advantage to their political opponents. They justify this stance by pretending that their opponents are deceitful and interested only in their own gain, not the well-being of the country. When the economic situation is finally serious enough to arouse public concern, political parties often continue to evade the issue by offering electoral bribes to distract voters from the real problems or, alternatively, as has been happening in New Zealand recently, try to divert public attention by casting accusations and unsub-

[1]First presented to the Mont Pelerin Society in Christchurch, NZ, 1989.

215

stantiated rumours of wrongdoing on the part of other people in the community.

None of this need be the case. I would argue, in direct contradiction to these beliefs, that political survival depends on making quality decisions; that compromised policies only lead to voter dissatisfaction; and that letting things drift is the equivalent of political suicide. Politicians can be politically successful while undertaking structural reform to benefit the nation. They do not have to wait until economic or social disaster forces their hand. The lessons learnt from New Zealand since 1984 are clear: where policies of real quality have been implemented — taxation, financial market reform, State-owned enterprises and labour market reform — the polls show continuing voter approval. Wherever the government stopped short of instituting policies of such rigorously high standard — in the reform of education, health and welfare — the polls show rising disapproval from the public.

Quality decisions are the key to the reforming of a country's infrastructure and to political success in government. New Zealand's story provides the evidence. The politicians who sought success through *ad hoc* solutions which evaded the real problems, damaged the nation and eventually destroyed their own reputations. Voters ultimately place a higher value on improving their medium-term prospects than on action that looks good in the short term but sacrifices larger and more enduring benefits. For any politician, the most basic of choices is always there. You can accept the initial costs and temporary discomfort in exchange for the good times that will come a few years ahead, or focus on immediate satisfaction and find yourself sandbagged by the accumulated costs at some unexpected time in the future.

These concepts are not foreign to the public. People accept low incomes as students to earn more later. They save for their old age and willingly invest in a better future for their children. When all the facts and information are made easily available, the ordinary people of any community show over and over again that they have a strong grip on reality and common sense. They want politicians to have guts and vision. The problem with so many politicians today is that they look for instant popularity as the key to power. Therefore, they look for policies with instant appeal. But there is no free lunch and every decision involves trade-offs which do not vanish just because some politician chooses to ignore them.

The problem with compromise policies is simple. Ultimately, they do not produce the right results for the public. So they come back to haunt the politicians responsible for them. As costs and distortions accumulate, the governments involved resort to misrepresenting and suppressing vital information about future economic prospects in order to warp the judgement of the voting public. Too often in the past they have ended up locking themselves and the public into their own nonsense. No one escapes until a major crisis liberates the suppressed information and consigns the politicians responsible to oblivion.

Objectives set on the basis of maximum benefit to the nation in the medium term, and the means to achieve them, must be tested against the best available economic analysis and all known facts before they are implemented. Traditional preconceptions or prejudices about means should not be allowed to prevent a thorough review of all the options and the selection of the approach most likely to achieve the chosen goals. Prejudice and preconceptions are obviously at work in welfare, health and education in many countries around the world today.

Political Lesson: If a solution makes sense in the medium term, go for it without qualification or hesitation. Nothing else delivers a result that will truly satisfy the public.

Decisions made on this basis do not treat problems separately. Instead, they take account of the way social and economic issues are linked and make use of those connections so that every action resulting from policy decisions improves the way the whole system works.

New Zealand's experience since 1984 provides an

important insight into the nature of political consensus which is widely misunderstood here and around the world. The conventional view is that consensus support for reform must exist before you start, otherwise the action taken will not prove to be politically sustainable at election time. The tendency instead is to seek consensus in advance with interested parties by compromising the quality of the decisions — bringing the benefits up front and either ignoring the costs or pushing them further down the track by some means or another.

But when the government compromises its decisions for immediate advantage, at the expense of the medium term, the public becomes more and more dissatisfied as time passes. The problem is that the interests of the many different groups in society are complex and diverse. None of them welcome the idea that their traditional privileges may be removed. If you try to get them together to agree to a programme, they will work instead to protect their respective interests at the expense of the taxpayer and consumer.

Political Lesson: Consensus among interest groups on quality decisions rarely, if ever, arises before they are made and implemented. It develops after they are taken, as the decisions deliver satisfactory results to the public.

Governments need the courage to implement sound policies, take the pain at the beginning, and be judged on the basis of the good results that follow later. Much of the tax reforms implemented by the Labour Government between 1984 and 1988, especially the introduction of GST, are good examples of that. By taking the approach we did, Labour won an increased majority in 1987 and remained in front in every opinion poll until the Prime Minister, David Lange, unilaterally reneged on government policy announcements, which included a flat tax rate of 23 cents in the dollar in personal tax and an asset sales programme of $14 billion. The government then dropped well behind and never recovered, despite the resignation of David Lange as Prime Minister in 1989. Once he lost the nerve required to take a consistent medium-term approach and to make quality decisions, the result of the 1990 election became a certainty — a huge and humiliating Labour loss.

There are 10 key principles for politically successful structural reform. This chapter looks at each of these 10 principles in detail.

FIRST PRINCIPLE: FOR QUALITY POLICIES, YOU NEED QUALITY PEOPLE

Policy starts with people. It emerges from the quality of their observation, knowledge, analysis, imagination and ability to think laterally so as to develop the widest range of options. Replacing people who cannot or will not adapt to the new environment is pivotal. Getting the incentives and structure right can also transform the performance of many dynamic and capable people who were not able to achieve the right results under the old system.

Since deregulation, management quality in the private sector has improved dramatically. The success of the public-sector reforms begun in New Zealand in 1984 has depended on people as much as policy. For example, in health, education and social welfare, the old public-service appeal system has been abolished and chief executives are appointed on merit and are accountable for performance, in much the same way as CEOs in the State-owned enterprises such as Electrocorp and New Zealand Post. However, top managers are not yet convinced that politicians have learned the limits of their role in the new system. They continue to fear that political interference in the running of departments could prejudice their ability to achieve the goals set for them. The full potential for reform in this area cannot be realised until ministers learn to play their new role correctly and let managers reach the agreed outcomes efficiently.

The biggest problem in New Zealand, however, is the calibre of the people attracted to and selected for political candidacy of both the Labour and National Parties. In a two-party system, the public interest cannot be met unless both parties adopt a broad spectrum approach that is widely representative of the community. For example, the

Labour Party tends to draw many of its active members from among trade unions, the teaching and legal professions and academe, while National draws mainly on farmers, lawyers and small-business people. This tendency towards a relatively narrow active membership base can create problems for both parties. They inevitably select people representative of their membership, not the wider community. Parties become, in a sense, closed societies. Candidate selection begins to tap into an inadequate gene pool. As a result, the quality of policy suffers. Those in the community with the capacity to break that closed-shop system find the parties too inward-looking to bother doing so. If people want to break that cycle, we will have to recognise that parties cannot and will not solve those problems for us. They are locked into their own inadequacies.

> *Political Lesson: There will only be a solution to the problem of poor-quality candidates if enough people with courage, education and vision are willing to do something worthwhile for their country in the political area.*

The low status of politicians in the community results from the short-sighted, excessively partisan approach so many take to their responsibilities. At the same time, too many high-calibre people are content just to criticise from the sidelines. As long as things continue this way, we will wait in vain for good government in democratic countries. Things will improve only if enough people take the trouble to get involved. They have a responsibility to ensure that good candidates are available in all parties. It is absolute nonsense to think that existing parties have a monopoly on quality ideas. If countries place quality at the heart of everything they do, they will break the old moulds which discredited politics and politicians and led too many countries into avoidable economic calamity.

SECOND PRINCIPLE: IMPLEMENT REFORM IN QUANTUM LEAPS, USING LARGE PACKAGES

> *Political Lesson: Do not try to advance a step at a time.*

Define your objectives clearly and move towards them in quantum leaps. Otherwise the interest groups will have time to mobilise and drag you down.

The political problems involved in making a conventional attack on protection are well understood. The benefits of protection are substantial in the hands of the favoured few who receive them. Such groups are usually well organised. They usually scream blue murder if anyone threatens to remove their privileges. They are capable of mobilising quite powerful opposition against reform. The problem is that the cost of protection, however large in total, is relatively small per person per item. It is widely dispersed across the rest of the economy and often invisible to the people paying the bills. Therefore, they are weak and disorganised allies of reform at best. At worst, their ignorance may be exploited by the interest groups in campaigns to convince them that reform will damage the general interest. This is happening at present in both education and health. In New Zealand, and the rest of the world, the conventional perception is that reformers are playing against a stacked deck.

Political Lesson: *Genuine structural reform is portrayed as equivalent to wilful political suicide. That rule holds good where privileges are removed one at a time in a step-by-step programme. Paradoxically, it ceases to apply when the privileges of many groups are removed in one package.*

In that case, individual groups lose their own privileges but simultaneously they no longer have to carry the cost of paying for the privileges of other groups in the economy. It is also harder to complain about damage to your own group when everyone else is suffering at least as much, and you benefit from their loss. Whatever its own losses, each group has a vested interest in the success of the reforms being imposed on all the other groups.

Packaging reforms into large bundles is not just a gimmick. The economy operates as an organic whole, not an unrelated collection of bits and pieces. Structural reform aims to improve the quality of the interactions within the whole. When reform is packaged in large bundles, the linkages in the system can be used to check that each action effectively enhances every other action. It also improves its selling potential.

> **Political Lesson:** *Winning public acceptance depends on demonstrating that you are improving opportunities for the nation as a whole, while protecting the most vulnerable groups in the community.*

Large packages provide the flexibility needed to demonstrate that the losses suffered by any one group are offset by worthwhile gains in other areas for the same group. The public will take short-term pain, if the gains are spelt out convincingly and the costs and benefits have been shared with obvious fairness across the community as a whole. Generally, fairness does not include compensation for those who are losing their past privileges, but even they make genuine gains after they come through the period of adjustment.

If insufficient consideration is given to these balances, the reactions of aggrieved people forced to take more than their share of the costs will end up tearing the reform process apart. In my view, the principle of quantum leaps and big packages provides the answer for New Zealand and other countries where opposition to reform has created problems recently.

THIRD PRINCIPLE: SPEED IS ESSENTIAL. IT IS ALMOST IMPOSSIBLE TO GO TOO FAST

Even at maximum speed, the total programme will take some years to implement. The short-term trade-off costs start from Day One. When reform has been delayed for many years, those costs are considerable. Tangible benefits take time to appear because of the time lags that are part of any system of reform. If action is not taken fast enough, the consensus that supports the general reform process can collapse before the results become evident, while the government is still only part-way through its reform programme.

There are serious dangers in seeking to hold back the rate of change in order to satisfy groups who claim a slower pace would give the community more time to adjust with less pain. Policy cannot be fine-tuned with enough precision to ensure that, for example, inflation will be reduced successfully by a modest and targeted amount every year over an extended period. If an attempt is made to do so, it takes only a modest error or miscalculation of external circumstances to end up going backwards instead of forwards, and destroying your credibility in the process. Vested interests seeking to preserve past privileges will always argue strongly for a slower pace of change. It gives them more time to mobilise public opinion against the reforms. On the other hand, vested interests cannot get the payoffs from change until the government has moved far enough to reduce the costs imposed on them by the privileges of other interest groups.

Political Lesson: Vested interests continuously underestimate their own ability to adjust successfully in an environment where the government is rapidly removing privilege across a wide front.

On closer analysis, many apparent demands for a slower pace are actually expressing powerful resentment that the government *is not moving fast enough* to abolish privileges enjoyed by other groups. In New Zealand, from 1984 on, farmers demanding a reduction in the rate of change regularly said they needed it because of the costs still imposed on them by excessive protection elsewhere in the economy. They cheered up whenever the government responded by announcing further and faster changes in the sectors where protection was still prejudicing their ability to act competitively. Properly understood complaints of that kind are reasonable. Farmers cannot be fairly asked to face up to their own adjustment costs if manufacturers of their supplies continue to enjoy the protection of high tariffs. Nor should they be asked to operate without subsidies and still be expected to afford to pay for the excessive costs of monopoly health and education systems.

> ***Political Lesson:*** *It is uncertainty, not speed, that*
> *endangers the success of structural reform programmes.*
> *Speed is an essential ingredient in keeping uncertainty down*
> *to the lowest possible level.*

When State trading departments were being transformed
into commercial corporations in New Zealand in 1987, it
became obvious that there would be large-scale
redundancies in the coal and forestry areas. Because some
of these activities were located in depressed areas, the
government took its time to make the final decision,
leaving thousands of employees in limbo for about six
months. Staff knew that some of them had no future in the
industry, but did not know which of them it would be. They
could not leave before the government made up its mind
because they might lose their redundancy pay-out. The
result was deep and intense bitterness, which the
government interpreted as hostility, primarily to the
policies themselves, and so further eroded its willingness to
take action. Once decisions were announced, the mood in
those regions improved rapidly. A lot of the people always
knew change was inevitable. The public often shows more
realism than the politicians. What they really wanted was
an end to the uncertainty, so that they could decide how to
get on with their lives.

A great deal of technical debate has gone on worldwide
about the best order for reform and the alleged sequencing
errors of governments, both here and elsewhere. Those
armchair theorists postulate the desirability of tackling the
labour market or the tradeable-goods market before
embarking on the deregulation of sectors such as finance,
for example. At a purely analytical level the debate is
entertaining but no clear-cut answers emerge. Moreover, as
a practitioner of reform, I find the question fundamentally
irrelevant. Before you can plan your perfect move in the
perfect way at the perfect time, the situation has already
changed. Instead of a perfect result, you wind up with a
missed opportunity. Some decisions take full effect the day
they are made. Others take two to five years of hard work
before they can be fully implemented. Perfect sequencing,

even if it existed, would not be achievable. If there is an opportunity to implement a reform that makes sense in the medium term, grab it before the moment passes. When an economy is stalled and failing, what matters is to get it moving towards a better future as soon as possible.

FOURTH PRINCIPLE: ONCE YOU BUILD THE MOMENTUM, DON'T LET IT STOP ROLLING

Political Lesson: Once the programme begins to be implemented, don't stop until you have completed it. The fire of opponents is much less accurate if they have to shoot at a rapidly moving target.

If you take your next decision while opponents are still struggling to mobilise against the last one, you will continually capture the high ground of national interest and force them to fight up hill. The government can develop public awareness of the key issues by structuring the content and sequence of its packages to dramatise the relevance of basic economic linkages.

By the end of 1985, for example, adjustment costs were biting quite deeply into pastoral farming which had lost some large subsidies and was also facing low international commodity prices. Land values were tumbling back from the inflated levels stimulated by the previous government's assistance measures, and equity problems of considerable magnitude had begun to emerge. Nevertheless, resource allocation in farming and forestry was still being distorted by large concessions that let people write off livestock and development costs against other taxable income. People buying livestock were happy to pay prices up to two or three times the value justified by market returns because they knew that the taxpayer was covering two-thirds of their costs.

Tax write-offs had led the wine industry to plant twice the acreage needed to satisfy the market, and boosted the amount of some varieties of wine held in stock to three years' supply against an international norm of half that. The government decided that, despite the adverse climate and the increased cost for those concerned, all such concessions had to be removed to promote the medium-term health of their industries.

To combat the inevitable outraged reaction, we moved the whole reform programme into a higher gear. In the same package, we announced an unprecedented onslaught on public-sector waste. State-owned businesses accounting for 12.5 per cent of GDP and 20 per cent of the nation's investment became corporations with commercial objectives and they were headed by directors of quality drawn from the private sector. They were to pay normal tax and dividends and raise their capital in the market, without the aid of government guarantees. The changes dwarfed any in our past public-sector history. Through corporatisation, Electricorp has cut costs by a real 20 per cent. Telecom did even better than that. Rail-freight rates are down by about 50 per cent in real terms. Coal prices to some major customers have been halved.

Farmers in New Zealand have traditionally loathed the Labour Party. But moves on that scale convinced them that we meant business in getting their costs down as well as removing their subsidies. Federated Farmers became one of the first major interest groups to endorse the principles behind our reforms. From then on, their aim was to ensure that the government lived up to its promises. The New Zealand Business Roundtable, representing large corporations forced to undergo massive and costly restructuring, also rapidly recognised the medium-term benefits to the nation. The underlying process is very important.

Political Lesson: Before you remove the privileges of a protected sector, it will tend to see change as a threat which has to be opposed at all costs. After you remove its privileges and make plain that the clock cannot be turned back, the group starts to focus on removing the privileges of other groups that still hold up its own costs.

Exactly the opposite process occurs wherever some favoured group is allowed to retain its privileges and is given ongoing protection from the broad thrust of the reforms. Anxiety levels in protected groups rise steadily as reform progresses through the rest of the economy. They fear their turn may come next. Their internal organisation improves dramatically. They raise their public profile and consolidate their opposition. To conceal their vested interest in exemption from reform, they will aim to dictate the rhetoric that governs all public debate — exactly what is happening in both the educational and health fields today. Efforts to improve the quality and quantity of health services for ordinary New Zealanders are portrayed as replacing public care with private profit at the expense of the ill and the elderly. The strategy of this rhetoric is to obliterate public awareness of all medium-term benefits, exaggerate the short-term costs and portray those costs as the objective and sole result of reform.

Those groups end up making strenuous efforts to gain control of the political process in the reforming party, and to stalemate any threat to themselves by terminating the total reform programme.

Political Lesson: Stop the rot before it begins. Remove privilege even-handedly across the board and give such groups, along with everyone else, a more constructive role in a better society.

FIFTH PRINCIPLE: CONSISTENCY + CREDIBILITY = CONFIDENCE

Untarnished credibility is essential to maintain public confidence in structural reform and minimise the costs. The key to credibility is consistency of policy and communications. The voting public has seen governments come and go, all of them promising low inflation, more jobs and higher living standards. But for years, life has gone on, exactly as it always used to. A government serious about reform must take the first step early, and make it a big one. You have to break the pattern of the past dramatically enough to convince the community that, this time, somebody really does mean business.

Political Lesson: When the government lacks credibility, people refuse to change until the clash between their old behaviour and the new policy imperatives has imposed large avoidable costs on the economy.

As the reform programme rolls forward, a lot of people start hurting. Their confidence depends on continuing to believe that the government will drive reform to a successful conclusion. Speed, momentum, the avoidance of *ad hoc* decisions and an unwavering consistency in serving medium-term objectives are the crucial ingredients in establishing the government's credibility. Resolution is particularly important when, notwithstanding the best intentions on the government's part, the community remains sceptical about its consistency.

By 1985, New Zealand had experienced a decade of high inflation. The previous government had over-stimulated the economy. The country was just emerging from a long wage-price freeze and a large devaluation. Nothing on earth could convince people that the new government would not validate a large wage rise, as the last one had. With interest rates at 20 per cent, people were still rushing out to buy houses. In situations like that, the government wins by informing, warning, holding its policy stance totally steady . . . and then waiting for experience to drive home the necessary lesson.

You know when you start to win the credibility battle: the media begin to put every government statement under a microscope, looking for inconsistent decisions and lapses of principle. People begin to grasp the idea that wherever a group manages to hold on to privilege and protection, an avoidable cost is imposed on those who are learning to adjust. Public opinion was outraged when the government granted a quite minor subsidy to New Zealand Railways to keep the Westland-Canterbury line open. The local political advantage of the action was buried by national criticism of the government for appearing to set aside the principles that it had promoted as basic to its reforms. One day the message from the public changes. It reads, 'Keep the reform process going, drive it to a successful conclusion, or you are dead at the next election.'

Political Lesson: *Structural reform has its own internal logic based on the linkages within the economy. One step* *inevitably requires and leads to another, to extract benefit for the population as a whole.*

Abolishing export assistance is fruitless unless exporters' costs are also reduced by lowering tariffs, deregulating internal transport and reforming ports and shipping services. The fiscal gains from corporatisation or privatisation will vanish without trace if expenditure in an un-reformed social-services sector is left to rise without regard for value. The redundancies created as production is rationalised to improve efficiency may turn into more or less permanent unemployment if an inflexible labour market protects insiders against outsiders. Where the logic of reform is not followed closely enough, the confidence of investors will be damaged and the ultimate growth rate may be less than it would have been.

Credibility takes a long time to win, but it can be lost almost overnight. Confidence then collapses. The costs of the adjustment rise. The time required to complete the process and bring in the gains expands. The political risk increases. In the wake of the sharemarket crash of 1987, for example, many countries sought to soften the political and financial impact on the community by easing back on their monetary policies. The dragon of inflation leapt back to life. Those countries have been faced with the costs involved in slaying the dragon for a second time.

Political Lesson: The battle for consistency and credibility is always ongoing and never finally won. It is central to every decision that comes before the government for consideration. Winning back lost credibility can take longer than winning it in the first place. If confidence starts to waver, push the reform programme forward the next big step, and do it quickly.

SIXTH PRINCIPLE: LET THE DOG SEE THE RABBIT

People cannot co-operate with the reform process unless they know where you are heading. Go as fast as you can but, where practicable, give the community notice in advance. Where programmes can or will be implemented in stages over time, publish the timetable up front. In this way you show that you know where you are going, commit the government to the process, let people know how fast they have to adjust, and reinforce the credibility of the whole programme. Such an approach is particularly important in areas such as the removal of import licensing and reductions in tariffs, which impose major changes in the way firms go about their business. Decision-makers must be able to see as much as possible of the total change affecting their businesses in the period ahead in order to plan effective adjustment.

In November 1984, the government indicated that in roughly two years' time wholesale sales tax would be abolished, GST would be introduced, and income-tax rates would be cut. By early 1988, the top marginal rate of income tax, which had been 66 per cent when Labour took office in 1984, had been reduced in two stages to 33 per cent and company tax had also been cut from 45 per cent in 1983/84 to 33 per cent. The December 1987 Economic Statement extended corporatisation of State trading enterprises into a large privatisation programme designed to help cut public debt by $14 billion by late 1992.

This approach has several very substantial advantages. First, the government was committed to perform in line with that target or lose valuable credibility. Secondly, the community's awareness of that factor was helpful to confidence. The release of such information also places professional analysts in a position to make their own independent evaluation of progress and government performance. They understand the importance of quality in decision-making and the benefits available in consistent medium-term policies. They are often trusted advisors of interest groups. As time passes, their objectivity, combined with their increasing goodwill towards the reform programme, becomes one of the major factors in creating a favourable climate of public opinion.

The confidence of the community is further increased if private-sector people, respected for their experience and capability, are involved in helping to fine-tune policies and improve management. Panels of experts appointed from the private sector, for instance, received public submissions on the government's major tax initiatives to help remove any administrative bugs from the new systems. Our programmed and principled approach to policy was welcomed by decision-makers and opinion-formers in particular because it contrasted so markedly with the previous government's approach. For example, the wage and price freeze imposed in 1982 seems to have been the result of a moment of inspiration by the then Prime Minister, which was thereupon implemented instantly without giving anyone a chance for second thoughts.

SEVENTH PRINCIPLE: NEVER FALL INTO THE TRAP OF SELLING THE PUBLIC SHORT

People out there in the community fight wars when they have to. They exchange short-term costs for long-term benefits every day of their lives. They take out mortgages and bring up children. Faced with the need for reform, normally responsible politicians will confide privately, 'I know it's needed but the people out there don't! Politics is the art of the possible.' Middle-of-the-road MPs maintain their political security by not taking too close or detailed a look at reality: 'Ups and downs are normal. Things will come right; they always do.' As the problems worsen, the demagogues and opportunists move in: 'We have just one problem — our political opponents are nuts! I can fix the lot with common sense and some No. 8 wire.' For years at a time, while the economy drifts on towards crisis or collapse, the public is offered nothing better by way of information or diagnosis. So they give the demagogue a go. Nobody stops to think that what people may really want is politicians with the vision and courage to help them create a better country for them and their children in the year 2000 and beyond. Do not mistake the fears of politicians for ignorance, lack of courage, or lack of realism on the part of the public.

> **Political Lesson:** *Successful structural reform does not become possible until you trust, respect and inform the electors. You have to put them in a position to make sound*

231

judgements about what is going on.

Tell the public, and never stop telling them:

❒ What the problem is and how it arose.
❒ What damage it is doing to their own personal interests.
❒ What your own objectives are in tackling it.
❒ How you intend to achieve those objectives.
❒ What the costs and the benefits of that action will be.
❒ Why your approach will work better than the other options.

People may not understand the situation in all its technical detail, but many of them can sift the wheat from the chaff. They know when key questions are being evaded. They can sense when they are being patronised or conned, and do not like it. They respect people who honestly answer their questions.

At the height of the rural crisis in 1986, I walked on to a platform in South Otago without a speech note in my hand, talked for 40 minutes and answered questions for two hours. The chairman wound up the meeting by saying that it took courage to do that and invited me to return in 12 months' time. The headline in the local paper read: Minister Puts Head Into Lion's Den. Audiences such as that one listen with interest and attention if you tell them simple truths that they are not used to hearing from politicians:

❒ There is no free lunch. The privilege of a favoured group is always paid for by the rest of the community. The group also has less need to perform, so the whole economy finally suffers.
❒ Subsidies always contain the seeds of destruction of the very industries they were meant to help. You end up investing in uneconomic production that damages your own market future.
❒ A lower exchange rate is not the way to safeguard exporters. Farmers were better off when the New Zealand dollar was worth US$1.35 than when it was worth US.43 cents in 1985.

❏ Where does it stop? When the New Zealand dollar is worth US.20 cents, or 10c or 5c? Those who argue for a lower dollar are worrying about the symptoms, not fundamentals such as getting their costs down.

❏ Inflation is what ruined the competitiveness of exporters in this country over the last 20 years. Unless we address that, exporters in New Zealand do not have a long-term future.

❏ Interest rates will always be inflation plus a margin. If inflation is 15 per cent, interest rates will be 15 per cent plus a margin; if it is 2 per cent, interest will be 2 per cent plus the margin.

❏ Easing monetary policy will not solve the problem of high interest rates. Six months out, instead of falling, inflation will take off again and interest rates will rise with it.

❏ For the last 100 years, ministers have thought they were running government departments. We now know that they had no idea what was really going on and no real control.

❏ For years, politicians in New Zealand have been under the illusion that they could pick winners better than the private sector. They wasted billions for zero or negative returns.

❏ You can have income tax at 20 cents without incentives, or tax at 40 cents with incentives and have government manage your investment. You choose.

❏ Import licensing did not create jobs. It gave State-guaranteed rip-off profits to selected people, regardless of their performance, at the expense of consumers and economic growth.

It is ridiculous to think that voters cannot absorb those messages.

EIGHTH PRINCIPLE: DON'T BLINK. PUBLIC CONFIDENCE RESTS ON YOUR COMPOSURE

Structural reform in New Zealand since 1984 has involved ministers in some of the most radical decisions announced to the public for 50 years or so. During major change, as the pressures from reform begin to affect the economy, the whole community starts watching every television appearance, looking for the least sign of government nervousness. Public confidence in and co-operation with the reform programme can be undermined by the least twitch. Visible uncertainty among key ministers spreads like a plague through the community.

Major reform demands a change in the ideas and attitudes that most people grew up with. Such demands inevitably cause discomfort and uncertainty in many people. Government research showed that people become hypersensitive to any signs of similar uncertainty in the politicians who are responsible for the reform programme. They attend meetings and watch the television news not just to find out what is happening and understand the ideas behind it, but also to probe the mood of the politicians at the helm. When they cannot understand the technical detail of the argument, they rely on their assessment of the speaker's mental and emotional condition as a basis for judgement.

It is another reason why it pays to make decisions of the highest quality. When you know you have it right, and know that the policies are on course, that comes out through people's TV screens. Knowing or believing that you have got it right provides a firm foundation for dealing with people in a relaxed, confident way when you come face to face with them, even at large meetings of quite angry people.

This is not intended to be a recommendation for arrogance. Listening to arguments from sources of every kind is enormously important to policy making, as well as to selling policies successfully. But all of that advice has to be measured against the government's medium-term goals. It is not arrogance to hold a sound course for objectives that benefit the country. I always regarded the speeches I made as Minister of Finance as a minor part of my meetings. The speech sets the framework for a question and answer session that follows it and lasts twice as long. The questions keep you fully attuned to the changing concerns of the general public. Relaxed answers are therapeutic for everyone.

Obviously people are not going to be convinced by every word. To achieve a flexible economy, the government has to implement policies over an extended period of time. Some people who are not convinced about the direction of policy will always leave the hall marvelling more at your inflexibility than the common sense of your answers. But it improves the confidence of the community as a whole to see the politicians responsible for structural adjustment face the music and deal with public fears in a gentle, reasonable, sensible way.

NINTH PRINCIPLE: INCENTIVES AND CHOICE VERSUS MONOPOLY – GET THE FUNDAMENTALS RIGHT

A sick economy cannot be regulated back to health. Economic dynamism is the liberated energy of people at every level personally choosing and using opportunities that benefit them. Government's role is to construct a framework that increases their choice, improves the incentives for productive activity and ensures that their gains also benefit society as a whole. In other words — remember whose side you are on. The purpose of economic activity is to satisfy the needs of consumers, to serve their interests and improve their lives. Government is not there to protect vested-interest groups, be they farmers, manufacturers, teachers or health workers, at the expense of the public. Its role is to ensure that vested interests cannot thrive except by serving the general public effectively.

In command economies, governments made all the important decisions on behalf of the general public, in order to protect people from vested interests. Since the revolution of 1917, that theory has been tested to extinction. The power government used to make those decisions was power taken away from the people themselves. Government became the most oppressive vested interest of all. Here in New Zealand, the government, in its past domination of areas such as coal mining, electricity, education, health and welfare, had gone a fair way in that direction. Our attention was focused on the supposed benefits of regulation without regard for the wider costs imposed. According to that kind of false and partial accounting, regulation will seem automatically to improve the public good.

> **Political Lesson:** *The abolition of privilege is the essence of structural reform. Wherever possible, use your programme to give power back to the people.*

No one should be surprised, therefore, that major deregulation was introduced in New Zealand by a Labour Government. Labour recognised that wherever power exists, vested interests will cluster, trying to convert it into privilege for themselves. Labour recognised that inefficiency created by monopoly privileges on the waterfront has exactly the same kind of adverse impact on the lives of working people as the privileges farmers or manufacturers might enjoy.

TENTH PRINCIPLE: WHEN IN DOUBT, ASK YOURSELF, 'WHY AM I IN POLITICS?'

Conventional politicians ignore structural reform because they think they are in power to please people, and pleasing people does not involve making them face the hard questions. They use the latest polls to fine-tune their image and their policies, in order to achieve better results in the next poll. In other words, their aim really is to be in perpetual power. Their adherence to policies which focus on their immediate problems, rather than the country's future opportunities, brings accumulating difficulties. It becomes increasingly clear to people that the problems have not been solved and that opportunities have been thrown away. And so, such governments are voted out.

Genuine structural reform carried out fairly and without compromise, delivers larger gains in living standards and opportunity than those achievable by any other political means. Conventional wisdom says that the unwelcome short-term costs that result from major reform make structural change a form of electoral suicide. However, in 1987, after the most radical structural reforms in 50 years, Labour fought the election on a platform that the job was only half done and that we alone had the courage and know-how to finish it. The government was returned with all the seats it won in the landslide 1984 election and took two more seats from the opposition. Voters wanted the job completed and they wanted it done right.

But after the election the government lost some of the momentum that had sustained the reform programme in its first three years. The vested interests were able to marshal a counter-attack. The then Prime Minister sought to re-establish a consensus by calling for a 'breather'. David Lange felt that some people needed time to catch up with the changes already made. He also feared that continuing reform would inevitably change some traditional social sector policies.

Protected groups within the community, looking for ways to arrest the process of change before it affected their interests, and if possible turn the clock back, seized their opportunity. The government became polarised internally between those who wanted to advance the process of reform a stage further, to bring even better results, and those who wanted to call a halt. A stalemate developed. The government lost its ability to take account of the 10 principles described here. Confidence was lost in public uncertainty about the future direction of policy. And so the inevitable happened — in the 1990 election Labour lost by an even greater margin than it had won in 1984 and 1987.

Credibility and consistency can be maintained only in the context of a disciplined Cabinet which works through the issues and stands behind every decision collectively taken. In my view, there is one force which is always capable of undermining the process of structural reform — the government itself when it loses sight of its own primary objectives. If the discipline of collective Cabinet decision-making and collective Cabinet responsibility breaks down, the way is open for interest groups to regain control of the game. Regrettably, that was what started to happen in New Zealand after David Lange began to set aside the collective decisions of Cabinet in January 1988.

11   Politics – Rhetoric or Substance?

The danger signs appear in this order: First, it becomes apparent that government is absorbing too great a share of the available talent and energy; there is a decline, therefore, in individual initiative and the spirit of inertia takes its place. Second, there is a decline in the sense of property, and the spirit of envy takes its place. Third, there is a decline of freedom, and the spirit of dependence takes its place. Fourth, there is a decline in the sense of purpose and the spirit of rebellion takes its place. All this adds up to a decline in the sense of individual responsibility, and so to a decline of individuality itself. And while the technical trend of the age goes to make the individual matter more, politically the trend is to make him matter less.

C. Northcote Parkinson, *The Law and the Profits*

There is a rumour, much perpetuated, that the process of reform is now complete in New Zealand. Apparently the job has been done and it is simply a matter of lying back, waiting for the good times to roll again and taking the tea break of a lifetime. But, like many rumours, particularly in politics, this one also is without foundation. The reality is quite different and can be found just by looking to the past.

For decades we were the worst performers in the OECD. The reforms initiated since 1984 may have raised our performance to an OECD average, but because we were the worst, we have to do more to recoup our previous losses. Until we recover a significant amount of that lost ground, we cannot say that we have provided adequately (let alone well) for the future well-being of our citizens. Moreover, the OECD average is no longer anything to be proud of. The group as a whole is performing badly at present. European growth rates are minimal, and the United States has a huge deficit and mounting productivity problems. Those countries are not examples we should be aiming to follow.

Unfortunately, since 1988, policy innovation in this country has diminished almost to vanishing point, except for a brief period of activity between the end of 1990 and early 1991. Our public debt is excessive. It puts living standards at serious risk from future economic shocks. Yet instead of reducing debt during the past two years, the government has increased it further, amplifying those risks. The government's tax take is rising too, at a rate above that of inflation, while progress in reducing the fiscal deficit has been stalled since 1990. The government persists in undertaking more than it can fund or manage efficiently. National's financial deficit continues to average 9 to 12 per cent of total revenue. Largely as a result of that fiscal failure, the net worth of the Crown is forecast to deteriorate by almost 60 per cent in the four years to 1994/95.

Instead of facing problems like these, the government has chosen to ignore them. It argues that remedial action might disrupt the process of economic recovery. In fact, it is its failure to act that has delayed and weakened the recovery by placing an ever-growing financial burden on individuals and enterprises of all kinds. In the microeconomic area, the present government has earned and deserves credit for private sector labour market reform. Although Labour had developed the underlying concepts before it left office, it proved incapable of taking this step towards increased employment and productivity because the party's constitution is designed specifically to protect the power, authority and financial gain of trade unions.

However, beyond labour market reform, the government has continuously adulterated, compromised, or botched in the process of implementation. For example, the concept of separating the funding of health care from its provision had been fully developed by early 1987. At that point, vested interests within the Labour Party, supported and promoted by senior ministers, successfully prevented real reform. Since 1990, there have been moves to turn provision into a competitive service, with the improvements in quality, cost and consumer choice that will inevitably follow. In the purchasing area, however, the government abandoned the core of the reform. Regional health authorities retain a totally unhealthy monopoly of public purchasing. Sick people are stuck with a system that is a licence for inefficiency. They have nowhere else to go if they are dissatisfied with what the RHAs purchase on their behalf.

The government's quest for a long-term retirement-income solution for an ageing population has become half-hearted as well. It now hopes to evade its responsibilities by seeking some short-term bipartisan agreement, instead of really facing up to the problem. There is no security in that for those who retire in the future. Changes in the benefit system since 1990 have been driven almost exclusively by the desire to contain current spending. Abuse has been attacked and the rewards of dependency have been pruned. But the government has not tackled the poverty traps which continue to keep thousands of decent people dependent on the State. National has tinkered round the edges of the old policies, without bothering to remedy their real perversions. Short of forcing people into desperate poverty, not even fiscal problems can be solved that way.

In the State-owned enterprises area, the government's track record is one of continuous failure to face up to its responsibilities to the national interest. Present legislation provides a clean mechanism for using SOEs to deliver social services. The principle is that they should be funded in the Budget, and purchased openly by the government, as Labour did with NZ Post, not hidden as cross-subsidies inside SOE accounts. But the present government has not wanted simply to provide efficient services at the lowest available cost to people in genuine need. It also wished to be able to give financial benefits to favoured interest groups in return for political support, even though that inevitably held up the cost of services. It has therefore forced SOEs to go on charging some customers millions of dollars a year above fair commercial rates to fund the losses they carry on uneconomically cheap services to those

241

special groups. As long as that practice continues, SOEs and their customers are being used by the government to buy votes.

Beyond the SOE model, privatisation plays a key role in creating a better future for New Zealand. When an SOE is privatised and subject to competition, it is forced to serve customers with maximum efficiency and for the lowest achievable price. Its long-term contribution to economic growth is much greater. But, as a result of the change in ownership, government loses the ability to tamper with business decisions in order to buy or retain electoral power. The process of privatisation, therefore, has been deliberately slowed to a crawl, despite its huge potential contribution to efficiency and the reduction of public debt. Elsewhere in the world it is proceeding at a pace — with renewed vigour now in Europe — while New Zealand is being left behind again.

Since 1988, in all these and many other areas, New Zealand has been going backwards, not forwards. During that time, both governments have preferred to put what they considered their own short-term political advantage ahead of the interests of the public and the nation. They are holding reform to the absolute minimum needed for New Zealand to scrape through for the next two to five years, and ignoring the future.

It is equally important to recognise that the thinking behind all current reform proposals was developed in the first half of the 1980s. We are running the country on intellectual capital that is now 10 years old. Moreover, 80 per cent of the policy implementation achieved to date had already been set in place by the end of 1987. Since then, no new policy concept development has taken place in the government, party or official political and bureaucratic systems. Thinking is now regarded by both parties as an embarrassment. If ideas are developed or promoted, they may find themselves obligated to do something.

This flight from constructive analysis is frightening in its repercussions. We all know from experience that there are long time lags between the implementation of reform and when the public sees the benefits. Those lags increase dramatically when politicians temporise. It has taken eight years to see concrete benefits from changes undertaken in 1984. Our prosperity in 2004 depends on the action we should be taking right now.

What, then, is the major parties' current thinking on future policy? Statements to date by the Labour Opposition talk about undoing some reforms already completed. Beyond that, fudge substitutes for analysis and rhetoric replaces policy. The party's Economic Statement earlier this year was virtually devoid of any policy, and every voter in the country was aware of that. More recently, the Prime Minister announced his party's *Vision for the Year 2010.* National hopes for annual growth of 5 per cent by:

❒ Emphasising the importance of parents as first teachers.
❒ Exhorting young people to stay at school longer.
❒ Talking about better tertiary education.
❒ Spending public money on infrastructure and technology.
❒ Listing five industries as potential sources of growth.

The government's vision does not pretend to have any credibility. The Prime Minister was careful to say that 5 per cent growth is not a target, merely something that New Zealand might, 'with a bit of luck', achieve in future. The government had only one real target — not growth but re-election. It hopes that touching buttons labelled *Vision* and *2010* may release a favourable reflex in worried people and lead them to vote blindly.

Not all MPs in the two major parties favour this approach to politics. The exceptions are an honourable minority crushed into submission by a majority of fellow Caucus members. With National and Labour both making an exceptionally poor showing in the polls, the parties are locked in a state of election psychosis. They know the public is profoundly dissatisfied with their performance, but they choose to think they are hated because they tried to reform the economy. Both are now desperately trying to avoid further constructive action. It is difficult to imagine a more ludicrous posture.

Obviously, New Zealanders are fed up. But they are not fed up with change. Nobody wants things to remain as they are today. What people are fed up with is change that fails to bring sufficient improvements. The present refusal by government to undertake positive reform is increasing, not reducing, the public's disgust and despair. They know both parties have restricted themselves to the most limiting of goals — winning power next November. To that end, Government and Opposition have said to voters, 'Look at the awful defects in our opponents.' In that, if in little else, the public agrees with them.

National is saying: 'Labour thrust you into recession. With a little help from us, a recovery is occurring. If we do almost nothing, it may continue for a while.' Labour retorts: 'National has destroyed almost everything you valued in the past. We will give a bit of it back to you, hopefully without destroying the recovery, at least for the next few years.' In fact, both parties intend if they win to make up policy as they go along by watching the polls and doing as little as possible — a haphazard response to future events. The similarities in their approach vastly outweigh any minor differences between them. Neither party has the least intention of taking the future seriously. Fixed solely on their own immediate political advantage, they are incapable of perceiving either the challenges or the opportunities open to New Zealand in the 10 to 20 years ahead. Choice between National and Labour has become irrelevant.

It is, perhaps, the ultimate irony that the only party and politician with a clear programme is the Alliance and Jim Anderton. For that, if for little else, they deserve respect and admiration. They know where they want to go — a shameless and wholehearted return to the interventionism and protectionism of the 1960s and 1970s. And they know how to get there: the recipe is set out in every history book. Because people know what they are talking about, the Alliance Party threatens National and Labour. In July 1993 it commanded up to a quarter of the total vote. If Jim Anderton and the Alliance became government, they undoubtedly would restore the policies of the sixties and seventies. Unfortunately, it is beyond their power to return the country to the level of debt, and the world markets to a condition which, for a brief period, allowed those policies to look like a viable economic option. If you want a real economic crash, and want it fast, then vote Alliance.

Virtually every voter, no matter what his or her point of view, knows that is how things stand currently. Surveys show that the public rates politicians only slightly above secondhand car salesmen for trustworthiness and credibility. The most popular MP in the country in mid-1993, Winston Peters, used that alienation, fear and contempt as the foundation for a national reputation. A few months out from the election, he was ahead of the field in the polls as preferred Prime Minister. The preference accorded him by 25 per cent of the voting population was not based on policy — he doesn't bother to offer policy to the public. He has none. What he has done instead is consistently and continuously identify and attack what he calls dishonesty and corruption in the established system. His penchant for character assassination is reminiscent of an earlier Prime Minister.

His monotonous allegations are unsupported by fact and are usually proved beyond doubt to be explicitly erroneous. Yet they set up a sympathetic resonance in many voters. The public feels instinctively that there is corruption somewhere deep in the system. And they are right. No evidence whatsoever exists that our politicians take bribes, but they do give bribes to vested interests, if votes can be won by using the economy to bankroll their election. At worst, in the past those bribes involved huge cash payments to particularly favoured groups. Walter Nash's £100 tax rebate promise made just before the 1957 election is just one flagrant example. Sir Robert Muldoon's 1976 national superannuation scheme was another low point, setting new records for notoriety. It has since cost the tax-paying public tens of billions of dollars and imposed a massive burden on generations to come. Since 1984, large cash bribes have been substantially discredited in New

Zealand. The bribing of special interests still survives but, since 1991, it has operated in a more sophisticated form.

For example, many National MPs would cheerfully abandon the SOE model entirely if that was the only way to protect farmers from an increase of 77 cents a week in their rural mail fees. Labour market reform has not reduced real wages but it did cut union power. Unions have an entrenched position in the constitution of the Labour Party, and Opposition parties unhesitatingly promise to turn back the clock for vested interests who have lost privileges in past reforms. Therefore, 'for the sake of the workers', Labour is committed to repeal the Employment Contracts Act. In fact, the only body to benefit will be the unions. The party's Economic Statement dedicated itself to government decision-making in collaboration with big business and the big trade unions. These two interest groups are at the heart of the traditional all-powerful State — socialist or fascist. Labour hasn't even noticed that the general public, the great mass of people it was set up to serve, has no place at this banquet table. Power politics is the grand obsession.

The public's feeling of disgust cannot be interpreted simply as a reactionary response to the pain of structural reform. It is a profound revulsion against self-serving politicians who consistently put their own political interests ahead of the national good. Nobody is offering an alternative that faces up to the future. In desperation, two-thirds of the voting public are now turning to proportional representation in the hope that it will break the existing political gridlock.

Unfortunately, the form of proportional representation under consideration has some serious disadvantages. Fifty per cent of MPs under that system would be appointed by and accountable to political parties rather than voters. The parties' memberships have shrunk dramatically in recent years: they currently stand at one-third of 1980 levels. Power to select those MPs would be placed with a very small number of people who do not necessarily reflect national interests. National Party branches are frequently dominated by elderly people from a narrow range of occupational classes. Labour has the trade unions. If we are not careful, we may introduce a form of proportional representation that increases rather than diminishes these people's power to direct the affairs of the nation. The unfortunate truth is that the problems involved in improving government performance are rather more difficult than most voters imagine.

As I see it, there are three prerequisites for major progress:

❒ A broad consensus on long-term goals for the nation.
❒ A reliable programme to achieve those goals.
❒ Quality people committed to achieve both.

Goals are primary. Until we form some coherent view about our destination, it is pointless to plague ourselves with questions about how to get there. In one sense, setting the right goals is not a real problem; many aspirations are common worldwide. What, then, are the factors that people consider critical for them and their families, to help them make the most of their lives? My suggested list is quite simple:

❒ Self worth
❒ Opportunity
❒ Initiative
❒ Independence
❒ Security
❒ Social responsibility
❒ A system fair to self and others.

In one sense, all the items on the list can be regarded as clichés. Politicians prate on about them all the time. But that does not alter the fact that they are the qualities most fundamental to a sense of human well-being. I may be wrong, but I do not think many people in this country would disagree with those goals. On the contrary, I believe people would be inspired and encouraged if they thought that a plan to achieve them had been put in action with the aim of delivering the goals in their lifetime. So how do we make those goals matter? How do we make them the foundation of a serious programme designed to transform New Zealand?

Once again, my suggestion is quite simple. We should ask ourselves what this country would be like if, 25 years from now, we could lead the world in those seven personal and social ambitions. It opens up a vision totally unlike anything currently being offered to New Zealanders by the present major or minor political parties. I consider it is a programme well worth fighting for. It also has an additional virtue. The economic and social policies needed to achieve those goals can be reliably defined. To be successful, we would also need to lead the world in high growth rates, high-quality education, high-quality health care, low debt, low tax rates, a highly competitive market-place and security in retirement. The disillusionment with politicians springs precisely from a realisation that no party is offering to deliver such a combination of policies at present. None of them provides us with a chance to say to our children a decade from now, 'I helped to vote those people in, and together we created a country I am proud to see you and your children inherit.'

Next in importance are the means capable of achieving the goals. Once we have a clear vision of the desirable objectives, we are free to think in new and fresh ways. For example, traditional analysis has always assumed that low tax rates are in conflict with quality education and health care for everyone. It was taken for granted that tax-funded schools and hospitals were the only means to provide universal service. So 'free' State provision came to be seen as the primary objective of the exercise, not simply one of several *means* available to achieve those goals.

Once a good education for everyone is made the central focus again, it becomes clear that there is more than one way to get universal education of quality. When the government takes money away from the public, then decides what schools to provide and what subjects to teach, it imposes a single standardised approach throughout the system. In giving up their money, parents also sacrifice the right to personal choice. In one alternative scenario, the State, instead of building schools and paying teachers, would simply ensure parents had the money to buy a good education for their children.

An average family on an average income is already paying, through taxes, the total cost of educating its children. If they kept their own money and paid schools personally, they could save on the deal by removing a lot of civil servants from the system. At the same time, they would have much more influence over the quality of education being provided to their children. Most parents care a great deal more than the State ever will about the education their children receive. Dissatisfied parents would begin to exercise a real discipline over school performance. Teachers could no longer afford to turn half their students into the world as educational failures. When parents and students hold the funds, they call the tune.

That principle applies to the billions of dollars a year which the government removes from the pockets of the public at present. The process is called 'churning'. The government takes your earnings from you, then gives it back in the form of monopoly services which deprive you of choice. Along the way, it deducts large sums of money to pay the civil servants who act as the middlemen in the process. You lose out twice: in monetary terms and in terms of personal independence.

This book has already demonstrated how much New Zealand could achieve by adopting different principles. If we choose to, we can:

❏ Balance the government's budget in three years, then move it into surplus.
❏ Cut government debt by 60 per cent in 10 years and eliminate it in 20 years.
❏ Reduce personal income, company and fringe benefit taxes to below 15 cents in 10 years, without increasing GST.
❏ Dramatically reduce or totally eliminate other indirect taxes or duties over a 20-year period.

❏ Slash government spending by 30 per cent in 10 years and 70 per cent in 35 years.

❏ Improve the standards and accessibility of good health care and education for everyone.

❏ Ensure security in retirement by introducing a sustainable contributory pension plan and health insurance to cover all costs above 5 per cent of annual income.

❏ Improve the security of low-income families by introducing a GMFI, providing education grants where needed and topping up pension and health insurance in retirement funds when necessary.

Supposing that a programme of this sort has appeal, how do we, as voters, deal with the problem that nothing of this kind whatsoever is on the agendas of the political parties?

The first crucial step is based on trust and information. The following is just one minor example. In June 1993, Dr Peter Troughton, the person responsible for hospital restructuring, told a select committee that some public hospitals in New Zealand were unsafe. That is not a controversial statement. Every doctor in the country is aware of it. Some of our smaller hospitals, for example, have been more or less consistently incompetent for years at a time as far as surgery is concerned. The resultant deaths are recorded in inquest findings and have caused a certain amount of public scandal in several regions. But when Peter Troughton said it, all hell broke loose. The government leapt to the conclusion that it might be blamed for any deficiencies, instead of praised for trying to fix them. The Minister of Health rushed to assert that all public hospitals in New Zealand are perfectly safe. Dr Troughton, he said, had merely been trying to explain that some failed to match certain New South Wales criteria. By New Zealand standards, there was nothing wrong with them. In any case, any deficiencies so identified had all been remedied.

The news media, blinded by politics, convicted Troughton publicly of a major gaffe which further damaged an already discredited and unnecessary health-reform process. The real gaffe was, of course, the government's. In a misguided effort to protect its own hide, it deliberately injured a man's reputation, and withheld information on why change is urgently needed. The government will never get decent people with the much-needed qualifications and integrity to work for them if they treat them with such scant regard; and experts hired to report on issues will quickly learn to tailor their findings to suit the prevailing attitudes in government. Meanwhile, everyone moves further and further from the truth, and any chance of finding a real solution becomes impossible.

The health saga then got sadder and sillier. The day the government rushed in to justify the status quo, the public learned that a woman had just died at a Palmerston North hospital because the wrong fluid had been put through her kidney dialysis machine by mistake. The same week, the government, concerned that people did not understand why it was reforming hospitals, launched a $2.5 million advertising campaign to justify itself. If it had been honest throughout in the first place, it could have had real credibility, and real public understanding, without wasting all that money.

I have always been amazed by the difference between what our senior politicians say on television during trips abroad, and what they say to their own voters. In front of foreign audiences, what they say is often simple, straightforward and sensible. But as soon as they step back on New Zealand soil, they resume their normal performance — distortions and evasion — as if clarity and credibility were their ultimate political nightmares.

The second step is to define clear goals and objectives that are fair and good for the country. People want to know where New Zealand is going. Enumerating the goals is not difficult; almost every politician can do that and make him or herself understood. What the constituency has to demand from politicians is the 'how'. If you cannot understand what politicians are saying about that, it is either because they don't understand themselves, there is nothing of real substance to understand, or they don't want you to understand. Whichever it is, the public is in trouble. Don't let politicians fudge the answers.

Therefore, the third step is to define a robust programme which, under the spotlight of professional scrutiny, is a visibly reliable means to achieve those goals and objectives. This book is a practical example of that. If goals are not supported by practical policies capable of achieving them, they are worse than nothing. I vividly recall publishing an ambitious programme in 1989, shortly after my resignation from the Finance portfolio and Cabinet. It set ambitious goals and the means to attain them by November 1993.

The government instantly adopted most of my goals to improve its own reputation, discarding every one of the policies that made them achievable. A practical reform programme was thereby transformed into an exercise in rhetoric that pretended New Zealand could achieve all those goals under Labour without any need for further reform.

A fourth requirement is equally important. Any programme of change will threaten and frighten those who feel ill-equipped to cope with it. Therefore, a major objective of the reform programme must be to show beyond doubt that such people are going to be kept safe throughout the transition period. Superannuation reform is a typical example of this need. If we move to a superannuation system based on personal savings, and personal ownership of those savings, young people have a lifetime in which to achieve that security. They have the capacity to live through such a change with advantage to themselves and their families, given appropriate State assistance to low-income people. Those who are already in retirement, or close to it, have no such opportunity. Their capacity to save is more or less exhausted. If they are not protected by adequate transition arrangements, then inevitably they will be forced to oppose change, even if it is clearly good for the nation in the longer term. Given reasonable protection, most older people would be only too happy to back a benefit for their grandchildren's future, rather than feeling forced to support policies which can only harm the young.

Given the short-sightedness, self-serving tendencies, persecutive anxieties and political psychoses that govern the behaviour of many of our MPs, how can such a programme ever make the transition to government policy and legislation? When my career as Finance Minister terminated in 1988, conditions within the Labour Party absolutely prevented me from further significant economic or social achievement. In my view, we take the critical step forward when we recognise that none of the existing parties offer New Zealanders a viable political path into a substantially better future. They are all absolutely committed, with minor variations, to the same old worn-out recipes for economic and social disaster. We waste our time trying to distinguish between them.

After that realisation finally sinks in, responsible people can begin to understand the task that now confronts those who really care about this country. It is a task that challenges all of us, from the highest-paid professionals to shop-floor workers and the unemployed. We need to understand that our desperate longing for a better country is a reasonable desire; and that we will not get it without further change. At the professional level, those who care will have to become vigorous and continuous advocates for sensible medium-term policies that put the country before vested interests and the status quo. Whenever politicians of any persuasion go on about vision and 5 per cent growth, others should be on radio and television next day demanding practical detail. We have to start making it politically dangerous for MPs and lobby groups to go on talking nonsense to the public.

Obviously there are personal risks involved in doing that. Governments control almost 40 per cent of GDP in New Zealand. They wield a lot of power and can behave with exceptional vindictiveness to individuals or firms who refuse to be silenced on matters that they consider may be dangerous to government popularity. But where the voice of reason is concerted and persistent, governments can be forced to improve accountability. I consider that important.

253

But it is not enough to transform the present parliamentary and party culture from the inside. The parties have monopoly control over the selection of political candidates and they are not putting enough quality people into Parliament. The process of candidate selection is under the almost absolute control of the existing culture of the parties. In most electorates on voting day, we get meaningless choices not merely between parties but also between candidates. The parties will not voluntarily mend their ways.

In my view, there are only three choices for people who want to demonstrate their concern for the future in a practical way: they invade the existing parties in sufficient numbers to change the old culture; they set up an organisation which will act as watchdog and ginger group; or, if these fail, they face the task of setting up a new political party with a new programme, based on changes designed to deliver a much better future. In all cases, the personal cost to the people involved in time, commitment, stress and risk, is much higher than just voting for any one of the competing parties on election day. But without that commitment, I find it hard to see New Zealand making the most of its opportunities in the future.

Which of those options — taking over an existing party, forming a monitoring organisation, or starting a new political party — is likely to prove most viable? My own experience in politics suggests that it is enormously difficult to transform an existing party from the inside. New entrants face an established culture supported and conditioned by resident special interests which have occupied the party turf for decades or generations. Some Labour Party branches are notorious for freezing out all members whose ideas differ from those of the incumbents accustomed to wielding local power. Some trade unions, used to their traditional incumbency and faced with a challenge to the power the party's constitution confers on them, do not hesitate to win by bussing in people whose faces have never been seen before at a Labour Party meeting. The Back Bone Club, a group within the party who supported the policy direction taken when I was Minister of Finance and actively backed it, was treated with enormous hostility by a narrow range of Labour people, especially the apparatchiks at head office. However, their supposedly sinister reputation and agenda were not treated seriously by general party members. Nevertheless, they were finally forced to disband 'for the good of the party' before the 1990 election. Many left the party in disgust.

Prospects within National Party branches are, for different reasons, not necessarily any better. Lively energetic reformers who have joined certain branches tell me that the stultifying atmosphere proved, in the end, to be an intolerable experience. For the sake of their own sanity, they gave up a hopeless battle and quit the field. National also has its own ways to 'cook the books' in candidate selections. Each branch delegate represents 20 members. When a faction wants to raise its voting strength, the group simply gets busy signing up new members for a negligible sum in order to increase the number of delegates backing its candidate. National at least has made some tentative moves to curtail such abuses.

Reforming an existing party is not impossible; but it will not happen through the existing membership of those parties. It is dependent on a large influx of determined people with totally new attitudes to political achievement. Their greatest problem would be in making the parties more democratic.

The next option is to set up a large and broadly based group who will not only monitor the utterances and performance of government and politicians, ask questions and challenge woolly or less-than-honest statements, but also put forward and promote alternative, workable and positive programmes of reform. Such a group would need to be highly organised, disciplined in their approach and consistent in their message. They would have to challenge the pressure groups and those factions who seek to obscure the argument and divert the debate in order to hide their real purpose — losing their exclusive place in the sun. If their work was done well, eventually the watchdog group would win public trust and support and at that point politicians and their parties would be forced to listen and act accordingly. But it would take time and fierce commitment as well.

The final option is a new party. More than half the voting population is seriously alienated from the major parties and neither the Alliance nor Winston Peters has a credible policy alternative. The first relies on nostalgia for the past, and the latter's message is all about personality and his insistence that he owns exclusive rights to truth and honesty. In other words, there is a vacuum waiting to be filled.

If a new party becomes inevitable because the existing parties refuse to change, it should, in my view, lay out ambitious but attainable medium-term economic and social goals which are in all New Zealanders' interests. Those goals would aim simultaneously at high growth rates and low taxation and would put an acceptable floor under the living standards of the disadvantaged. The government's role would be clearly defined. Its concern would be with the legal and regulatory framework governing the activity of the nation. For example, it would establish the priorities and set the framework for education, health, investment and retirement income. These would include sharing between individuals through taxation, to help the poor, the weak and the disadvantaged. In other words, government would aim to assist people in their access to all those services but would not provide them itself through State monopolies.

It is surprising how quickly people forget what life was like in the 1960s and 1970s when this was essentially a State-run, State-controlled country. And there is a new generation growing up now that has had little or no first-hand experience of it. In June 1993, businessman Bob Matthew, in an address to a group of graduates at Otago University, described some of the daily facts of life back then. He began by recalling the two American millionaires whose applications to come and live here and set up businesses (one a shipyard in Whangarei employing 25 people) were turned down in the 1970s. In one case, the man made the mistake of putting 'millionaire' as his occupation, which turned out not to be on the approved list, unlike carpenters or electricians. The other was refused residency because he was not married to the young crew member who helped him sail his boat from the USA. Bob Matthew went on:

> They were strange days. Daily life was a patchwork of controls, regulations and State interventions. Hotels closed at 6 p.m. Only the government was allowed to broadcast television programmes. Interest rates were set by the government. If you wanted to bring in Italian tiles or German beers or an American car you needed a government licence. Workers were obliged to belong to a trade union. Your earnings were circumscribed by a top rate of tax which reached 66 cents in the dollar. In those days it took three to six weeks to have a business telephone connected. Movies took nine to 18 months to arrive here. There were just two sorts of refrigerator — both made by the same manufacturer to the same specifications.
>
> If you wanted to rent a television you were obliged by law to put down six months' rent in advance. If you wanted to invest in or set up a business overseas you had to renounce your nationality to get your money out of the country. You needed a permit to subscribe to an overseas journal. You were not allowed to truck goods more than 40 miles and then 150 kilometres without the permission of the Railways. It was illegal to sell petrol below a minimum price. Jarvad Miandad said this year that when he first came here in 1979 he couldn't get anything to eat after 5 or 6 o'clock. It was against the law to make carpets from anything other than wool. To buy margarine, you had to have a doctor's prescription.

To most 1993 eyes, the list is ludicrous and appalling. Yet, if in 20 years' time, someone compiled a list of today's rules and regulations, I suspect it would be considered equally amazing.

Given its inefficiency as an owner-operator, government confers most benefit when it confines its role to setting the right goals, priorities and rules in place, and lets others get on with the business of providing competitive services.

However, the ultimate question, the one of paramount

importance for the future, revolves around the quality of the people in Parliament. They have to be people willing to study the evidence and take the facts on board, instead of dismissing them. They need the ability to think laterally, in the interests of the nation, beyond the boundaries which those with vested interests in the status quo try continually to impose on them. If such a group ever comes together, I see no reason whatever why they should not attract some experienced and good MPs from both sides of the present House. Within both the National and Labour parties, the best MPs are now the most frustrated and helpless. Party discipline locks them into positions contrary to their own convictions.

A new party founded on all the principles just outlined would need to understand from the start what it was running against. The accumulated bile of all the existing parties and all the interests they presently serve would be mobilised to distort and misrepresent the new programme. Nor could the new party expect assistance from the news media, despite their continuous expressions of disgust for the existing system. Journalism is driven by an ethic of impartiality. Good ideas must not be reported more prominently or favourably than bad ideas. As far as possible, both kinds will be presented as if they had equivalent value.

Journalists have no mechanism, short of polling, by which they can consult the general public. Their major sources of news are the organised pressure groups in society. The same limited list of vested interest groups is continuously promoted. They are, as far as journalists are concerned, the established authorities in their field, the people whose views really count in society. Impartiality operates within the existing social, political and cultural climate, in favour of the status quo. Therefore, new ideas which challenge or change the status quo will get the hardest time in the daily news media, no matter where they originate. All of the established authorities with a particular interest in the existing state of affairs will be sedulously consulted. Their views, no matter how stupid or self-serving, will be fully reported as the authorised version of the true situation.

Governments trying to introduce valuable new policies inevitably take a heavy beating as a result of this process. But governments have a significant advantage that helps to protect their position. In any country, they are the major source of daily news. Most journalists are willing to offend them only up to a certain intangible point. Beyond that, independence of thought or analysis could start to close off their own access to government information. In that sense, therefore, most political journalists operate more like Elizabethan courtiers than modern, independent news analysts. Like courtiers, they are happy to gossip, often maliciously, about politics and politicians, but only within the accepted limits of established political convention. Good-quality thinking has very little to do with this process. Incumbents are always heavily favoured over new entrants, until the opinion polls finally make it clear that the incumbent is on the way out. At that point, but not until then, the flavour of news coverage finally starts to change.

The news media in New Zealand, contrary to their own view of themselves, continuously condition the public and the politicians to regard change as obnoxious in principle. They are now the voice of conservatism. As I see it, attack is the best means of defence in those circumstances. Any new party would need to be totally upfront about its goals and its programme — the benefits, transitional problems and the safeguards — to handle those problems.

For many people, the programme in this book will be made to look quite terrifying by vested interests, at least at first. They have been bred into dependency by the State for most of the last 60 years. The government today devotes the largest proportion of its expenditure to keeping them in a state of dependency. Parents almost universally are dependent on State education; patients on State health care; and elderly people on State retirement income. They have forgotten, in most cases, that their own earnings are paying for those services.

259

The greatest fear will undoubtedly be among those who are substantially dependent on the State, even for food and housing, and who see no prospect of changing their situation. It would be particularly important for the new party to demonstrate clearly that those people would be better off, not worse off, in the future. For retired people dependent on national superannuation, for example, the book's programme locks in a State income with the security of government bonds. The programme will not be fair unless it provides disadvantaged people with a balance of hope and security which improves their confidence in life.

I believe those involved in politics should start to seriously consider entrenching some of its basic principles in statute. The Reserve Bank Act was a pioneering example of such legislation in New Zealand. It requires the bank, as its primary duty, to ensure the stability of the currency. That Act has played a fundamental role in the reliable delivery of low inflation to the benefit of the public and the economy. Certainly governments retain the power to instruct the bank to disregard that purpose and to encourage or permit levels of inflation which are not compatible with a stable currency. But the Act forces government to take such action right out in the open, in full view of the public, with debate in the community. That discipline has greatly improved the quality of economic management.

There is absolutely no reason, given present levels of public debt, why legislation should not impose a similar obligation on governments to balance their revenue and expenditure. A similar legal obligation could just as fruitfully be imposed on local government. Such laws would help to make it clear to voters and politicians that balanced budgets are the normal, sound and sensible way to run their accounts. Deficit budgeting would not be prohibited, but special obligations would be imposed to spell out both costs and benefits to the public, before deficit budgets could be regarded as legal.

Similarly, I see no reason why legislation should not specify new provisions designed to safeguard the public when major policy is introduced and prior to its implementation. Governments could very reasonably be required to publish White Papers which spell out their proposals in detail, as Labour did before introducing GST, and to set up working parties to study the reforms, headed by someone recognisably independent. One of the best examples was Labour's appointment of Dr Don Brash, an economist who had been a National Party candidate in the 1981 election, to chair the committees on GST, primary sector taxation and accrual tax treatment. The costs and benefits of proposals are then subject to audit by an independent body which reports to the public. Such safeguards might help to prevent fiascos like the present government's health charges regime, which promised to save $95 million but cost an extra $9.5 million a year instead.

Further scope obviously exists to place some legislative safeguards around the election manifestos of political parties. At present, each party conceals the cost of its own promises and exaggerates the costs of promises by opponents. The public votes with no idea what the bill may finally be. Some discipline could be introduced into that situation by legislation requiring all parties to submit their manifestos to an independent body for a published cost/benefit audit. Voters could then make decisions on reliable information.

Finally, it seems particularly important to consider setting legislative rules in place to govern the selection of politicians by political parties. Both major parties have become small, closed societies. Nothing at present prevents candidate selection from being gerrymandered by even smaller cliques of people who are not democratically accountable, either to party or public. That situation already contributes significantly to the pathetically inadequate quality of many current candidate selections.

If the polls are right, and multiple proportional representation is adopted in New Zealand, political parties will be appointing half the MPs. Without sound regulations governing candidate selection, the situation may deteriorate instead of improving, at huge cost to the nation's future. The same legislation should establish mandatory minimum standards of democracy for all political party constitutions. I see no reason why parties complying with those standards should not enjoy some government funding.

Unless pressure is brought to bear from outside, and from within the parties themselves, we cannot expect such legislation from any of our existing parties. Their deliberately sloppy approach to the way they think and develop policy gives them a reason to hold on to the way things are. But a new party could greatly improve its own credibility and the trust of the public in a serious long-range programme, by providing those visible safeguards.

In the end, it is over to New Zealanders. None of these are matters that we can afford to put aside. Too many people are sitting on the sidelines, complaining. Everything I have been talking about doesn't just apply to political leaders. It is just as true for the average citizen. They all have to see past their fear and look unflinchingly at the problems.

People will always pursue their own self-interests, if not in one place, then another. But the policy framework which regulates society should be constructed in such a way that even when people are working only for themselves, they are still helping wider interests. Farmers, trade unionists, teachers, doctors and others will come to see the opportunities being offered them, but must also accept that with those opportunities come demands and responsibilities. Everyone will be expected to make a contribution, even those on unemployment. The country's older citizens should be asking the government to follow what comes naturally to that generation, instead of running up more debt: they would not dream of mortgaging their own children's and grandchildren's futures. In return, government and society must accept that it is our responsibility to look after them, to provide the security they no longer have time to provide themselves.

Archibald MacLeish once asked:

> *What is freedom? Freedom is the right to choose: the right to create for oneself the alternatives of choice. Without the possibility of choice and the exercise of choice a man is not a man but a member, an instrument, a thing.*

I would like New Zealand to be a country where that freedom can be readily exercised and where the individual Northcote Parkinson referred to at the beginning of this chapter has his and her rights and powers returned, without diminishing the rights of the communal whole. If we really want that country, it is there for the making.

12   Sum Totals

*I place economy among the first and most important virtues,
and public debt as the greatest of dangers to be feared ... To
preserve our independence, we must not let our rulers load us
with public debt ... we must make our choice between
economy and liberty or confusion and servitude ...*

*If we run into such debts, we must be taxed in our meat
and drink, in our necessities and comforts, in our labor and
in our amusements ... If we can prevent the government
from wasting the labor of the people, under the pretense of
caring for them, they will be happy.*

Thomas Jefferson

This chapter pulls together Chapters 4 to 8 and sets out in
detail the financial results which would come from
implementing the measures outlined there. It is laid out so
that anyone who is interested can check for themselves, in
a series of tables, the assumptions made and the numbers
which flow from them. (Overseas readers should be able to
see whether the results would apply equally in their
countries.)

Section One summarises the main economic assumptions upon which the separate parts of the government
budget have been prepared.

Section Two summarises the main consequences of
implementing the changes outlined in Chapters 4 to 8.
Readers will be able to verify these outcomes by referring
to the tables which follow in Section Three.

Section Three puts the three budget parts in table form,
from 1993 until the year ending June 2020. It highlights
the main results of each budget table, the assumptions
made and the possible risks and upsides to the budgets as
shown. Finally, it draws together the three parts to show
the overall fiscal situation for each year.

Section Four describes how the changes affect different groups throughout their lives — the impacts, both short and long term, and how transitional issues have been dealt with.

SECTION ONE: ECONOMIC ASSUMPTIONS

The economic assumptions used to prepare the various budget parts (which are set out in detail in Section Three) are as follows:

❏ A real increase in Goods and Services Tax (GST) revenue of 2.5 per cent a year.
❏ An inflation rate of 3 per cent.
❏ A real growth rate in personal income of 2 per cent.
❏ A real earning rate on superannuation and health savings scheme funds of 3 per cent.

These are modest economic assumptions given the changes which have already taken place in New Zealand and those proposed in this book. Higher real economic growth of 4 per cent and lower inflation of 1 per cent, which I would expect under the policies proposed, would bring forward the benefits outlined in this chapter by a number of years and make the transition less onerous than it is.

SECTION TWO: MAIN OUTCOMES AND CHANGES

The main results shown in the budget tables and which come from implementing the policies in Chapters 4 to 8 are:

1. A balanced government fiscal budget by Year 3 and thereafter a surplus each year (revenue exceeds expenditure).
2. Government debt, now standing at around $47 billion, is totally eliminated inside 20 years, having been cut by more than 60 per cent within 10 years.
3. Personal income tax, company taxation and fringe benefit tax are eliminated within 20 years. The top rate of personal and company tax falls to 13 cents in the dollar in Year 11.

4. The existing superannuation tax surcharge is eliminated in Year 11, having been phased down by 1 cent a year for 10 years.

5. GST remains at 12.5 per cent for 22 years, drops to 10 per cent in Year 23 and thereafter steadily declines.

6. Remaining stamp duties are abolished by the end of Year 5.

7. Other indirect taxes or duties are either reduced dramatically or eliminated altogether over a 20-year period. Those remaining are largely of a user-pay nature.

8. Government expenditure is reduced in real terms by over $22 billion, or more than 70 per cent over a 35-year period, and by more than 30 per cent in the first 10 years.

9. Personal Income Tax.

(i) Families with children at school: The immediate introduction of a tax-free level of income for families with children at school — for 1 child, $32,000, plus an extra $10,000 for each additional child at school. The tax-free income levels are adjusted each year by the rate of inflation. Family income, earned by parents with children at school, beyond the tax-free income level applying in that year (e.g., Year 1, 2 children — $42,000) is to be taxed at the highest marginal tax rate applying to personal income that year.

(ii) Other taxpayers: In the year the new policies are introduced (1993/94 for the purposes of the calculations used here) taxpayers other than those with children at school have the income that is taxed at 15 cents in the dollar rise from $9500 to $12,000. As a result, those who earn $12,000 or more annually have their tax reduced by $325 a year. Thereafter, the 15 cents in the dollar income-tax bracket rises each year by $1000, from the $12,000 level that applies in 1993/94, until annual tax reductions have lowered the top personal tax rate from 28 cents in the dollar in 1993/94 to 15 cents in the dollar in 2001/02. At that point there is a flat tax rate of 15 cents in the dollar.

10. Superannuation and health care in retirement are provided for through a compulsory saving scheme introduced from 1/7/93 for those retiring after that date. It

has the following benefits:

❒ An individual pension of $10,000 a year (1993/94 terms) on retirement at 65. A lower pension applies to anyone retiring under the age of 65 until the normal retirement age becomes 65.

❒ Insurance to cover the cost of health care above 5 per cent of the income of a person in retirement.

11. The introduction of a compulsory yearly health insurance policy for every New Zealander who has not reached the age of retirement. It will look after any health care costs that exceed 5 per cent of family income.

12. The introduction of a compulsory employers' levy which is 3 per cent of the payroll for the first 7 years, 2 per cent of the payroll for the next 10 years and ceases after that. The revenue this brings in goes towards the retirement cost of superannuation and health care.

13. Education is paid for directly by parents or students. Families with income below the tax-free income limit (outlined in Note 9) are eligible for negative tax payments in the form of an education cash grant (voucher) of $1 for every $3 shortfall in income, to ensure they are able to purchase their children's educational requirements.

14. A Guaranteed Minimum Family Income (GMFI) of $380 per week in the hand is paid to couples (one of whom works full time) with one child, or $390 per week where both adults earn income. Payments are made every two months.

15. A GMFI of $340 per week is payable to a single person working full time.

16. The level of GMFI for people qualifying under Notes 14 and 15 above is increased by $25 a week for each additional child.

17. The GMFI payments are indexed to inflation each year.

18. From 1/7/93, individual social security benefits are set at the current before-tax level.

19. An 8 per cent deduction is made from these inflated benefits to cover the cost of compulsory superannuation, health, ACC and sickness insurance.

20. Means-tested beneficiaries and those eligible for the

GMFI automatically receive an education cash grant sufficient to enable them to pay for their children's education.

21. An asset sales programme of $20 billion over the next 10 years starts immediately.

SECTION THREE: THE GOVERNMENT BUDGET

During the transition period the government budget is divided into three parts:

Part 1 — A Base Ongoing Budget: This covers all government expenditure items except health, superannuation and interest payments on government debt. Expenditure items, other than those just mentioned, are financed from GST revenue and other indirect and miscellaneous taxation or government revenues.

Part 2 — A Transitional Budget: This covers existing expenditure on health superannuation and interest on government debt. These items are financed by personal taxation revenue until the year 2013/14 when their cost will have become relatively insignificant and they can therefore be financed directly from GST and any other remaining indirect taxation revenue.

Part 3 — A Superannuation and Health Retirement Budget: This sets down the retirement costs associated with fully funding the superannuation and health care requirements of those retiring on or after 1 July 1993, and the transitional revenue that needs to be raised as a result.

Government Overall Budget: The three parts of the budget are then drawn together in one budget table to show the overall financial position of the government each year from 1993/94 to 2019/20. However, before looking at the overall budget and the three parts which go to make it up, it is worthwhile itemising what government costs us as individuals and as a family (two adults, two children).

Current cost of government (1993/94) — pop. 3,408,600

Education expenditure	$ 4,950 million or $1,452	per head
Health	$ 3,950 million or $1,159	per head
Superannuation	$ 4,500 million or $1,320	per head
Interest on debt	$ 4,600 million or $1,350	per head
Other expenditure	$11,500 million or $3,374	per head
(excludes tax on benefits and family support payments)		
Total expenditure	$29,500 million or $8,655	per head

The anticipated cost of government per head of population for 1993/94, therefore, is $166.44 a week, or $665.77 a week (and $34,620 a year) for a family of four. In these circumstances, how can some politicians and providers claim that education and health care, for example, are free?

❒ Education, at $5808 a year or $111.69 a week for a family of four is not free.
❒ Clearly health care at $4636 a year or $89.15 a week is not free.
❒ Nor is pay-as-you-go superannuation at $5280 a year or $101.54 a week.
❒ Nor can the interest costs on the yearly deficits and/or accumulated debt be classed as free at $5400 a year or $103.85 a week.

Not only are they not free, they cannot even be said to be very cheap. Politicians' claims to the contrary are nonsense and need to be treated as such by voters. Equally, the claim by politicians that they can do away with user charges or spend more money on this or that item without cost to the taxpayer is an absolute lie. It is also clear that running deficits each year, as we have been doing for years, is not free, particularly in relation to the costs it imposes on future generations.

Under the policies proposed in this book, the cost of government for a family of four will decline over time to $9392 a year or $180.62 a week, a saving of $25,228 a year and $485.15 a week. This lower annual cost, once the policy changes are fully implemented (and assuming the same population), is made up as follows:

Proposed cost of government

Education — cash grants	$ 600 million or	$ 176 per head
Health — govt. admin.	$ 20 million or	$ 6 per head
Education — govt. admin.	$ 10 million or	$ 3 per head
Superannuation/		
Health retirement costs	$ 800 million or	$ 235 per head
Interest on debt		
Other expenditure	$6570 million or	$1928 per head
Total expenditure	$8000 million or	$2348 per head

Part 1: Base Ongoing Budget — Revenue
The following points should be noted in relation to this budget:

1. The Model Year base revenue position (the ultimate government revenue position) is set out in Column 1. A comparison with Column 2 — the expected revenue position for the first year (1993/94) — indicates the first of the changes in government revenue collections that will take place over a 25-year period. In addition, the year-by-year revenue figures are set out and enable the reader to see when the anticipated reductions in collected revenue take place.
2. Income for the starting year 1993/94, Column 2, has been taken from a written answer in the House of Representatives, on 27 August 1992. Some minor amendments have been made which reduce the overall projected income for the year to $58 million below the Minister of Finance's figures.
3. The GST revenue estimate of $6667 million for 1993/94 translates into a gross taxable GST figure of $60 billion (i.e., one-ninth of $60 billion).

4. A growth factor of 2.5 per cent real has been applied to the 1993/94 GST revenue to calculate yearly revenue. In the following years this should prove to be a modest rate of increase in GST revenue, given the lower personal tax rates and the expected rate of real economic growth, both of which will increase disposable income and therefore GST revenue.

5. To the extent that GST revenue exceeds or falls below the revenue projections set out in Table 1, the timing of any planned reductions in other indirect taxes could be either brought forward or delayed, in order to keep total revenue in line with the estimates.

6. While estimates of this nature are always hazardous when budgeting so far in advance, given that both the National and Labour parties are predicting a real growth rate of 4 per cent in the years to come under what can only be described as static policy settings, the estimate adopted in this book of 2 per cent real growth in personal income should prove to be on the low side. The policies outlined are much more conducive to growth than those currently in force. GST projections, therefore, are likely to be on the low side over the 25-year period covered. This conservative approach to budgeting has been deliberately adopted throughout, so the costs of transition highlighted in this chapter are likely to be less than those set out.

These budgets were based on government estimates in 1992 and do not incorporate the actual Budget figures for 1993. Therefore, they tend to overstate expenditure, particularly government interest payments, and to underestimate revenue, which gives a conservative bias of about $1 billion in Year 1.

7. The difference between Revenue Table 1 and Expenditure Table 2 is shown at the bottom of Table 1, and it is these amounts that are transferred to Table 7 to help produce the overall yearly fiscal position.

271

Table 1: Base Ongoing Budget — Revenue (all amounts in millions)

Column	1	2	3	4	5	6
Revenue	Model Year	1993/94	1994/95	1995/96	1996/97	1997/98
Goods & Services Tax	6500	6667	6833	7004	7179	7359
Petroleum	400	840	840	840	840	840
Motor Vehicle & Road User	350	450	450	450	450	450
Gaming and Royalties		110	110	110	110	110
Energy levies	100	100	100	100	100	100
Customs	250	600	600	600	600	550
Tobacco	200	560	550	550	550	520
Alcohol		430	430	430	430	400
Stamp duty		110	110	110	110	110
Interest		470	450	425	375	300
Profits & Dividends		570	550	525	475	400
Misc.	200	500	500	500	450	400
Income	8000	11407	11523	11644	11669	11539
Expenditure (from Table 2)	7150	13297	12854	12240	11890	11435
Surplus (transfer to Table 7)	850	-1890	-1331	-596	-221	104

Column	1	16	17	18	19	20
Revenue	Model Year	2007/08	2008/09	2009/10	2010/11	2011/12
Goods & Services Tax	6500	9420	9655	9897	10144	10398
Petroleum	400	400	400	400	400	400
Motor Vehicle & Road User	350	350	350	350	350	350
Gaming and Royalties						
Energy levies	100	100	100	100	100	100
Customs	250	300	250	250	250	250
Tobacco	200	400	300	300	300	300
Alcohol						
Stamp duty						
Interest						
Profits & Dividends						
Misc.	200	300	200	200	200	200
Income	8000	11270	11255	11497	11744	11998
Expenditure (from Table 2)	7150	7915	7460	7430	7400	7370
Surplus (transfer to Table 7)	850	3355	3795	4067	4344	4628

7	8	9	10	11	12	13	14	15
1998/99	1999/00	2000/01	2001/02	2002/03	2003/04	2004/05	2005/06	2006/07
7543	7731	7925	8123	8326	8534	8747	8966	9190
840	840	840	840	700	400	400	400	400
450	450	450	450	350	350	350	350	350
110	110	100						
100	100	100	100	100	100	100	100	100
500	500	500	500	450	450	450	400	400
500	500	500	500	500	500	500	500	500
400	300	200	200	200	200	200	100	
200	100							
300	200	100	100	50				
350	300	300	300	300	300	300	300	300
11293	11131	11015	11113	10976	10834	11047	11116	11240
11080	10705	10280	9905	9420	9045	8720	8545	8190
213	426	735	1208	1556	1789	2327	2571	3050

21	22	23	24	25	26	27	28
2012/13	2013/14	2014/15	2015/16	2016/17	2017/18	2018/19	2019/20
10658	10924	11197	9390	9625	9866	10112	10365
400	400	400	400	400	400	400	400
350	350	350	350	350	350	350	350
100	100	100	100	100	100	100	100
250	250	250	250	250	250	250	250
300	300	300	300	300	300	300	300
200	200	200	200	200	200	200	200
12258	12524	12797	10990	11225	11466	11712	11965
7340	7310	7280	7250	7230	7210	7190	7170
4918	5214	5517	3740	3995	4256	4522	4795

Table 2: Base Ongoing Budget — Expenditure (all amounts in millions)

Column	1	2	3	4	5	6	7	8	9	10	11	12	13	14	15
Expenditure	Model Year	93/94 Budget	1993/94	1994/95	1995/96	1996/97	1997/98	1998/99	1999/00	2000/01	2001/02	2002/03	2003/04	2004/05	2005/06
Administration															
Audit		3.6													
Conservation	100	111.0	110	105	100	100	100	100	100	100	100	100	100	100	100
Crown Law	14	14.0	14	14	14	14	14	14	14	14	14	14	14	14	14
Cultural Affairs	20	56.2	50	50	50	30	20	20	20	20	20	20	20	20	20
Customs	30	39.6	40	40	35	30	30	30	30	30	30	30	30	30	30
Govt. Super		721.6	720	710	700	680	660	640	600	560	520	480	440	400	360
Inland Revenue	180	383.9	380	360	360	350	340	330	320	300	300	280	280	280	280
Internal Affairs	50	101.7	100	90	80	70	60	50	50	50	50	50	50	50	50
Justice	530	564.8	560	550	540	530	530	530	530	530	530	530	530	530	530
Maori Development	70	106.2	100	100	90	80	70	70	70	70	70	70	70	70	70
Office Clerk	10	12.4	12	12	10	10	10	10	10	10	10	10	10	10	10
Office Ombudsman	3	3.2	3	3	3	3	3	3	3	3	3	3	3	3	3
Parl Counsel	2	2.1	2	2	2	2	2	2	2	2	2	2	2	2	2
Parl Service	70	98.1	100	100	100	100	100	70	70	70	70	70	70	70	70
Parl Commission	1	1.2	1	1	1	1	1	1	1	1	1	1	1	1	1
Police	660	681.0	680	670	660	660	660	660	660	660	660	660	660	660	660
PM & Cabinet	13	13.4	13	13	13	13	13	13	13	13	13	13	13	13	13
SIS	10	10.3	10	10	10	10	10	10	10	10	10	10	10	10	10
Serious Fraud Off.	5	5.0	5	5	5	5	5	5	5	5	5	5	5	5	5
State Services		23.5	23	20											
Statistics	30	36.6	35	32	30	30	30	30	30	30	30	30	30	30	30
Survey & Land	15	16.4	15	15	15	15	15	15	15	15	15	15	15	15	15
Treasury	70	78.3	75	70	70	70	70	70	70	70	70	70	70	70	70
Valuation		3.7	3												
Women's Affairs	1	4.9	5	1	1	1	1	1	1	1	1	1	1	1	1
Youth Affairs	1	7.2	7	1	1	1	1	1	1	1	1	1	1	1	1
Environment	15	24.6	24	20	15	15	15	15	15	15	15	15	15	15	15
ADMINISTRATION	1900	3124.5	3087	2994	2905	2820	2760	2690	2640	2580	2540	2480	2440	2400	2360
Foreign Relations															
Defence	900	1239.0	1200	1100	1000	900	900	900	900	900	900	900	900	900	900
External	280	332.5	330	320	310	300	300	300	280	280	280	280	280	280	280
Govt Communications	20	20.0	20	20	20	20	20	20	20	20	20	20	20	20	20
FOREIGN	1200	1591.5	1550	1440	1330	1220	1220	1220	1200	1200	1200	1200	1200	1200	1200
Industry															
A&F	50	89	80	75	70	60	50	50	50	50	50	50	50	50	50
Commerce	20	79	75	20	20	20	20	20	20	20	20	20	20	20	20
Forestry	10	21	20	15	10	10	10	10	10	10	10	10	10	10	10
Labour	100	494	480	450	400	400	350	350	350	300	300	250	250	200	200
Research	200	275	270	260	250	240	230	220	210	200	200	200	200	200	200
INDUSTRY	380	958	925	820	750	730	660	650	640	580	580	530	530	480	480
Housing		16	15	10											
National Library	45	46	45	45	45	45	45	45	45	45	45	45	45	45	45
Pacific Is. Aff.	5	5	5	5	5	5	5	5	5	5	5	5	5	5	5
Transport Dept	40	40	40	40	40	40	40	40	40	40	40	40	40	40	40
Transit NZ	700	700	700	700	700	700	700	700	700	700	700	700	700	700	700
Inland Rev. Fam. Spt		493													
SUNDRY ADMINISTRATION	790	1300	805	800	790	790	790	790	790	790	790	790	790	790	790
EDUCATION	10	4949	10	10	10	10	10	10	10	10	10	10	10	10	10
HEALTH	20	3966	20	20	20	20	20	20	20	20	20	20	20	20	20
DEBT		4619													
Social Welfare															
Administration	300	492	490	480	470	460	450	440	430	420	400	390	380	370	360
GRI		5135													
AUST Benefit		30													
Rest Home		160	150	140	130	120	110	100	90	80	70	60	50	40	30
Sickness		251	250	200	150	100	50								
Taxes on Benefit		641													
GMI	100		100	100	100	100	100	100	100	100	100	100	100	100	100
Unemployment Benefit	400	1542	1800	1750	1700	1650	1600	1500	1400	1300	1200	1000	900	800	700
DPB	400	1087	1300	1300	1250	1250	1200	1100	1000	900	750	750	600	600	600
Other	700	927	1100	1100	1050	1050	1000	1000	1000	950	900	850	800	800	800
War Vets		90	90	80	75	70	65	60	55	50	45	40	35	30	25
Accommodation	200	220	220	220	210	200	200	200	200	200	200	200	200	200	200
Education Grants	600		1200	1200	1100	1100	1000	1000	900	900	900	800	800	700	700
Superannuation Contrib.	150		200	200	200	200	200	200	230	200	200	200	190	180	170
SOCIAL WELFARE	2850	10575	6900	6770	6435	6300	5975	5700	5405	5100	4765	4390	4055	3820	3685
TOTAL EXPENDITURE	7150	31083	13297	12854	12240	11890	11435	11080	10705	10280	9905	9420	9045	8720	8545

Column	1	16	17	18	19	20	21	22	23	24	25	26	27	28	29
	Model Year	2006/07	2007/08	2008/09	2009/10	2010/11	2011/12	2012/13	2013/14	2014/15	2015/16	2016/17	2017/18	2018/19	2019/20
Expenditure															
Administration															
Audit															
Conservation	100	100	100	100	100	100	100	100	100	100	100	100	100	100	100
Crown Law	14	14	14	14	14	14	14	14	14	14	14	14	14	14	14
Cultural Affairs	20	20	20	20	20	20	20	20	20	20	20	20	20	20	20
Customs	30	30	30	30	30	30	30	30	30	30	30	30	30	30	30
Govt. Super		320	280	240	220	200	180	160	140	120	100	80	60	40	20
Inland Revenue	250	250	250	250	240	230	220	210	200	190	180	180	180	180	180
Internal Affairs	530	50	50	50	50	50	50	50	50	50	50	50	50	50	50
Justice	70	530	530	530	530	530	530	530	530	530	530	530	530	530	530
Maori Development	10	70	70	70	70	70	70	70	70	70	70	70	70	70	70
Office Clerk	3	10	10	10	10	10	10	10	10	10	10	10	10	10	10
Office Ombudsman	2	3	3	3	3	3	3	3	3	3	3	3	3	3	3
Parl Counsel	70	2	2	2	2	2	2	2	2	2	2	2	2	2	2
Parl Service	1	70	70	70	70	70	70	70	70	70	70	70	70	70	70
Parl Commission	1	1	1	1	1	1	1	1	1	1	1	1	1	1	1
Police	660	660	660	660	660	660	660	660	660	660	660	660	660	660	660
PM & Cabinet	13	13	13	13	13	13	13	10	13	13	13	13	13	13	13
SIS	10	10	10	10	10	10	10	10	10	10	10	10	10	10	10
Serious Fraud Off	5	5	5	5	5	5	5	5	5	5	5	5	5	5	5
State Services															
Statistics	30	30	30	30	30	30	30	30	30	30	30	30	30	30	30
Survey & Land	15	15	15	15	15	15	15	15	15	15	15	15	15	15	15
Treasury	70	70	70	70	70	70	70	70	70	70	70	70	70	70	70
Valuation															
Women's Affairs	1	1	1	1	1	1	1	1	1	1	1	1	1	1	1
Youth Affairs	1	1	1	1	1	1	1	1	1	1	1	1	1	1	1
Environment	15	15	15	15	15	15	15	15	15	15	15	15	15	15	15
ADMINISTRATION	1900	2290	2250	2210	2180	2150	2120	2090	2060	2030	2000	1980	1960	1940	1920
Foreign Relations															
Defence	900	900	900	900	900	900	900	900	900	900	900	900	900	900	900
External	280	280	280	280	280	280	280	280	280	280	280	280	280	280	280
Govt Communications	20	20	20	20	20	20	20	20	20	20	20	20	20	20	20
FOREIGN	1200	1200	1200	1200	1200	1200	1200	1200	1200	1200	1200	1200	1200	1200	1200
Industry															
A&F	50	50	50	50	50	50	50	50	50	50	50	50	50	50	50
Commerce	20	20	20	20	20	20	20	20	20	20	20	20	20	20	20
Forestry	10	10	10	10	10	10	10	10	10	10	10	10	10	10	10
Labour	100	150	150	100	100	100	100	100	100	100	100	100	100	100	100
Research	200	200	200	200	200	200	200	200	200	200	200	200	200	200	200
INDUSTRY	390	430	430	380	380	380	380	380	380	380	380	380	380	380	380
Housing															
National Library	45	45	45	45	45	45	45	45	45	45	45	45	45	45	45
Pacific Is. Aff.	5	5	5	5	5	5	5	5	5	5	5	5	5	5	5
Transport Dept	40	40	40	40	40	40	40	40	40	40	40	40	40	40	40
Transit NZ	700	700	700	700	700	700	700	700	700	700	700	700	700	700	700
Inland Rev. Fam. Spt															
SUNDRY ADMINISTRATION	790	790	790	790	790	790	790	790	790	790	790	790	790	790	790
EDUCATION	10	10	10	10	10	10	10	10	10	10	10	10	10	10	10
HEALTH	20	20	20	20	20	20	20	20	20	20	20	20	20	20	20
DEBT															
Social Welfare															
Administration	300	350	340	300	300	300	300	300	300	300	300	300	300	300	300
GRI															
AUST Benefit															
Rest Home		20	10												
Sickness															
Taxes on Benefit															
GMI	100	100	100	100	100	100	100	100	100	100	100	100	100	100	100
Unemployment Benefit	400	600	500	400	400	400	400	400	400	400	400	400	400	400	400
DPB	400	600	500	400	400	400	400	400	400	400	400	400	400	400	400
Other	700	800	800	700	700	700	700	700	700	700	700	700	700	700	700
War Vets		20	15												
Accommodation	200	200	200	200	200	200	200	200	200	200	200	200	200	200	200
Education Grants	600	600	600	600	600	600	600	600	600	600	600	600	600	600	600
Superannuation Contrib.	150	160	150	150	150	150	150	150	150	150	150	150	150	150	150
SOCIAL WELFARE	2850	3450	3215	2850	2850	2850	2850	2850	2850	2850	2850	2850	2850	2850	2850
TOTAL EXPENDITURE	7150	8190	7915	7460	7430	7400	7370	7340	7310	7280	7250	7230	7210	7190	7170

Part 1: Base Ongoing Budget — Expenditure

The following points should be noted in relation to this budget:

1. The Model Year base expenditure position (the government's ultimate position) is set out in Column 1. A comparison with Column 2, the expected expenditure totals for Year 1 (1993/94), indicates the first of the ultimate reductions or increases in expenditure that will take place over a 25-year period.

2. Expenditure estimates for the year 1993/94, based on current policies, are set out in Column 2. These have been taken directly from published government forward projections with some minor amendments.

3. Proposed expenditure under the new policies for 1993/94 and subsequent years is set out in detail from Column 3 onwards.

4. Major changes in government expenditure under the new policies are as follows:

(i) Administration down by $1224 million over 25 years. The major items of reduced government expenditure in administration are Government Superannuation ($722 million) and Inland Revenue ($204 million). The remaining items of administration expenditure are reduced by $300 million over 25 years, as shown in Table 2.

(ii) Government expenditure on Foreign Relations is down by $392 million over 25 years. The major reductions in expenditure are Defence ($339 million) and External Affairs ($52 million).

(iii) Government expenditure on industry is down by $578 million over 25 years. The major item of reduced expenditure is Labour ($394 million) with other expenditure items ($184 million).

(iv) Sundry administration spending is down by $510 million over 25 years. The major reductions are in Inland Revenue Family Support ($403 million) and other expenditure items ($107 million).

(v) Education expenditure is down by $4939 million.

(vi) Health expenditure is down by $3946 million.

(vii) Interest on debt expenditure is down by $4619 million.

(viii) Social Welfare expenditure is down by $7725 million. Major items here are superannuation expenditure, down by $5135 million and taxes on benefits, down by $641 million. The reductions in other benefits include unemployment expenditure ($1142 million), DPB expenditure ($227 million), sickness benefit expenditure ($251 million), other benefits ($227 million), other items (including social welfare administration ($700 million).

There would also be a number of major new items of expenditure under Social Welfare:

GMFI $100 million
Educational grants $600 million
Government superannuation contributions $150 million

5. From the numbers given above it can be seen that expenditure on the four main items of current government expenditure (Column 2) —

Health $3946 million
Education $4939 million
Interest on debt $4619 million
Superannuation $5135 million

— has been reduced to zero or close to zero over time (Model Year, Column 1). For the path of these reductions, refer to Table 4 for health, superannuation and interest on debt. The difference between the expenditure starting point in Table 4 and the figures above reflect Day One (1/7/93) reductions in government expenditure.

In the case of education, any remaining expenditure has been included in Table 2 and has been reduced to $10 million for administration. The sum of $1200 million has been placed under Social Welfare in Year 1 for educational cash grants, and the balance of education expenditure is purchased directly by parents and students as a result of the tax-free income allowance and consequential reductions in income tax.

This reduction in four items of current budget expenditure results from adopting the policies in Chapters 5 to 8 and therefore is virtually immutable. The reason for this is that after 1/7/93 health and superannuation costs in retirement are fully funded on the day people retire, and education will be paid for by parents or students in future. In these circumstances, with a full 60 per cent of budget expenditure set on a predictable reduction path, an expenditure blowout is highly unlikely. The other 40 per cent of government expenditure, apart from benefits, is relatively easy to control and has not been the major cause of the government's budget problems during the last 20 years.

6. There is one remaining significant item of government expenditure where some variability and therefore risk could occur. It is the planned reductions in the cost of benefits such as unemployment and DPB. The risk is that the drop in the number of people on those benefits might be slower than forecast. The chances of this happening are relatively low because of the following factors:

❐ The improved incentives to earn income as opposed to staying on the benefit as a result of the introduction of the GMFI and lower personal tax rates.

❐ The increased employment opportunities in a deregulated labour market and the suggested changes to minimum wage laws.

❐ The proposed changes to the education system.

❐ The proposed crackdown on fraud, particularly within the cash economy.

❐ The tighter criteria applying to DPB payments.

❐ The higher growth levels which can be confidently predicted.

❐ The higher investment levels and thereby employment opportunities that will undoubtedly flow from the dramatically lower taxation rates that will apply in New Zealand compared to other countries.

❐ The improved competitiveness of New Zealand producers, especially compared to Australia, and the consequential shift in manufacturing and other production to New Zealand.

❐ Higher savings levels coming from the compulsory superannuation and health schemes.

7. In practice, there may well be room for further

substantial savings that are not identified in Table 2, e.g., Justice, Inland Revenue Department, Treasury, Parliamentary Services. The fact that spending on these and some other items is likely to be lower than given here helps give a conservative bias to the tables.

Part 2: Transitional Budget — Revenue
There are several points to note in this budget:

1. The base individual income used to calculate the amount of personal taxation which the government is likely to receive during the first year of the new policies (1993/94) is $51 billion (Table 3, Column 2). This $51 billion has been calculated according to the answer to Parliamentary Question No 16, 27/8/92:

Wages & Salaries	$ 38,800	million
Interest	$ 3,200	million
Dividend Income	$ 800	million
Rents, etc	$ 600	million
**Company Income now taxed in hands of individuals	$ 6,600	million
**Non-Resident Income	$ 600	million
*Growth in Income 1993/94	$ 1,400	million
	$ 52,000	million

* Expected growth in personal income tax for the year ending 1993/94 over 1992/93 has been multiplied by three to calculate a growth in the tax base of $1400 million (Parliamentary Question No. 146, 27/8/92).
** Estimated tax revenue from companies and non-resident income has been multiplied by three to calculate the contribution to the tax base from these items for 1993/94 (Parliamentary Question No. 146, 27/8/92).

As 33 cents in the dollar is the highest personal income tax rate in New Zealand, the estimate of base income at $52 billion is itself likely to be conservative. For example, had

Table 3: Personal income tax (all amount in billions).

Column	1	2	3	4	5
Year	Growth in Base Income	Personal Income Tax Base	Tax-Free Education Allowance	Adjusted Personal Income Tax Base	Personal income to be taxed at 15c in dollar
1993/94	100.00	51.0	9.0	42.0	11
1994/95	105.00	53.6	9.5	44.1	12
1995/96	110.25	56.2	10.0	46.2	13
1996/97	115.76	59.0	10.5	48.5	14
1997/98	121.55	62.0	11.0	51.0	15
1998/99	127.63	65.1	11.5	53.6	16
1999/00	134.01	68.3	12.0	56.3	17
2000/01	140.71	71.8	12.5	59.3	18
2001/02	147.75	75.4	13.0	62.4	
2002/03	155.13	79.1	13.5	65.6	
2003/04	162.89	83.1	14.0	69.1	
2004/05	171.03	87.2	14.5	72.7	
2005/06	179.59	91.6	15.0	76.6	
2006/07	188.56	96.2	15.5	80.7	
2007/08	197.99	101.0	16.0	85.0	
2008/09	207.89	106.0	16.5	89.5	
2009/10	218.29	111.3	17.0	94.3	
2010/11	229.20	116.9	17.5	99.4	
2011/12	240.66	122.7	18.0	104.7	
2012/13	252.70	128.9	18.5	110.4	
2013/14	265.33	135.3	19.0	116.3	

Rate of growth = 2%   Inflation = 3%

Column	6	7	8	9	10
Year	Tax rate on other income	Personal income to be taxed at other than 15c	Personal income tax total for year	Fringe benefit & surcharge for year	Total personal taxation for year (to Table 5)
1993/94	28	31.0	10.330	0.61	10.940
1994/95	28	32.1	10.774	0.61	11.384
1995/96	27	33.2	10.921	0.61	11.531
1996/97	25	34.5	10.735	0.59	11.325
1997/98	23	36.0	10.528	0.57	11.098
1998/99	21	37.6	10.294	0.55	10.844
1999/00	19	39.3	10.026	0.53	10.556
2000/01	17	41.3	9.715	0.34	10.055
2001/02	15	62.4	9.353	0.26	9.613
2002/03	14	65.6	9.186		9.186
2003/04	13	69.1	8.980		8.980
2004/05	12	72.7	8.727		8.727
2005/06	11	76.6	8.425		8.425
2006/07	10	80.7	8.067		8.067
2007/08	9	85.0	7.648		7.648
2008/09	7	89.5	6.267		6.267
2009/10	6	94.3	5.660		5.660
2010/11	3	99.4	2.982		2.982
2011/12	2	104.7	2.095		2.095
2012/13	1	110.4	1.104		1.104
2013/14	0	116.3	0.000		0.000

25 cents been taken as the average tax paid on growth in income 1993/94 (instead of 33 cents), the $1400 million tax base income increase would have been around $1850 million — an extra $450 million.

A starting point of $51 billion for the personal income-tax base is therefore doubly conservative and provides a built-in safety margin of $1 billion when calculating the level of personal taxation in any year.

2. The base figure for personal income taxation calculations of $51 billion has been adjusted each year by a growth factor of 2 per cent real and an inflation factor of 3 per cent for the purposes of establishing the year-by-year tax base (Table 3, Column 2).

3. The tax-free family educational income allowance (Column 3) has been deducted from the base figure of $51 billion before any calculations have been made on the level of personal taxation in any year. The educational allowance has been calculated to equal $9 billion for 1993/94 and has been subsequently adjusted by $500 million a year. (See Annex 2 for the calculations on the tax-free family educational income allowance, at the end of this chapter.)

4. Once we have the adjusted personal income tax base for 1993/94 of $42 billion (Column 4), the next step is to determine the amount of income to be taxed at 15 cents in the dollar and the amount to be taxed at 28 cents in the dollar for Year One. (See Annex 3, at the end of this chapter, for the basis by which the level of $11 billion dollars of taxable income at 15 cents is arrived at. This $11 billion has been adjusted by $1 billion a year until the top marginal personal income-tax rate has been reduced to 15 cents in the dollar in 2001/02.)

5. Once these calculations have been made it is a simple matter to work out the amount of personal income tax the government will receive in any year (see Columns 5, 6, 7, 8). Fringe benefit tax and any income from any remaining tax surcharge is then added to the Column 8 figures to give the total personal income-tax figure in Column 10. This figure is then transferred to Table 5.

Part 2: Transitional Budget — Expenditure

Table 4: Expenditure: Health, Superannuation and Interest (all amounts in millions)

Column	1	2	3	4
Year	Health	Super	Interest	Total (to Table 5)
1993/94	1700	4234	4600	10534
1994/95	1674	4170	4480	10324
1995/96	1645	4097	4209	9952
1996/97	1613	4018	3762	9394
1997/98	1579	3932	3319	8829
1998/99	1542	3841	2852	8236
1999/2000	1503	3743	2276	7521
2000/01	1460	3637	1934	7031
2001/02	1415	3525	1463	6404
2002/03	1367	3405	1169	5940
2003/04	1318	3283	1010	5611
2004/05	1266	3152	827	5245
2005/06	1211	3017	652	4880
2006/07	1154	2875	531	4561
2007/08	1096	2731	377	4204
2008/09	1038	2586	191	3816
2009/10	967	2409	19	3395
2010/11	916	2282	159	3040
2011/12	855	2129	-190	2794
2012/13	793	1976	-208	2562
2013/14	733	1825	-226	2331
2014/15	671	1670	-252	2090
2015/16	612	1523	-318	1817
2016/17	553	1376	-306	1623
2017/18	496	1235	-330	1401
2018/19	441	1099	-396	1144
2019/20	391	973	-504	860

There are four points to note in this budget:

1. Table 4 sets out the cost to government of the phase-out of existing health, superannuation and interest costs for

the period 1993/94 to 2019/20.

2. Health — The starting point for this expenditure is $1700 million, the estimated cost to government of health care for those currently retired. People who have not yet retired would be insuring themselves from 1/7/93. This figure of $1700 million is added to each year by the assumed 3 per cent rate of inflation and then reduced each year by the number of people in the original retired population at 1/7/93 who have died during the year. (See Annex 4, at the end of this chapter.)

Note: People retiring after 1/7/93 will be fully funded for their health care needs in retirement. (See Table 6.)

3. Superannuation — The starting point for this expenditure is $4234 million, the estimated net cost to government of superannuation for those people currently in retirement. This figure of $4234 million is added to each year by the assumed 3 per cent rate of inflation and then reduced each year by the number of people who were part of the retired population at 1/7/93 who have died during the year. (See Annex 5, at the end of this chapter.)

Note: People retiring after 1/7/93 will be fully funded for their superannuation needs in retirement. (See Table 6.)

4. Interest — The starting point is $4600 million, the expected cost to government for the 1993/94 year. Interest costs decline as set out in this table as a result of asset sales and fiscal surpluses after 1997. (See Table 8.)

Part 2: Transitional Budget — Difference

Table 5: Difference between Revenue and Expenditure

Column	1	2	3	4
Year	Income Tax from Table 3	Expenditure from Table 4	Net Transitional Fiscal Position	Fiscal Position Real Terms (to Table 7)
1993/94	10940	10534	406	406
1994/95	11384	10324	1060	1029
1995/96	11531	9952	1579	1489
1996/97	11325	9394	1931	1767
1997/98	11098	8829	2269	2016
1998/99	10844	8236	2608	2250
1999/2000	10556	7521	3034	2541
2000/01	10055	7031	3024	2459
2001/02	9613	6404	3209	2533
2002/03	9186	5940	3246	2488
2003/04	8980	5611	3369	2507
2004/05	8727	5245	3483	2516
2005/06	8425	4880	3545	2487
2006/07	8067	4561	3506	2387
2007/08	7648	4204	3444	2277
2008/09	6267	3816	2451	1573
2009/10	5660	3395	2265	1411
2010/11	2982	3040	-58	-35
2011/12	2095	2794	-700	-411
2012/13	1104	2562	-1458	-832
2013/14	0	2331	-2331	-1291
2014/15	0	2090	-2090	-1129
2015/16	0	1817	-1817	-962
2016/17	0	1623	-1623	-847
2017/18	0	1401	-1401	-726
2018/19	0	1144	-1144	-595
2019/20	0	860	-860	-457

There are several points to note regarding this budget:

1. Table 5 sets out the sizes of the yearly surplus or deficit both in dollar-of-the-day terms and real terms, i.e., 1993/94 dollars.

Column 1 sets down personal income tax received by government. These figures have been taken directly from Table 3.

Column 2 sets down total government expenditure on health, superannuation and interest. These figures have been taken from Table 4.

Column 3 sets down the difference between Column 1 (Revenue) and Column 2 (Expenditure).

Column 4 deflates Column 3 to real terms, i.e., it takes out the 3 per cent inflation factor.

2. It is the amounts set down in Column 4 which are transferred to Table 7 to help produce the overall yearly fiscal position.

Part 3: Superannuation and Health Care in Retirement Budget

Table 6: Superannuation and health care in retirement budget (all amounts in millions)

Column	1	2	3	4	5	6	7
	Contributions to Health Care & Super for People Retiring Each Year		Income Available from Individual Plus Employer	Cost of Fully Funding		Total Expenditure on Pensions & Health Care	Budget Cost
Year	Individual	Employer	Employer	Pension	Health		
1993/94	27	1290	1317	1678	559	2237	920
1994/95	55	1316	1371	1666	555	2221	850
1995/96	81	1342	1423	1617	539	2156	733
1996/97	110	1369	1479	1605	535	2140	661
1997/98	143	1396	1539	1642	547	2189	650
1998/99	185	1424	1609	1617	539	2156	547
1999/2000	227	1453	1680	1617	539	2156	476
2000/01	272	988	1260	1605	535	2140	880
2001/02	668	1008	1676	3357	1119	4476	2800
2002/03	792	1028	1820	3467	1156	4623	2803
2003/04	949	1048	1997	3626	1209	4835	2838
2004/05	1134	1069	2203	3847	1282	5129	2926
2005/06	1364	1091	2455	4128	1376	5504	3049
2006/07	1510	1113	2623	4116	1372	5488	2865
2007/08	1605	1135	2740	3957	1319	5276	2536
2008/09	1834	1157	2991	4116	1372	5488	2497
2009/10	2128	1181	3309	4361	1454	5815	2506
2010/11	2520	-	2520	4741	1580	6321	3801
2011/12	2990	-	2990	5182	1727	6909	3919
2012/13	3339	-	3339	5341	1780	7121	3782
2013/14	3520	-	3520	5268	1756	7024	3504
2014/15	3820	-	3820	5304	1768	7072	3252
2015/16	4130	-	4130	5341	1780	7121	2991
2016/17	4410	-	4410	5329	1776	7105	2695
2017/18	4800	-	4800	5415	1805	7220	2420
2018/19	5200	-	5200	5500	1833	7333	2133
2019/20	5700	-	5700	5660	1886	7546	1846

The following points should be noted in relation to the costs of superannuation and health care for those retiring after 1/7/93:

1. In Table 6 the revenue columns 1, 2 and 3 set out the contributions which go towards fully funding superannuation and health costs in retirement.

2. Column 1 sets down the personal contribution of people retiring each year from 1993/94 onwards. While the amount contributed during the early years by those retiring is small, it builds momentum quickly. (Annex 6, at the end of this chapter, provides the basis on which the calculations have been made for retirees' contributions.)

3. Column 2 sets down the income government would receive each year from employers towards the cost of fully funding superannuation and health care in retirement. This is one of the transitional requirements involved in moving from an unfunded method of financing superannuation and health care in retirement to fully funding those requirements. (Annex 7, at the end of this chapter, provides the basis for calculating the level of income to government.) It is worth remembering the following points:

(i) It is a transitional contribution.

(ii) The rate of employer contributions has been kept as low as possible — at 3 per cent for the first 7 years, then 2 per cent for 10 years, and nil thereafter. The highest rate payable is only a third of what Australian employers will be expected to contribute by the year 2000 towards the superannuation requirements of their employees.

(iii) The costs involved — 3 per cent of employee incomes — are offset immediately by a reduction in the top personal tax rate and the company withholding tax rate of 5 cents in the dollar, down from 33 cents to 28 cents.

(iv) Continuing reductions in company and personal taxation will mean that companies paying withholding tax and other employers will soon find the cost of any contribution made towards superannuation and health care is more than offset by reductions in the taxation they would otherwise have had to pay.

(v) The rate of return on the investment (in this case any additional cost to the employer of funding the transition to a fully funded health and superannuation system at the time of retirement) will be very high indeed for most employers, given the move to zero taxation on personal and company income over 20 years.

4. Column 3 simply adds Columns 1 and 2 together to give the total revenue from individuals and employers.

5. Columns 4 and 5 set out the cost involved in fully funding superannuation and health care in retirement. (For details of how those amounts were calculated, refer to Annex 8 at the end of this chapter.) Column 6 totals the expenditure cost of both superannuation and health care costs in retirement.

6. Column 7 is the difference between the revenue and expenditure and sets out the cost of fully funding superannuation and health care from the date of retirement which has to be met elsewhere from the government budget, i.e., primarily from savings in existing superannuation and health care costs. It is these figures in Column 7 that are transferred to Table 7 to help produce the overall government fiscal position on a year-by-year basis.

Government Overall Budget

Table 7: Government overall budget — fiscal position year by year (all amounts in millions)

	Part 1	Part 2	Part 3	
Year	Base Budget Position (Tables 1 & 2)	Transitional Budget Position (Table 5)	Superannunation & Health Savings Budget (Table 6)	Overall Government Fiscal Position
1993/94	-1890	406	-920	-2404
1994/95	-1331	1029	-850	-1152
1995/96	-596	1489	-733	160
1996/97	-221	1767	-661	885
1997/98	104	2016	-650	1470
1998/99	213	2250	-547	1916
1999/2000	426	2541	-476	2491
2000/01	735	2459	-880	2314
2001/02	1208	2533	-2800	941
2002/03	1556	2488	-2803	1241
2003/04	1789	2507	-2838	1458
2004/05	2327	2516	-2926	1917
2005/06	2571	2487	-3049	2009
2006/07	3050	2387	-2865	2572
2007/08	3355	2277	-2536	3096
2008/09	3795	1573	-2497	2871
2009/10	4067	1411	-2506	2972
2010/11	4344	-35	-3801	508
2011/12	4628	-411	-3919	298
2012/13	4918	-832	-3782	304
2013/14	5214	-1291	-3504	419
2014/15	5517	-1129	-3252	1136
2015/16	3740	-962	-2991	-213
2016/17	3995	-847	-2695	453
2017/18	4256	-726	-2420	1110
2018/19	4522	-595	-2133	1794
2019/20	4795	-457	-1843	2495

Points to note:

1. This table simply brings together the yearly balances (surpluses or deficits) from the three budget parts.

❐ Part 1, Base Budget — The amounts shown in Column 1 are the difference between Revenue Table 1 and Expenditure Table 2, as shown at the bottom of Revenue Table 1.

❐ Part 2, Transitional Budget — The amounts shown in Column 2 are taken directly from Table 5.

❐ Part 3, Superannuation and Health Care Budget — The amounts shown in Column 3 are taken directly from Table 6.

2. The amounts shown in Columns 1, 2 and 3 are added to give the total shown in Column 4 in order to establish the overall yearly fiscal position for the years 1993/94 to 2019/20. The yearly fiscal position in Column 4 is then transferred to Table 8 in order to calculate New Zealand's yearly debt position. Having determined the level of debt for any year, the interest cost on that debt is then calculated.

Debt and Interest Costs

Table 8: Debt and interest costs (debt given in billions)

Column	1	2	3	4	5	6	7
Year	Debt at Start of Year	Asset Sales	Fiscal Deficit/ Surplus	Debt at End of Year	10% Debt	6% Debt	Cost (in $ Millions)
1993/94	47.0	1.8	-2.4	47.6	47	0.0	4600
1994/95	47.6	4.6	-1.2	44.2	45	2.6	4480
1995/96	44.2	3.3	0.2	40.7	39	5.2	4209
1996/97	40.7	2.5	0.9	37.3	33	7.7	3762
1997/98	37.3	2.3	1.5	33.5	27	10.3	3319
1998/99	33.5	1.7	1.9	29.9	21	12.5	2852
1999/20	29.9	1.2	2.5	26.2	12	17.9	2276
2000/01	26.2	2.0	2.3	21.9	9	17.2	1934
2001/02	21.9	1.5	0.9	19.5	3.7	18.2	1463
2002/03	19.5	1.4	1.2	16.8		19.5	1169
2003/04	16.8	1.6	1.5	13.8		16.8	1010
2004/05	13.8	1.0	1.9	10.9		13.8	827
2005/06	10.9		2.0	8.9		10.9	652
2006/07	8.9		2.6	6.3		8.9	531
2007/08	6.3		3.1	3.2		6.3	377
2008/09	3.2		2.9	0.3		3.2	191
2009/10	0.3		3.0	-2.7		0.3	19
2010/11	-2.7		0.5	-3.2		-2.7	-159
2011/12	-3.2		0.3	-3.5		-3.2	-190
2012/13	-3.5		0.3	-3.8		-3.5	-208
2013/14	-3.8		0.4	-4.2		-3.8	-226
2014/15	-4.2		1.1	-5.3		-4.2	-252
2015/16	-5.3		-0.2	-5.1		-5.3	-318
2016/17	-5.1		-0.4	-5.5		-5.1	-306
2017/18	-5.5		1.1	-6.6		-5.5	-330
2018/19	-6.6		1.8	-8.4		-6.6	-396
2019/20	-8.4		2.5	-10.9		-8.4	-504

Points to note:

1. Column 1 sets down the expected debt position at the beginning of each financial year, beginning with $47 billion for the 1993/94 year.

2. Column 2 sets down the expected yearly revenue (in billions) to government from asset sales. (For details of assets that make up the sale programme, see Chapter 8.)

3. Column 3 sets down the overall government fiscal surpluses or deficits for each year taken directly from Table 7.

4. Column 4 sets down the outstanding debt at the end of the year, having taken into account asset sales and the year's fiscal position.

5. Columns 5 and 6 calculate the quantity of debt that is subject to one interest rate or another:

❐ Column 5 — The interest on the quantity of debt shown in this column has been calculated at 10 per cent, except for the first two years where Government estimates have been used. A 10 per cent interest rate is likely to be on the high side, resulting in interest payments higher than actual and again providing a conservative bias to the budget.

❐ Column 6 — The interest on the quantity of debt in this column has been calculated at 6 per cent. The amount of debt is the estimated lump-sum savings held to the credit of people who retire after 1/7/93. Government has used the money to retire existing debt and replaced it with debt owning to retirees after 1/7/93. The interest rate of 6 per cent is based on the real rate of return required by superannuation and health care funds of 3 per cent plus the assumed inflation factor of 3 per cent.

6. Column 7 sets out the total interest cost to the government, year by year, which is then used in Table 4.

ANNEX 1:

GOODS & SERVICES TAX

Column	1	2	3	4
Year	Tax Base (billion)	Real Growth (2.5%)	Rate (%)	Revenue (million)
1993/94	60.00	100.00	12.5	6.667
1994/95	61.50	102.50	12.5	6.833
1995/96	63.04	105.06	12.5	7.004
1996/97	64.61	107.69	12.5	7.179
1997/98	66.23	110.38	12.5	7.359
1998/99	67.88	113.14	12.5	7.543
1999/2000	69.58	115.97	12.5	7.731
2000/01	71.32	118.87	12.5	7.925
2001/02	73.10	121.84	12.5	8.123
2002/03	74.93	124.89	12.5	8.326
2003/04	76.81	128.01	12.5	8.534
2004/05	78.73	131.21	12.5	8.747
2005/06	80.69	134.49	12.5	8.966
2006/07	82.71	137.85	12.5	9.190
2007/08	84.78	141.30	12.5	9.420
2008/09	86.90	144.83	12.5	9.655
2009/10	89.07	148.45	12.5	9.897
2010/11	91.30	152.16	12.5	10.144
2011/12	93.58	155.97	12.5	10.398
2012/13	95.92	159.87	12.5	10.658
2013/14	98.32	163.86	12.5	10.924
2014/15	100.77	167.96	12.5	11.197
2015/16	103.29	172.16	10.0	9.390
2016/17	105.88	176.46	10.0	9.625
2017/18	108.52	180.87	10.0	9.866
2018/19	111.24	185.39	10.0	10.112
2019/20	114.02	190.03	10.0	10.365

Note: The estimated GST revenue for 1993/94 is $6664 million according to the answer to Question No. 146, 27/8/92, in the House of Representatives, Hon Ruth

Richardson. The starting tax base is $60 billion and I have applied a real growth rate of 2.5 per cent.

Annex 2:

CALCULATION OF TAX-FREE INCOME OF FAMILIES WITH CHILDREN AT SCHOOL

No. of Full-time Equivalents	Student Numbers
Pre-School	64,081
Primary	431,471
Secondary	234,510
Tertiary	48,795
University	68,717
Total	847,574

(*Source:* Parliamentary Question No. 7, 27/8/92.)

Less — Number of students (full-time equivalents) eligible for the full cash grant (voucher) scheme (see Parliamentary Question No. 5, 27/8/92 and Note 1 below) — 338,779.

— Number of eligible students (full-time equivalents) falling within families who are able to take advantage of the tax-free allowance (see Note 1 below) — 460,000. (These children are presupposed to come from 200,000 families, i.e., an average of 2.3 children per family.)

Cost of Tax-Free Income (see Note 2):

200,000 families at $32,000 each	$6400 million
260,000 students at $10,000 each	$2600 million
Total tax-free allowance	$9000 million

Note:

1. The number of students in the cash grant (voucher) scheme or tax-free income allowance is made on a best-estimate basis (Parliamentary Question No. 5, 27/8/92).
2. The financial numbers given above are on a best-estimate basis (Parliamentary Question No. 5, 27/8/92).
3. A partial allowance has been made for university and tertiary students, who will be required to fund themselves over time.

Annex 3:

CALCULATION OF INCOME TO BE TAXED AT 15 CENTS IN THE DOLLAR

Current level of personal income which falls below $12,000 (Parliamentary Question No. 165, 27/8/92)	$25,500 million
Less:	
1. Means-tested benefits and national superannuation payments	$ 9,500 million
2. Portion of $9000 million tax-free family educational allowance included in $25,500 million	$ 4,200 million
3. Estimated portion of income below $12,000 not eligible for 15 cents in the dollar tax rate	$ 800 million
Income subject to 15 cents in the dollar rate	$11,000 million

Annex 4 points to note:

1. Column 1 sets out the number of people in the retired population on 1 July 1993 who are still alive at the beginning of each succeeding year (Parliamentary Question, August 1992).

2. Column 2 expresses the number of people still alive each year as a percentage of the original retired population.

3. Column 3 increases the cost of health care each year by a factor of 3 per cent.

4. Column 4 calculates what the cost of health care for the original population would have been each year.

5. Column 5 deflates the cost of health care shown in Column 4 by the number of people who have died in order to provide the cost of health care for those retired at the start of the new programme and still alive each succeeding year.

Annex 4:

HEALTH (all amounts in millions)

Column	1	2	3	4	5
Year	Number of People Alive That Year	% Alive	Inflation Factor	Cost in $ of Day (Pop. 508,733)	Cost In $1993/94 (No. still alive)
1993/94	508 733	100.0	100.00	1700	1700
1994/95	486 438	95.6	103.00	1751	1674
1995/96	464 058	91.2	106.09	1804	1645
1996/97	441 848	86.9	109.27	1858	1613
1997/98	419 738	82.5	112.55	1913	1579
1998/99	398 128	78.3	115.93	1971	1542
1999/2000	376 655	74.0	119.41	2030	1503
2000/01	355 278	69.8	122.99	2091	1460
2001/02	334 350	65.7	126.68	2154	1415
2002/03	313 523	61.6	130.48	2218	1367
2003/04	293 488	57.7	134.39	2285	1318
2004/05	273 610	53.8	138.42	2353	1266
2005/06	254 220	50.0	142.58	2424	1211
2006/07	235 243	46.2	146.85	2497	1154
2007/08	216 915	42.6	151.26	2571	1096
2008/09	199 470	39.2	155.80	2649	1038
2009/10	180 355	35.5	160.47	2728	967
2010/11	165 925	32.6	165.28	2810	916
2011/12	150 285	29.5	170.24	2894	855
2012/13	135 418	26.6	175.35	2981	793
2013/14	121 393	23.9	180.61	3070	733
2014/15	107 890	21.2	186.03	3163	671
2015/16	95 505	18.8	191.61	3257	612
2016/17	83 788	16.5	197.36	3355	553
2017/18	72 978	14.3	203.28	3456	496
2018/19	63 063	12.4	209.38	3559	441
2019/20	54 203	10.7	215.66	3666	391

Annex 5:

SUPERANNUATION (all amounts in millions)

Column	1	2	3	4	5
Year	Number of People Alive That Year	% Alive	Inflation Factor	Cost in $ of Day (Pop. 508,733)	Cost In $1993/94 (No. still alive)
1993/94	508 733	100.0	100.00	4234	4234
1994/95	486 438	95.6	103.00	4361	4170
1995/96	464 058	91.2	106.09	4492	4097
1996/97	441 848	86.9	109.27	4627	4018
1997/98	419 738	82.5	112.55	4765	3932
1998/99	398 128	78.3	115.93	4908	3841
1999/20	376 655	74.0	119.41	5056	3743
2000/01	355 278	69.8	122.99	5207	3637
2001/02	334 350	65.7	126.68	5364	3525
2002/03	313 523	61.6	130.48	5524	3405
2003/04	293 488	57.7	134.39	5690	3283
2004/05	273 610	53.8	138.42	5861	3152
2005/06	254 220	50.0	142.58	6037	3017
2006/07	235 243	46.2	146.85	6218	2875
2007/08	216 915	42.6	151.26	6404	2731
2008/09	199 470	39.2	155.80	6596	2586
2009/10	180 355	35.5	160.47	6794	2409
2010/11	165 925	32.6	165.28	6998	2282
2011/12	150 285	29.5	170.24	7208	2129
2012/13	135 418	26.6	175.35	7424	1976
2013/14	121 393	23.9	180.61	7647	1825
2014/15	107 890	21.2	186.03	7876	1670
2015/16	95 505	18.8	191.61	8113	1523
2016/17	83 788	16.5	197.36	8356	1376
2017/18	72 978	14.3	203.28	8607	1235
2018/19	63 063	12.4	209.38	8865	1099
2019/20	54 203	10.7	215.66	9131	973

Points to note:

1. Column 1 sets out the number of people in the retired population on 1 July 1993 who are still alive at the

beginning of each succeeding year (Parliamentary Question, August 1992).

2. Column 2 expresses the number of people still alive each year as a percentage of the original retired population.

3. Column 3 increases the cost of superannuation each year by a factor of 3 per cent.

4. Column 4 calculates what the cost of superannuation for the original population would have been each year.

5. Column 5 deflates the cost of superannuation shown in Column 4 by the number of people who have died in order to provide the cost of pensions for those retired at the start of the new programme and still alive each succeeding year.

Annex 6:

RETIREES' CONTRIBUTION TOWARDS FULLY FUNDING SUPERANNUATION AND HEALTH CARE IN RETIREMENT

Year	Number of People Retiring (Thousands)	Contributions ($millions)
1993/94	13.7	27
1994/95	13.6	55
1995/96	13.2	81
1996/97	13.1	110
1997/98	13.4	143
1998/99	13.2	185
1999/2000	13.2	227
2000/01	13.1	272
2001/02	27.4	668
2002/03	28.3	792
2003/04	29.6	949
2004/05	31.4	1134
2005/06	33.7	1364
2006/07	33.6	1510
2007/08	32.3	1605
2008/09	33.6	1834
2009/10	35.6	2128
2010/11	38.7	2520
2011/12	42.3	2990
2012/13	43.6	3339
2013/14	43.0	3520
2014/15	43.3	3820
2015/16	43.6	4130
2016/17	43.5	4410
2017/18	44.2	4800
2018/19	44.9	5200
2019/20	46.2	5700

Note: The contributions per person are based on 7 per cent of the average wage up to 1997 and 9 per cent thereafter. The average wage has been taken as $28,000 for 1993 and increases by 2 per cent per annum. Some people will obviously be contributing 7 per cent or 9 per cent on income above or below the average wage.

Annex 7:

EMPLOYER CONTRIBUTION TOWARDS FULLY FUNDING SUPERANNUATION AND HEALTH CARE IN RETIREMENT

Column Year	1 Payroll Tax Base ($millions)	2 Payroll Tax Rate (%)	3 Payroll Tax Revenue ($millions)
1993/94	43,000	3	1290
1994/95	43,860	3	1316
1995/96	44,737	3	1342
1996/97	45,632	3	1369
1997/98	46,545	3	1396
1998/99	47,475	3	1424
1999/2000	48,425	3	1453
2000/01	49,393	2	988
2001/02	50,381	2	1008
2002/03	51,389	2	1028
2003/04	52,417	2	1048
2004/05	53,465	2	1069
2005/06	54,534	2	1091
2006/07	55,625	2	1113
2007/08	56,738	2	1135
2008/09	57,872	2	1157
2009/10	59,030	2	1181

Points to note:

1. Wages and salaries $39,000 million
Means-tested benefits $ 4,000 million
Payroll base 1993/94 $43,000 million
2. The 1993/94 base is adjusted by 2 per cent real each year.

Annex 8:

COST OF PROVIDING PENSIONS AND HEALTH CARE FOR THOSE RETIRING EACH YEAR

Column	1	2	3
Year	Number of People Retiring (thousands)	Pension @ $122,500 per Person (millions)	Health Care @ $40,833 per Person (millions)
1993/94	13.7	1678	559
1994/95	13.6	1666	555
1995/96	13.2	1617	539
1996/97	13.1	1605	535
1997/98	13.4	1642	547
1998/99	13.2	1617	539
1999/2000	13.2	1617	539
2000/01	13.1	1605	535
2001/02	27.4	3357	1119
2002/03	28.3	3467	1156
2003/04	29.6	3626	1209
2004/05	31.4	3847	1282
2005/06	33.7	4128	1376
2006/07	33.6	4116	1372
2007/08	32.3	3957	1319
2008/09	33.6	4116	1372
2009/10	35.6	4361	1454
2010/11	38.7	4741	1580
2011/12	42.3	5182	1727
2012/13	43.6	5341	1780
2013/14	43.0	5268	1756
2014/15	43.3	5304	1768
2015/16	43.6	5341	1780
2016/17	43.5	5329	1776
2017/18	44.2	5415	1805
2018/19	44.9	5500	1833
2019/20	46.2	5660	1886

Points to note:

1. The year begins on 1 July.

2. The number of people expected to retire each year has been taken from the answer to Parliamentary Question No. 163, 27/8/92.

3. The lump-sum amount required to fund superannuation has been calculated actuarially while the $40,833 is the sum required, based on the cost of $1700 million to fund those retired at 1/7/93.

SECTION FOUR: HOW PEOPLE ARE AFFECTED BY THE PROPOSED POLICY

With Policy Fully Implemented

1. There will be large increases in disposable income for those in employment as personal income tax has been abolished.

2. Indirect taxes will have been abolished or tax rates reduced substantially, including the reduction of GST to below 10 per cent.

3. These taxes will have been replaced by a compulsory savings scheme in which people save 9 per cent of their income until their savings reach a level which will ensure a minimum pension of $10,000 a year in 1993/94 terms and an adequate level of health care in retirement. Once minimum savings levels are reached, the 9 per cent compulsory savings levy becomes voluntary.

4. Parents and students will become responsible for their own educational needs. It will be compulsory for parents to ensure that their children attend a registered school up to a set age.

5. Low-income families will receive special assistance to ensure that they are not disadvantaged in the process:

(i) Any shortfall in the amount saved by those on low incomes will be made up by the government in the year they retire, thereby ensuring they have access to the same minimum pension and health care as others in retirement.

(ii) The educational cash grant (voucher) will be provided to low-income families to ensure they can purchase adequate education for their children.

(iii) The GMFI scheme will ensure that low-income

families with one partner in the full-time workforce have a weekly income substantially above the unemployment benefit.

Transitional Impacts

1. For the retired population:

(i) Security is provided as a result of capping the existing superannuation payment levels by fully funding all future retirees; and by confining the direct health-care costs of government just to the current retired population and not the entire population.

(ii) There is dignity in knowing that this is being done without placing an increasing burden on future generations.

2. For those within 25 years of retirement:

(i) There is security in the knowledge that both an improved superannuation payment level and adequate health care will be available to them when they retire, partly as a result of their own and their employers' contributions which have made both items affordable and sustainable.

(ii) There is the incentive to save beyond the level required to provide the minimum levels of superannuation and health care as the superannuation surcharge is reduced and then eliminated.

(iii) There is fairness in the knowledge that having saved towards their own superannuation and health care in retirement during their remaining working life, they are assured that their contribution will be topped up to provide an improved superannuation payment and adequate health care.

3. For 20- to 40-year-olds:

(i) There will be the incentive of very low income-tax rates for most of their working life.

(ii) There will be the widest choice in their children's education, the health care providers they use and the superannuation and health funds they join.

(iii) There will be security knowing that New Zealand will not be burdened by crippling government debt during their old age and that therefore they will be able to look forward to higher levels of disposable income and more incentive to invest in business.

(iv) There will be security in the knowledge that adequate superannuation and health care will be available when they retire as a result of their own savings.

(v) There will be security in knowing that if anything unexpected happened to them, adequate provision would be available for their children's care, for their education and health and the other necessities of life.

4. For the disadvantaged:

(i) There is incentive, in that to the extent that it is possible for them to provide for themselves, they should do so.

(ii) There is more choice available to them in education and health as there is already for better-off New Zealanders.

(iii) There is security in the knowledge that New Zealand's better economic situation — lower debt and fiscal surpluses — means that assistance to the disadvantaged is more affordable and thereby sustainable.

(iv) There is dignity is the knowledge that even when they are on a benefit, they are saving towards their retirement and that as a percentage of income, their contribution is similar to other New Zealanders.

(v) There is also dignity in being treated as an individual who is able to make his or her own decisions and is trusted to do so.